CHILTON'S REPAIR & TUNE-UP GUIDE
TEMPEST GTO 1968-73

Tempest 1968-70 • Le Mans 1968-73 • T-37 1971 • GTO 1968-73

Managing Editor KERRY A. FREEMAN, S.A.E.
Senior Editor RICHARD J. RIVELE, S.A.E.
Editor EUGENE P. NICOLO

President WILLIAM A. BARBOUR
Executive Vice President JAMES A. MIADES
Vice President and General Manager JOHN P. KUSHNERICK

CHILTON BOOK COMPANY
Radnor, Pennsylvania
19089

SAFETY NOTICE

Proper service and repair procedures are vital to the safe, reliable operation of all motor vehicles, as well as the personal safety of those performing repairs. This book outlines procedures for servicing and repairing vehicles using safe, effective methods. The procedures contain many NOTES, CAUTIONS and WARNINGS which should be followed along with standard safety procedures to eliminate the possibility of personal injury or improper service which could damage the vehicle or compromise its safety.

It is important to note that repair procedures and techniques, tools and parts for servicing motor vehicles, as well as the skill and experience of the individual performing the work vary widely. It is not possible to anticipate all of the conceivable ways or conditions under which vehicles may be serviced, or to provide cautions as to all of the possible hazards that may result. Standard and accepted safety precautions and equipment should be used when handling toxic or flammable fluids, and safety goggles or other protection should be used during cutting, grinding, chiseling, prying, or any other process that can cause material removal or projectiles.

Some procedures require the use of tools specially designed for a specific purpose. Before substituting another tool or procedure, you must be completely satisfied that neither your personal safety, nor the performance of the vehicle will be endangered.

Although information in this guide is based on industry sources and is as complete as possible at the time of publication, the possibility exists that the manufacturer made later changes which could not be included here. While striving for total accuracy, Chilton Book Company cannot assume responsibility for any errors, changes, or omissions that may occur in the compilation of this data.

PART NUMBERS

Part numbers listed in this reference are not recommendations by Chilton for any product by brand name. They are references that can be used with interchange manuals and aftermarket supplier catalogs to locate each brand supplier's discrete part number.

ACKNOWLEDGMENTS

Chilton Book Company wishes to express its appreciation to the Pontiac Motor Division, General Motors Corporation, Pontiac, Michigan 48053 for their generous assistance in the preparation of this book.

Manufactured in the United States of America
      90   2

Chilton's Repair & Tune-Up Guide: Tempest, GTO and LeMans 1968–73
ISBN 0-8019-5809-1
ISBN 0-8019-5905-5 pbk.
Library of Congress Catalog Card No. 73-10219

Contents

1 · General Information and Maintenance

Introduction

This book covers repair and maintenance procedures that the owner with an average set of tools can perform. The use of special tools has been kept to a minimum and, wherever possible, conventional tools substituted in their place. Jobs that require special factory tools, such as automatic transmission overhaul, should be referred to your authorized Pontiac dealer.

Whenever the left side of the car is referred to, it is meant to specify the driver's side of the car. Likewise, the right side of the car means the passenger's side of the car. Most screws and bolts are removed by turning counterclockwise and tightened by turning clockwise unless indicated otherwise.

All Pontiac Tempest, LeMans, T-37, and GTO models are covered. The tune-up and troubleshooting section is especially designed to enable the owner to diagnose and correct minor problems before they become major repair jobs. A section is devoted to each operating system and includes repair and overhaul procedures. Read through the section you are working on completely before attempting the actual work.

Serial Number Identification

VEHICLE

The Vehicle Identification Plate is secured to the upper left corner of the instrument panel. This plate is visible through the windshield and consists of six (1968–71) or seven (1972–73) sets of numbers and letters; each is significant in the identification of the car.

1968–71

The first number represents the Pontiac Motor Division of General Motors that produces the car. The Pontiac Division is represented by the number 2. The second number indicates the specific series of Pontiac. For example the number 42 is the series number for GTO, 33 for the Tempest and T-35, T-37 for the LeMans (1970–71). See the "Vehicle Identification Chart" for a complete listing of the series numbers. The third number is the body style code number. This number identifies the car as a sports-coupe, 4-door sedan, 4-door hard-top, or station wagon. The fourth number is the last number of the model year. The next symbol is a letter which represents the particular factory where the car was

1

The final set of numbers is the serial number.

A typical vehicle identification number might be: 2 42 37 1 B 100001. The two signifies that it is a Pontiac, 42 denotes that it is a GTO, 37 means a hardtop coupe and 1 for the year 1971. The B shows that the car was built in Baltimore and equipped with an eight-cylinder engine.

1972–73

In 1972 and 1973 an additional letter was added to the identification plate. This letter appears between the style number and the model year number. It represents a particular engine, exhaust, and carburetor combination.

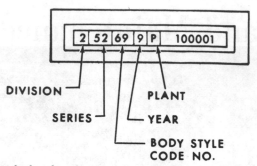

Vehicle identification plate, 1968–71 (© Pontiac Div., G.M. Corp.)

Vehicle Identification Chart

Year	Series	Model	Style Number
1968	Tempest 23300	Sports Coupe	23327
		4 Door Sedan	23369
	Tempest Custom 23500	Sports Coupe	23527
		Hardtop Coupe	23537
		4 Door Hardtop	23539
		4 Door Sedan	23569
		Convertible	23567
		Station Wagon	23535
	LeMans 23700	Sports Coupe	23527
		Hardtop Coupe	23537
		4 Door Sedan	23739
		Convertible	23767
	Tempest Safari 23935	2 Seat Station Wagon	23935
	GTO 24200	Hardtop Coupe	24237
		Convertible	24267
1969	Tempest 23300	Sports Coupe	23327
		4 Door Sedan	23369
	Custom S 23500	Sports Coupe	23527
		4 Door Sedan	23569
		Hardtop Coupe	23537
		4 Door Hardtop	23539
		Convertible	23567
		Station Wagon	23535
	LeMans 23700	Sports Coupe	23727
		Hardtop Coupe	23737
		4 Door Hardtop	23739
		Convertible	23767
	LeMans Safari 23935	2 Seat Station Wagon	23935

Vehicle Identification Chart (cont.)

Year	Series	Model	Style Number
1969	GTO 24200	Hardtop Coupe	24237
		Convertible	24267
1970	Tempest 23300	Sports Coupe	23327
		4 Door Sedan	23369
	LeMans 23500	Sports Coupe	23527
		4 Door Sedan	23569
		Hardtop Coupe	23537
		4 Door Hardtop	23539
		Convertible	23567
		Station Wagon— Single-Action Gate	23535
		Station Wagon— Dual-Action Gate	23536
	LeMans Sport 23700	Sports Coupe	23727
		Hardtop Coupe	23737
		4 Door Hardtop	23739
		Convertible	23767
		2 Seat Station Wagon	23736
	GTO 24200	Hardtop Coupe	24237
		Convertible	24267
1971	T-37 23300	Sports Coupe	23327
		2 Door Hardtop	23337
		4 Door Sedan	23369
	LeMans 23500	Sports Coupe	23527
		4 Door Sedan	23569
		Hardtop Coupe	23537
		4 Door Hardtop	23539
		2 Seat Station Wagon	23536
		3 Seat Station Wagon	23546
	LeMans Sport 23700	Hardtop Coupe	23737
		4 Door Hardtop	23739
		Convertible	23767
	GTO 24200	Hardtop Coupe	24237
		Convertible	24267

Year	Series	Model	Style Number	V.I. Model Number
1972	LeMans 23500	2 Door Sedan	23527	2D27
		2 Door Hardtop	23537	2D37
		4 Door Sedan	23569	2D69
		2 Seat Station Wagon	23536	2D36
		3 Seat Station Wagon	23546	2D46
		2 Door Convertible	23567	2D67
	Luxury LeMans 24400	2 Door Hardtop	24437	2G37
		4 Door Hardtop	24439	2G39

Vehicle Identification Chart (cont.)

Year	Series	Model	Style Number	V.I. Model Number
1973	LeMans 2AD00	4 Door Notch Back Sedan Hardtop	2AD29	2D29
		4 Door Station Wagon 2 Seat	2AD35	2D35
		2 Door Notch Back Hardtop Coupe	2AD37	2D37
	LeMans Sport 2AF00	2 Door Notch Back Hardtop Coupe	2AF37	2F37
	Luxury LeMans 2AG00	4 Door Notch Back Sedan Hardtop	2AG29	2G29
		2 Door Notch Back Coupe Hardtop	2AG37	2G37

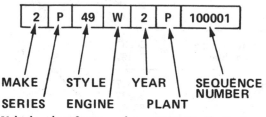

MAKE   STYLE   YEAR   SEQUENCE NUMBER

SERIES   ENGINE   PLANT

Vehicle identification plate, 1972–73 (© Pontiac Div., G.M. Corp.)

ENGINE SERIAL NUMBER

Six-Cylinder

1968–69

The engine code is stamped on the engine block, at the point where the cylinder head contacts the engine block. It is located behind the oiler filler tube.

Engine serial number location, 6 cylinder, 1968–69 (© Pontiac Div., G.M. Corp.)

1970–73

On these cars the engine code was stamped on the right side of the engine block on the distributor mounting plate.

Engine serial number location, 6 cylinder, 1970–73 (© Pontiac Div., G.M. Corp.)

Eight Cylinder

1968–73

The engine code on the V8 engines is located on a pad on the right side of the front of the engine block directly below the production engine number.

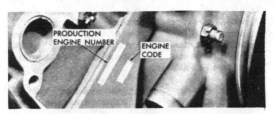

Engine serial number location, 8 cylinder, 1968–70 (© Pontiac Div., G.M. Corp.)

Engine serial number location, 8 cylinder, 1970–73 (© Pontiac Div., G.M. Corp.)

TRANSMISSION

Two-speed Automatic

1968–69

The identification number can be found on the right side of the transmission on the lower servo cover.

1970–73

The identification number can be found on the right side at the front of the transmission.

Turbo Hydramatic (M-38)

The identification number of this transmission is located in the middle of the right side of the transmission. The serial number begins with the letter J and is followed by another letter that shows the particular engine with which it is used. A two-digit number denoting the model year, completes the transmission identification number.

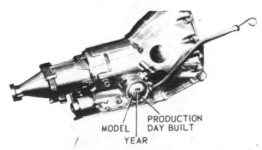

Two speed automatic transmission serial number location, 1968–69 (© Pontiac Div., G.M. Corp.)

Two speed automatic transmission serial number location, 1970–73 (© Pontiac Div., G.M. Corp.)

Turbo Hydramatic (M40)

The identification number for this transmission is located on the right side of the transmission case. The number begins with the letter P meaning Pontiac, followed by the engine code letter and completed with a two-digit number signifying the model year.

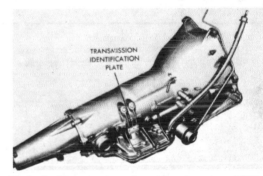

Turbo-hydra-matic serial number location, 1968–73 (© Pontiac Div., G.M. Corp.)

Turbo-hydra-matic serial number location, 1969–73 (© Pontiac Div., G.M. Corp.)

Engine and Transmission Identification Chart
1968

Displacement	Horsepower	Engine Code	Trans		Carb			Comp Ratio					Camshaft						Standard Distributor								Valve Springs			
			Manual	Automatic	1-bbl	2-bbl	Quadrajet	8.6	9.0	9.2	10.5	10.75	9777254	9779067	9779068	9785744	9790826	9792539	1110430	1110431	1111281	1111282	1111447	1111272	1111270	1111449	Single	Std Two	H-D Two (spec.)	Ram Air
250 cu in. (six)	175	ZK	X		X				X								X		X								X			
	175	ZN		X	X				X								X		X								X			
	215	ZO	X			X					X								X	X							X			
	215	ZE	X			X					X								X	X							X			
350 cu in. (V8)	265	WD	X			X			X				X							X							X			
	265	YN		X		X			X				X							X							X			
	320	WR	X				X				X		X										X				X			
	320	YP		X			X				X		X											X			X			
400 cu in. (V8)	265	XM	X		X		X						X												X		X			
	360	WT	X			X					X			X										•	•				X	
	350	YS	X			X					X			X										•	•				X	
	360	WS	X			X					X					X								•	•				X	
	350	YZ	X			X					X			X										•	•				X	
	360	XS	X			X					X					X								•	•					X
	360	XP				X					X				X									•	•					X

• With 60 PSI Oil Pump Spring
All Cars Use CCS

595463 YN

1969

Horsepower	Engine Code	Displacement			Trans		Carb			Comp Ratio					Camshaft								Distributor									Valve Springs					Cyl Head	
		250	350	400	Manual	Automatic	1 bbl (MV)	2 bbl (2GV)	4 bbl (4MV)	8.6:1	9.0:1	9.2:1	10.5:1	10.75:1	9790826	9792539	9796327	9777254	9785744	9779067	9779068	9794041	1110474	1110475	1111940	1111946 (b)	1111942	1111952 (b)	1111941 (b)	1111960	Single	Std-Dual	H-D Dual	H-D Spec-Dual	Ram Air IV-Dual	Small Valve	Large Valve
175	ZK[a] ZC	X			X		X				X					X									X							X				X	
175	ZN[a] ZF	X				X	X				X					X									X							X				X	
230	ZD[a] ZH	X			X			X				X					X						X									X				X	
215	ZE[a] ZL	X			X			X				X			X								X									X				X	
265	XR[a] XS		X		X			X			X							X										X					X			X	X
265 (c)	YN[a] YU		X		X			X			X							X										X					X			X	X
265	WP[a] WU		X		X			X			X							X																	X	X	X
330	XU		X		X			X			X									X						(d)								X		X	X
330	WV		X		X			X			X								X									(e)						X		X	X
350	YS			X	X	X		X					X						X						X							X					X
350	WT			X	X	X		X											X									X				X					X
366	YZ			X	X	X		X					X						X						X								X				X
366	WS			X	X	X		X		X										X					X				X				X				X
265	XM[a] XX		X		X		X	X		X										X				X									X			X	X
370	XP			X	X	X		X		X			X								X								X					X	X	X	X
370	WW			X	X	X		X		X										X					X				X					X	X	X	X

(a) Early production (small valve) engines with 30° intake valve seat angle. Later production (small valve) engines use 45° intake valve seat. NOTE: All large valve engines use 30° intake valve seat.

(b) Uses hardened drive gear for use with 60 psi oil pump and high tension distributor points.

(c) Two speed (M31) if equipped with A/C; Turbo-Hydra-matic (M38) optional without A/C.

(d) Uses distributor 1111965

(e) Uses distributor 1111966

1970

Horsepower	Engine Code	Displacement				Trans		Carb			Comp Ratio					Camshaft					Distributor									Valve Springs				Cyl Head	
		250	350	400	455	Manual	Automatic	1 bbl (MV)	2 bbl (GV)	4 bbl (4MV)	8.5:1	8.8:1	10.0:1	10.25:1	10.5:1	9772254 (U)	9779066 (N)	9779067 (P)	9779068 (S)	9794041 (T)	1110463	1110464	1112008	1112007	1111148④	1111176④	1112009④	1112012④	1112011 •	Single	Std-Dual	H-D Spec-Dual	Ram-Air-IV-Dual	Small Valve	Large Valve
155	ZB①	X						X	X		X												X								X			X	
155	ZG①	X							X	X	X													X							X			X	
255	WU		X			X		X				X				X										X						X			X	
255	YU		X				X	X				X				X										X						X			X	
366	WS②			X		X				X					X					X										†			X			X
350	WT			X		X	X			X				X					X								X						X			X
370	WW③			X		X				X						X					X								X						X		X
370	XP③			X			X			X						X					X								X						X		X
265	XX				X		X		X		X						X									X						X			X	
330	XV				X		X			X			X					X								X						X			X	
350	YS				X		X			X			X						X								X					X				X
366	YZ②				X		X			X					X					X							X						X			X
370	WA				X	X				X					X					X									X				X			X
370	YC				X		X			X					X			X										X					X			X

① L-6 camshaft usage is 3864897 for both manual and automatic transmissions.
† WS Engine uses 1112024 Distributor.
② Ram Air III
③ Ram Air IV
④ Uses hardened drive gear for use with 60 psi oil pump and high tension distributor points.
• Uses cadmium gear for use with R.A. IV only.

1971

Engine Code	Engine No. (Last Two Digits)	Horsepower	"A" Series	250 L-6	350 V8	400 V8	455 V8	Manual (3 Speed)	Manual (4 Speed)	Automatic	MV (1 bbl)	2GV (2 bbl)	4MV (4 bbl)	8.5 : 1	8.0 : 1	8.2 : 1	8.4 : 1	Pressed-In	Threaded	Single	Dual (Std)	Dual (H-D)	Small	Large	3864897	483355 (W)	9779066 (N)	9779067 (P)	9779068 (S)	High-Ball (Std)	High-Ball °	Low-Ball	1110489	1112069	1112068	1112070	1112072	1112073	1112083	1112089	1112090
ZB	63	145	X	X				X			X			X				X		X			X		X					X			X								
ZC	64	145	X	X						X	X			X				X		X			X		X					X			X								
WR	94	250	X		X			X				X			X			X			X		X			X				X									X		
WN	90	250	X		X					X		X			X			X			X		X			X				X											X
WU	92	250	X		X			X				X			X			X			X		X			X				X									X		
YP	98	250	X		X					**		X			X			X			X		X			X				X									X		
YU	96	250	X		X				**			X			X			X			X		X			X				X				X							
WP	97	250	X		X					**		X			X			X			X		X			X				X											X
XR	95	250	X		X				**			X			X			X			X		X			X				X				X							
YN	99	250	X		X					X		X			X			X			X		X			X				X					X						
WT	78	300	X			X		X					X			X			X				X		X				X			X				X					
WK	74	300	X			X			X				X			X			X				X		X				X			X				X					
XX %	73	265	X			X				X		X				X			X			X			X			X			X					X					
YX	71	265	X			X				X		X				X			X			X			X			X			X					X					
YS	79	300	X			X				X			X			X			X			X			X		X				X					X					
WL †	18	335	X				X		X				X				X		X			X			X				X			X				X		X		
WC †	15	335	X				X	X					X				X		X			X			X				X			X						X		
YC +	19	325	X				X			X			X			X			X			X			X			X		X							X			
YE †	16	335	X				X			X			X				X		X			X			X				X			X				X		X		

* Lifter Body with Cast-Iron Foot
** "YU" is used with M35 transmission; "XR" is used with M38 transmission.

† 455 H.O. Engine
% Man Trans Models use WS engine code
+ Man Trans Models use WJ engine code

1972

Engine Code	Model Usage	Displacement				Trans			Carb				Comp. Ratio				Rkr Arm Stud		Valve Spring		Valve Size		Camshaft							Valve Lifter		Distributor													
	"A" Series	250 L-6	350 V8	400 V8	455 V8	Manual (3 Speed)	Manual (4 Speed)	Automatic	MV (1 bbl)	WGD (2 bbl)	2GV (2 bbl)	4MV (4 bbl)	8.5 : 1	8.0 : 1	8.2 : 1	8.4 : 1	Pressed-In	Threaded	Single	Dual	Small	Large	3844497	626809	3896929	483355 (W)	9779066 (N)	9779067 (P)	9779068 (S)	High-Ball	Low-Ball	1110489	1112005	1112039	1112118	1112119 ⓓ	1112121	1112122	1112127 %	1112133 %	1112140	1112145	1112126	1112143
W6	X	X				X			X				X				X		X		X	X	X							X	X	X												
Y6	X	X					X	X	X X				X				X		X		X		X							X	X	X												
CBA*	X	X				X			X				X		X		X		X		X			X						X	X	X												
CSD*	X	X				X		X X	X X		X		X				X		X		X			X						X	X	X												
YU**	X		X					X			X			X	X		X			X	X	X				X				X															X
YR	X		X			X		X			X			X			X			X	X					X				X					X									
WR	X		X			X X	X	X		X				X			X			X	X					X				X											X			
YX	X			X				X			X			X			X	X		X	X					X				X						X								
WS	X			X		X						X		X			X	X		X	X	X						X	X	X							X							
WK	X			X			X					X		X			X	X		X	X	X						X	X	X							X							
YS	X		X					X				X		X			X	X		X	X	X						X	X	X							X							

ZS ▲	X		X				X	X	X		X	
ZX *	X		X	X		X	X	X		X		X	
YC	X	X	X	X		X	X	X		X	X		X
WM &	X	X		X		X	X	X	X		X	X	
YB &	X	X	X	X		X	X	X		X	X	X	

* Available California only: "CBA" and "CSD" equipped with A.I.R.
** Available California only A&F Series and nationwide B Series.
† California cars with manual transmission use "CAY" engine code.
†† California cars with M-35 use "CAZ" engine code.
▲ Replaced by "YS" engine code

% Unit distributor
& 455 H.O. engine
@ 1112189 2nd Type
& Man Trans Models use WG engine code

Routine Maintenance

AIR CLEANER

The air cleaner assembly consists of the air cleaner and a flame arrestor located in the base of the air cleaner. If your Pontiac is equipped with the paper element, it should be replaced once every 12,000 miles or 12 months, whichever comes first. Inspections and replacements should be more frequent if the car is operated under dusty conditions. To check the effectiveness of your paper element, remove the air cleaner assembly and, if the idle increases, the element is restricting air flow and should be replaced. Cars equipped with the Overhead Cam (OHC) six-cylinder engine use a polyurethane air cleaner element that must be replaced or cleaned and re-oiled at each 12,000 mile or 12 month interval. If you choose to clean it, do so with kerosene or another suitable solvent. Soak it in the solvent, then squeeze it dry. Allow it to soak in engine oil and then squeeze out the oil using a clean, dry cloth to remove the excess. The flame arrestor, located at the base of the air cleaner, should be cleaned in solvent once every 12,000 miles. Some cars are equipped with a dual-stage, heavy-duty air cleaner. The inner element is paper and must be replaced every 12,000 miles or 12 months while the outer element is polyurethane and must be washed as previously described.

POSITIVE CRANKCASE VENTILATOR (PCV)

Once every 12,000 miles or 12 months, check the PCV hoses and replace them if they are clogged. A ventilation filter is located in the air cleaner. This filter must be cleaned and oiled after 12,000 miles or 12 months and the PCV valve must be replaced at this time. The PCV service interval for 1972 and 1973 cars is increased to 24,000 miles or 24 months, whichever comes first.

EVAPORATIVE CANISTER

The Evaporative Control System, standard equipment since 1970, should be inspected once every 12 months or 12,000 miles, whichever comes first. The filter at

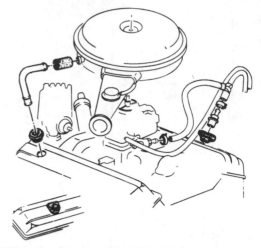

PCV valve location, V8, 1970–73 (© Pontiac Div., G. M. Corp.)

the bottom of the canister should be replaced and the canister inspected.

Replacing canister filter (© Pontiac Div., G.M. Corp.)

FLUID LEVEL CHECKS

Engine Oil

The engine oil level is checked with the dipstick, which is located at the left side of the engine block on a V8 and on the right side of the engine on a 6-cylinder. NOTE: *The oil should be checked before the engine is started or five minutes after the engine has been shut off. This gives the oil time to drain back to the oil pan and prevents an inaccurate oil level reading.*
Remove the dipstick from its tube, wipe it clean, and insert it back into the tube. Remove it again and observe the oil level.

It should be maintained between the "full" and "add" marks without going above "full" or below "add."

CAUTION: *Do not overfill the crankcase. It may result in oil-fouled spark plugs or oil leaks caused by oil seal failure.*

Transmission Fluid

MANUAL TRANSMISSION

Remove the filler plug from the side of the transmission. The oil should be level with the bottom edge of the filler hole. This should be checked at least once every 6,000 miles and more often if any leakage or seepage is observed. Fill with SAE 80 or 90 Multipurpose Gear lubricant.

AUTOMATIC TRANSMISSION

Run the engine until it reaches normal operating temperature. Park the car on a level surface. With the transmission in Park and the engine idling, the fluid level on the dipstick should be between the "full" mark and 1/4 inch below "full" mark. Replace the dipstick making sure that it is pushed fully into the filler tube.

CAUTION: *Do not overfill the automatic transmission. Use Dexron® automatic transmission fluid or any other equivalent fluid. One pint raises the level from "add" to "full."*

Brake Master Cylinder

Once every 6,000 miles or four months, check the brake fluid level in the master cylinder. The master cylinder is mounted on the firewall and is divided into two reservoirs and the fluid level in each reservoir must be maintained at 1/4 inch below the top edge.

Coolant

Check the coolant level when the engine is cold. The level of coolant should be maintained 2 in. below the bottom of the filler neck.

CAUTION: *Allow the engine to cool considerably and then add water while the engine is running.*

Rear Axle

STANDARD DIFFERENTIAL

The rear axle oil level should be checked when the chassis is lubricated. Remove the plug from the side of the housing. The lubricant level should be maintained at the bottom of the filler plug

Capacities Chart

| Year | Engine Displacement | Engine Crankcase (qts) | | Transmission (pts) | | | Drive Axle (pts) | Gasoline Tank (gals) | Cooling System (qts) |
		With Filter	Without Filter	Manual 3-spd	4-spd	Automatic			
1968	250	5.0	4.0	3.5	3.5	15.0	3.0	21.5	12.1
	350	5.0	4.0	3.5	2.5	15.0	3.0	21.5	18.6
	400	5.0	4.0	2.8	2.5	19.0①	3.0	21.5	17.8
1969	250	4.5	3.5	2.8	3.5	15.0	3.0	21.5	12.0
	350	5.0	4.0	3.5	2.5	15.0	3.0	21.5	19.5
	400	5.0	4.0	3.5	2.5	19.0	3.0	21.5	18.5
1970 thru 1972	250	4.0	3.0	3.5③	2.5	20.0	3.0②	21.5	19.5
	350	5.0	4.0	3.5	2.5	19.25④	3.0②	21.5	19.5
	400	5.0	4.0	2.8	2.5	19.0	3.0②	21.5	19.5
	455	5.0	4.0	2.8	2.5	19.0	3.0②	21.5	19.5
1973	250	4.0	3.0	3.5	——	19.2	3.0②	21.5	12.4
	350	5.0	4.0	2.8	2.5	19.2	3.0②	21.5	20.2
	400	5.0	4.0	2.8	2.5	19.2	3.0②	21.5	18.6
	455	5.0	4.0	——	2.5	19.2	3.0②	21.5	18.0

① 350 Trans—20
② 5 pts. with 8.875 in. ring gear
③ Saginaw 3 speed; Muncie 2.8

④ M-38 Hydra 21.0 (V8), M-38 Hydra 19.25 (6 cylinder)

hole. When replacing oil, use SAE 80 or 90 multipurpose hypoid gear lubricant.

SAFE-T-TRACK DIFFERENTIAL

Lubricant level should be checked at each chassis lubrication and maintained at the bottom of the filler plug hole. Special Safe-T-Track oil must be used in this differential.

CAUTION: *Never use standard differential lubricant in a Safe-T-Track differential.*

Steering Gear

Check the lubricant by removing the center bolt on the side cover of the steering gear. Grease must be up to the level of this bolt hole.

Power Steering Reservoir

Maintain the proper fluid level as indicated on the cap of the reservoir. Check this level with the engine off and warm. Use GM power steering fluid or automatic transmission fluid.

Battery

The electrolyte level in the battery should be checked about once every month and more often during hot weather or long trips. If the level is below the bottom of the split ring, distilled water should be added until the level reaches the ring.

DRIVE BELTS

Check the drive belts every 6,000 miles for evidence of wear such as cracking, fraying, and incorrect tension. Determine the belt tension at a point halfway between the pulleys by pressing on the belt with moderate thumb pressure. The belt should deflect about ¼ inch at this point. If the deflection is found to be too much or too little, loosen the mounting bolts and make the adjustments.

TIRES

Tire Rotation

Tires should be rotated every 6,000 miles. Rotate the tires as shown in the diagram. When you rotate the tires check for uneven wear, bulging, cuts, or punctures.

Tire Pressure

Tire pressure varies with the size of the car or tire and how much load the car is

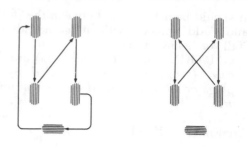

5 WHEELS   4 WHEELS

Tire rotation (© Pontiac Div., G.M. Corp.)

carrying. Check the decal located on the glove compartment door for recommended pressures.

FUEL FILTER

The filter element should be replaced every 12 months or 12,000 miles. To replace, follow these procedures:

1. Using an open-end wrench (preferably a line wrench), disconnect the fuel line connection from the larger fuel filter nut.

2. Remove the larger nut from the carburetor with a box-end wrench or a socket.

3. Remove the filter element and spring from the carburetor.

4. Check the bronze element for dirt blockage by blowing on the cone end. If the element is good, air should pass through easily.

5. If the car has a paper element instead of a bronze element, check by blowing into the fuel inlet end. If air does not pass

Removing fuel filter (paper type) (© Pontiac Div., G.M. Corp.)

through easily, replace the element. Do not attempt to clean these elements.

6. Install the spring and then the element into the carburetor, making sure the small end of the bronze cone is facing outward.

7. Install a new gasket on the large nut and tighten securely.

8. Insert the fuel line and tighten the nut with a line wrench.

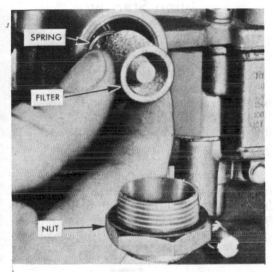

Removing fuel filter (bronze type) (© Pontiac Div., G.M. Corp.)

Lubrication

ENGINE

Engine oil should be changed once every four months or every 6,000 miles, whichever comes first. New Pontiacs arrive from the factory containing a high quality SE oil and not a thin, short-life "break-in" oil as some people believe. Because of this, it is not necessary to change this factory oil before the first 6,000 miles or four months. Certain types of driving require the interval between oil changes not to exceed two months or 3,000 miles. These include:

1. Operating the car under dusty conditions or during a dust storm. A dust storm may necessitate an immediate oil change.
2. Long periods of idling.
3. Trailer hauling.

4. Short trips at freezing temperatures when the engine hasn't had time to warm up sufficiently.

5. Commercial driving such as that performed by patrol cars, taxicabs, or limousines.

These recommended oil change intervals are based upon the assumption that a high quality SE oil is used; otherwise, the intervals have to be made shorter. Long engine life, low maintenance, and good performance cannot be ensured if these oil changes are not performed at the proper intervals. Oil left in the crankcase too long will begin to deteriorate due to dilution by gas vapors and water condensation. Leakage of gasoline into the oil pan usually occurs when the engine is warming up and not hot enough to thoroughly vaporize and burn the fuel. Water vapor enters the crankcase oil through engine ventilation and exhaust blow-by and condenses during the engine warm-up. This water combines with the gasoline and exhaust gases to form harmful acids in the oil pan. The acidic oil is then pumped throughout the engine where it will pit moving parts and result in rapid engine wear and eventual engine failure. A good oil with an SE rating will help in fighting this condition but the source of the trouble is often found to be water in the fuel system, excessive engine blow-by, a faulty or improperly adjusted carburetor or automatic choke, a low-temperature thermostat, or too many short trips at freezing temperatures resulting in cold engine operation.

OIL CHANGES

Engine

The engine oil should be drained from the crankcase after the engine has reached normal operating temperature. Hot, faster moving oil will remove much more of the dirt and sludge from the engine. Be sure not to tighten the drain plug too tightly.

Transmission

Remove the drain plug and remove the transmission fluid. Refill the transmission with automatic transmission fluid to the proper level. Manual transmission oil should only be replaced after overhaul; fill the transmission through the inspection hole.

OIL FILTER

The oil filter should be removed before draining the oil pan. Spin-on filters may require the use of an inexpensive filter wrench (available at auto supply stores) for removal. To remove, turn the filter counterclockwise. Before installing a new filter, make sure that the surfaces are clean and then lightly coat the gasket with fresh oil. Tighten the new filter by hand. Do not use the wrench.

CHASSIS GREASING

Chassis greasing can be performed with a pressurized grease gun or it can be performed at home by using a hand-operated grease gun. Wipe the grease fittings clean before greasing in order to prevent the possibility of forcing any dirt into the component.

WHEEL BEARINGS

Once every 12 months or 12,000 miles, clean and repack wheel bearings with a wheel bearing grease. Use only enough grease to completely coat the rollers. Remove any excess grease from the exposed surface of the hub and seal.

It is important that wheel bearings be properly adjusted after installation. Improperly adjusted wheel bearings can cause steering instability, front-end shimmy and wander, and increased tire wear. For complete adjustment procedures, see the "Wheel Bearings" section in Chapter Eight.

Pushing, Towing, and Jump Starting

Pushing

AUTOMATIC TRANSMISSION

If your Pontiac is equipped with an automatic transmission, do not try to start the engine by pushing it; use battery jumper cables instead.

MANUAL TRANSMISSION

Manual transmission equipped cars can be started by pushing. Turn on the ignition key, push in the clutch, place the transmission in Second gear, and release the clutch at a speed of 10–15 mph.

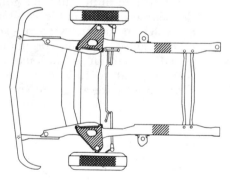
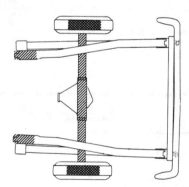

DRIVE ON HOIST

BUMPER JACK AT FRAME ATTACHMENT ONLY

FLOOR JACK OR HOIST LIFT

Lift point locations (© Pontiac Div., G.M. Corp.)

Towing

The car can be towed safely (with the transmission in Neutral) from the front at speeds of 35 mph or less. The car must either be towed with the rear wheels off the ground or the driveshaft disconnected if:

    a. towing speeds are to be over 35 mph;

    b. towing distance is over 50 miles;

    c. transmission or rear axle problems exist.

When towing the car on its front wheels, the steering wheel must be secured in a straight-ahead position. Tire to ground clearance should not exceed 6 in. during towing.

Jacking

Your Pontiac may be lifted on the frame side rails. The car may also be lifted at the bottom of the front and rear axles.

2 · Tune-Up and Troubleshooting

Tune-Up Procedures

SPARK PLUGS

Beginning in 1969, all Pontiacs used resistor spark plugs, in addition to resistor wires, to reduce radio and television interference.

In addition to performing their basic function of igniting the air-fuel mixture, spark plugs can also serve as very useful diagnostic tools. Once removed, compare your spark plugs with the samples in the "Troubleshooting" section at the back of this chapter. Typical plug conditions are illustrated along with their causes and remedies. Plugs which exhibit only normal wear and deposits can be cleaned, gapped, and reinstalled. Before removing the spark plug leads, number the towers on the distributor cap with tape. Trace the No. 1 lead and then proceed in the firing order. Use the firing order illustrations in Chapter Three if you get lost. This prevents mix-ups when reinstalling the leads and also comes in handy when you're replacing wires or the distributor cap. Grasp each spark plug boot and pull it straight out.

Install the spark plug socket on the plug's hex and remove it. If removal is difficult, loosen the plug only slightly and drip some light oil onto the threads. Allow the oil to penetrate and then unscrew the spark plug. Proceeding this way will prevent damaging the threads in the cylinder head. Be sure to keep the socket straight to avoid breaking the ceramic insulator. Inspect the plugs using the "Troubleshooting" section illustrations and then clean or discard them according to their condition.

New spark plugs come pregapped, but double check the setting or reset them if you desire a different gap. Recommended spark plug gap is given in the "Tune-Up Specifications Chart." Use a spark plug wire gauge for checking the gap. The wire should pass through the electrodes with just a slight drag. Using the electrode bending tool on the end of the gauge, bend the side electrode to adjust the gap. Never attempt to adjust the center electrode. Lightly oil the threads of the replacement plug and install it.

BREAKER POINT AND CONDENSER

Removal and Replacement

SIX CYLINDER

1. Remove distributor cap from the distributor and place it out of the way.
2. Remove the rotor.
3. Remove the wires from the contact point terminal.
4. Remove the mounting screws and lift the point set and condenser from the breaker plate.

5. Clean the breaker plate.

6. Install a new point set onto the breaker plate.

7. Install a new condenser and connect the primary and condenser lead wires to the contact point terminal.

8. Check the points for alignment. Contact surfaces must align with each other. If alignment is necessary, bend only the stationary contact support and not the movable lever.

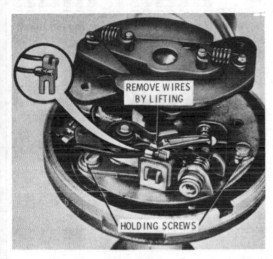

Contact breaker points (© Pontiac Div., G.M. Corp.)

9. Using a flat feeler gauge, set the point opening at 0.019 in. for new points, 0.016 in. for used points. Observe the points while an assistant lightly activates the ignition switch. Turning the ignition key to the START position will rotate the distributor shaft and cause the points to open and close. When the points open completely (this occurs when the rubbing block is resting on the high point of the cam lobe), TURN THE IGNITION KEY OFF and check the space between the open points. This space or gap should be 0.019 in. for new points. If not, slightly loosen the point set mounting screw and, using a screwdriver to move the point support, adjust the gap until correct. Tighten the mounting screw.

10. Install the rotor and distributor cap.

11. Start the engine, check the dwell angle and then the ignition timing.

V8

Point alignment is pre-set at the factory and requires no adjustment. Point sets using the push-in type wiring terminal should be used on those distributors equipped with an R.F.I. (radio frequency interference) shield (1970–73). Those points using a lock screw type terminal may short out due to the shield contacting the screw.

1. Remove the distributor cap.

2. Remove the rotor.

3. If so equipped, remove the two piece R.F.I. shield.

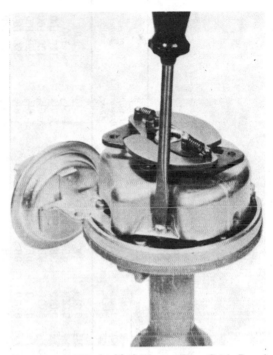

Removing R.F.I. shield (© Pontiac Div., G.M. Corp.)

4. Loosen the two mounting screws and slide the contact point set from the breaker plate.

5. Remove the primary and condenser leads from the terminal.

6. Loosen the condenser bracket screw and slide the condenser from the bracket.

7. Install the new point set and condenser and then tighten the mounting screws.

8. Install the wires to the terminal so that they will not interfere with the cap, weight base, or breaker advance plate.

9. Make an initial point setting of 0.019 in. at this time.

10. The cam lubricator (if so equipped) must be replaced after 12 months or 12,000 miles. The end of the lubricator should be adjusted to just touch the cam lobes. Additional grease should not be applied to the lubricator.

Tune-Up Specification Chart

Year	Engine Cu In. Displacement	Spark Plugs Type	Gap (in.)	Distributor Point Dwell (deg)	Point Gap (in.)	Ignition Timing (deg) MT	AT	Intake Valve Opens (deg)	Fuel Pump Pressure (psi)	Compression Pressure (psi)	Idle Speed (rpm) MT	AT
'68	250 OHC	44N	0.035	32½	0.019	TDC	TDC	14	4-5½	140	700①/500	600①/500
	250 OHC	44N	0.035	30	0.019	5B	5B	14	4-5½	140	800①/600	600①/500
	350	45S	0.035	30	0.019	9B	9B	22	5-6½	120–160	700①/500	600①/500
	350	45S	0.035	30	0.019	9B	9B	23/30	5-6½	120–160	850①/650	650①/500
	400	44S	0.035	30	0.019	9B	9B	22	5-6½	120–160	800①/500	600①/500
	400	44S	0.035	30	0.019	9B	9B	31/23	5-6½	120–160	850①/650	650①/500
	400	44S	0.035	30	0.019	9B	9B	31/23	5-6½	120–160	1000①/650	650①/500
	400 Ram Air	44S	0.035	30	0.019	9B	9B	38/31	5-6½	120–160	1000①/650	650①/500
'69	250 OHC	R-44NS	0.035	32½	0.019	TDC	TDC	14	4-5½	140	700①/500	600①/500
	250 OHC	R-44NS	0.035	32½	0.019	5B	5B	22/14	4-5½	140	850①/600	600①/500
	250 OHC	R-44NS	0.035	32½	0.019	5B	5B	22/14	4-5½	140	850①/600	600①/500
	350	R-46S	0.035	30	0.019	9B	9B	22	5-6½	120–160	850	650
	350	R-45S	0.035	30	0.019	9B	9B	38/23	5-6½	120–160	1000	650
	400	R-46S	0.035	30	0.019	9B	9B	22	5-6½	120–160	850	650
	400	R-45S	0.035	30	0.019	9B	9B	23	5-6½	120–160	1000	650
	400	R-45S	0.035	30	0.019	9B	9B	23	5-6½	120–160	1000	650
	400 Ram Air	R-45S	0.035	30	0.019	15B	15B	23	5-6½	120–160	1000①/650	650①/500
	400 Ram Air	R-44S	0.035	30	0.019	15B	15B	42	5-6½	120–160	1000①/650	650①/500
'70	250	R46T	0.035	32½	0.019	TDC	4B	16	4-5	140	830①/750	630①/600
	350	R46S	0.035	30	0.019	9B	9B	22	5-6½	120–160	800	650
	400	R46S	0.035	30	0.019	9B	9B	22	5-6½	120–160	800	650
	400	R45S	0.035	30	0.019	9B	9B	30	5-6½	120–160	950	650
	400	R-46S	0.035	30	0.019	9B	9B	23	5-6½	120–160	950	650
	400 Ram Air	R-46S	0.035	30	0.019	9B	9B	31	5-6½	120–160	950	650
	400 Ram Air	R-46S	0.035	30	0.019	15B	15B	40	5-6½	120–160	1000/650	750/500
	455	R-46S	0.035	30	0.019	9B	9B	31/23	5-6½	120–160	950	650

Year	Engine	Spark Plug	Plug Gap	Dwell	Point Gap	Timing	Timing				Idle Speed	Idle Speed
'71	250	R-46TS	0.035	32½	0.019	4B	4B	16	4-5	140	850①/550	650①/500
	350	R-47S	0.035	30	0.019	12B	12B	26/30	5-6½③	120-160	800	600
	400	R-47S	0.035	30	0.019	—	8B	26	5-6½③	120-160	—	600
	400	R-46S	0.035	30	0.019	12B	12B	23	5-6½③	120-160	1000/600①	700①
	455	R-46S	0.035	30	0.019	—	12B	23	5-6½③	120-160	—	650①
	455	R-46S	0.035	30	0.019	12B	12B	31	5-6½③	120-160	1000/600①	700①
'72	250	R-45T	0.035	32½	0.019	4B	4B	16	4-5	140	700/450①	600/450
	350	R-46TS	0.035	30	0.019	8B	10B	26/30	5-6½	120-160	800	625
	400	R-46TS	0.035	30	0.019	—	10B	23/26	5-6½	120-160	—	625
	400	R-46TS	0.035	30	0.019	8B	10B	23	5-6½	120-160	1000/600①	700/500
	455	R-45TS	0.035	30	0.019	—	10B	23	5-6½	120-160	—	650/500
	455	R-45TS	0.035	30	—	8B	10B	31	5-6½	120-160	1000/600①	700/500
'73	250	R-46TS	0.040	32½	0.019	4B	4B	16	4-5	140	700/450①	600/450
	350 SE	R-46TS	0.040	30	0.019	8B	12B	26/30	5-6½	120-160	900/600	650
	350 DE	R-46TS	0.040	30	0.019	8B	12B	26/30	5-6½	120-160	900/600①	650
	400 SE	R-46TS	0.040	30	0.019	8B	12B	23/26	5-6½	120-160	—	650
	400 DE	R-46TS	0.040	30	0.019	8B	12B	23/26	5-6½	120-160	650/450①	650
	400 SE	R-46TS	0.040	30	0.019	8B	12B	23/26	5-6½	120-160	650/450①	650
	400 DE	R-46TS	0.040	30	0.019	8B	12B	23/26	5-6½	120-160	—	650
	455 SE	R-46TS	0.040	30	0.019	8B	12B	31	5-6½	120-160	—	650
	455 DE	R-46TS	0.040	30	0.019	8B	12B	31	5-6½	120-160	—	650
	455 S.D. DE	R-46TS	0.040	30	0.019	8B	12B	31	5-6½	120-160	1000/600①	650

SE Single Exhaust
DE Dual Exhaust
① Lower figure indicates idle speed with solenoid disconnected
③ 6½-8 with A/C

B Before Top Dead Center
TDC Top Dead Center
— Not applicable

11. Start the engine and check the point dwell and the ignition timing.

DWELL ANGLE

Dwell angle is the amount of time (measured in degrees of distributor cam rotation) that the contact points remain closed. Initial point gap (0.019 in.) determines dwell angle. If the points are set too wide they open gradually and dwell angle (the time they remain closed) is small. This wide gap causes excessive arcing at the points and, because of this, point burning. This small dwell doesn't give the coil sufficient time to build up maximum energy and so coil output decreases. If the points are set too close, the dwell is increased but the points may bounce at higher speeds and the idle becomes rough and starting is made harder. The wider the point opening, the smaller the dwell and the smaller the gap, the larger the dwell. Adjusting the dwell by making the initial point gap setting with a feeler gauge is sufficient to get the car started but a finer adjustment should be made. A dwell meter is needed to check the adjustment.

SIX CYLINDER

1. Perform Steps 8 and 9 in the above procedure ("Breaker Points and Condenser Replacement") and then check the dwell angle with a dwell meter. Compare the reading on the meter with that listed in the "Tune-Up Specifications Chart" and adjust if necessary. If the dwell angle is less than the specified minimum, check for misaligned points or worn distributor cam lobes. Accelerate the engine to 1,750 rpm and check for dwell variation. If the dwell angle changed more than three degrees from idle to 1,750 rpm, then check for a worn distributor shaft, shaft bushing, or a loose breaker plate.

IMPORTANT: *After changing the dwell angle, it will be necessary to set the ignition timing. Changing the dwell changes the ignition timing although changing timing does not affect the dwell angle. Therefore, when performing both settings, dwell angle adjustment must be done before timing.*

V8

1. Run the engine to normal operating temperatures and then let it idle.
2. Raise the adjusting window on the distributor cap and insert a small allen wrench into the adjusting screw.
3. Turn the adjusting screw until the specified dwell angle is obtained on the dwell meter.

IGNITION TIMING

SIX CYLINDER AND V8

1. Disconnect and plug the distributor vacuum advance hose.
2. Start the engine and run it at idle speed.
3. Connect the timing light and, with the engine running at an idle, aim it at the timing tab on the front engine cover.

Timing marks—V8 engine (© Pontiac Div., G.M. Corp.)

Timing marks—6 cylinder engine (© Pontiac Div., G.M. Corp.)

NOTE: *It may be necessary to clean off the tab and slash mark on the crankshaft pulley before proceeding any further. To further improve visibility, take a piece of chalk and fill in the slash mark on the crankshaft pulley. The "0" marking on the tab is TDC and all the BTDC (before top dead center) settings are on the "before" (advance) side of the "0" or, on the 1970 6 cylinder, on the "A" (advance) side of the "0". On the 1968 and 1969 six cylinder models, the BTDC settings are on the + (advance) side of the "0".*

4. Loosen the distributor clamp bolt and turn the distributor until the slash on the crankshaft pulley lines up with the specified timing mark on the tab. Once the timing is correct, tighten the distributor clamp bolt and recheck the timing.

5. Turn off the engine, remove the timing light, and connect the vacuum advance hose.

VALVE LASH

IMPORTANT: *Before adjusting the valves, thoroughly warm-up the engine.*

OVERHEAD CAM SIX CYLINDER

The OHC six cylinder engine is equipped with automatic valve lash adjusters. No adjustment is necessary or possible.

1970–73 6 CYLINDERS AND V8s (EXCEPT RAM AIR AND S. D.)

The purpose of the hydraulic valve lifter is to maintain zero clearance in the valve train. It does this by expanding to take up additional clearance created as the lifter moves onto the base circle of its camshaft lobe. To perform properly, the lifter must be adjusted half-way between its fully extended position and its collapsed position. If the lifter is adjusted too loosely, the valve will not open fully; if adjusted too lightly, any number of major mechanical failures may result.

When a rocker arm is loosened or removed, the lifter will expand to its fully extended position. Upon reassembly, it is necessary to be sure that the lifter is on its camshaft lobe base circle before adjusting the lifter. This is the purpose of the preliminary valve adjustment. Perform the final valve adjustment after the engine is running.

Preliminary Valve Adjustment

1. Rotate the crankshaft until no. 1 piston is at TDC on the compression stroke and the distributor rotor points to no. 1 spark plug wire cap tower. The timing mark should be aligned with zero (0°) on the timing cover.

2. Tighten the adjusting nut until the play just disappears. Adjust both valves. On Ram Air and Super Duty engines, adjust the valves to obtain a 0.008 in. clearance between the rocker arms and valve stems, then tighten the adjusting nut an additional ⅛ turn and tighten the locknut.

3. On V8s, rotate the crankshaft 90°, in the normal direction of rotation, to bring the next piston in firing order to TDC on the compression stroke. Repeat step two until all of the valves are done. On six-cylinder engines, bring each cylinder to TDC on its compression stroke and repeat step two.

Final Valve Adjustment

1. Start the engine and retighten the rocker arm on any valve that is clattering. Tighten until the noise disappears.

2. Allow the engine to run until normal operating temperature is reached, then loosen each rocker arm adjusting nut until clattering begins. Retighten the nut until the noise disappears. On all V8s tighten the nut, very slowly, to 20 ft lbs. On the

Adjusting valve lash, V8 and 6 cylinder engines (© Pontiac Div., G.M. Corp.)

1970–72 six-cylinder engines, tighten the nut ½–1 revolution further, very slowly.

NOTE: *The purpose of tightening the adjusting nut slowly is to give the lifter time to adjust its height.*

RAM AIR IV AND SUPER DUTY V8's

With this engine, it is not possible to adjust the valves by tightening the rocker

arm adjusting nut until it seats on the shoulder of the rocker arm. To adjust these limited travel lifters with the engine installed in the car, proceed as follows. If the engine has been removed, use the second procedure.

Engine Installed

1. Tighten the rocker arm adjusting nuts so that the pushrods will not jump out of place when the engine is started.

2. Start the engine and retighten the rocker arm on any valve that is clattering. Tighten just until the noise disappears.

3. Allow the engine to run until normal operating temperature is reached, then loosen each rocker arm adjusting nut until the clattering begins. Retighten the nut until the noise disappears (this brings the pushrod slightly into the top of lifter travel) and, with the adjusting nut in this position, tighten the locknut to 30–40 ft lbs.

Engine Out of Car

1. Rotate the crankshaft until the No. 1 piston is at TDC on the compression stroke and the distributor rotor points to the No. 1 spark plug wire cap tower. The timing mark should be aligned with the "0" on the timing cover.

2. Tighten the rocker arm adjusting nuts on the No. 1 cylinder rockers to obtain 0.008 in. clearance between the rocker arms and the valve stems.

3. Tighten the adjusting nuts an additional ⅛ turn, then tighten the locknuts to 30–40 ft lbs.

4. Rotate the crankshaft 90° in the normal direction of rotation to bring the next piston in the firing order (No. 8) to TDC on the compression stroke, then complete Steps 2 and 3.

5. Continue as in Step 4 for the rest of the cylinders; firing order is 1-8-4-3-6-5-7-2.

CARBURETOR

Idle Speed and Mixture

1968–69, 6 CYLINDER

NOTE: *Make these adjustments with the air cleaner installed.*

1. Turn in the mixture screws until they lightly seat, then back them out five turns.

2. Start the engine, connect the tachometer, and allow the engine to warm up to normal operating temperature. On auto-

matic transmission cars, place the selector in Drive and turn off the A/C, if so equipped.

3. Adjust the idle stop solenoid screw to obtain 610 rpm for automatic transmission (1 bbl and 4 bbl), 730 rpm for manual transmission (4 bbl), or 880 rpm for 1969 manual transmission (4 bbl).

4. Turn the mixture screws clockwise to obtain 600 rpm for automatic transmission (1 bbl and 4 bbl), 700 rpm for manual transmission (1 bbl), 800 rpm for 1968 manual transmission (4 bbl), or 850 rpm for 1969 manual transmission (4 bbl).

5. Disconnect the idle stop solenoid and adjust the idle speed screw on the carburetor to obtain 600 rpm for manual transmission (4 bbl) and 500 rpm for all others.

NOTE: *Don't disturb the idle mixture screws or stop the solenoid after this point.*

6. Reconnect the solenoid and adjust the fast idle speed.

1968–69, V8

1. Turn in the idle mixture screws until they are lightly seated, then back them out four turns (2 bbl) or six turns (4 bbl).

2. Connect a tachometer, start the engine, and allow it to warm up to normal operating temperature. On cars with automatic transmission and A/C, turn off the A/C.

3. Place the car in Drive (automatic) or Neutral (manual). With the idle stop solenoid energized, adjust the mixture screws for the best lean idle speed.

4. Adjust the idle stop solenoid screw to obtain the specified idle speed for all 1968 and only 1969 Ram Air; use the idle screw for all other 1969 cars.

5. Disconnect the idle stop solenoid, then adjust the idle speed screw on the carburetor to obtain 650 rpm idle for manual transmission (4 bbl), 500 rpm for all others.

6. Place the fast idle lever on the top step of the cam and adjust the fast idle speed.

1970

NOTE: *Make this adjustment with the air cleaner installed.*

1. On California cars, remove the fuel filler cap.

2. Disconnect and plug the distributor vacuum advance hose.

3. Plug the hot idle compensator on all automatic transmission V8's with the Quadrajet (4MV) carburetor except the Ram Air III and IV. Also plug the compensator on all L-6 and V8 2 bbl with automatic transmission and A/C.

With the car in Drive (automatic) or Neutral (manual), adjust the curb idle speed as follows:

L-6 and Ram Air IV

a. With the idle stop solenoid energized, adjust the solenoid screw to obtain 830 rpm for the L-6, 1,000 rpm for the Ram Air IV, 630 rpm for the automatic L-6, and 750 rpm for the automatic Ram Air IV.

b. Adjust the mixture screws equally to obtain lean best idle at 1,000 rpm for the Ram Air IV (manual), 750 rpm for the automatic Ram Air IV, 750 rpm for the manual L-6, and 600 rpm for the automatic L-6.

c. Disconnect the solenoid wire and adjust the carburetor idle speed screw to obtain 400 rpm for the L-6, 500 rpm for the Ram Air IV (automatic) and 650 rpm for the Ram Air manual.

350, 400, 455 Engines

a. Back out the mixture screws 3–5 turns from the lightly seated positions.

b. Adjust the carburetor idle speed screw to obtain 850 rpm for the manual 350 and 400 bbl, 1,050 rpm for the manual 400 and 455 4 bbl, or 675 rpm for all automatic 350, 400, 455 engines.

c. Lean the mixture screws equally (turn in) to obtain 800 rpm for manual 350 and 400 2 bbl, 950 rpm for manual 400 and 455 4 bbl, or 650 rpm for all automatic 350, 400, 455 engines.

1971

NOTE: *Adjust with the air cleaner installed.*

The idle stop solenoid is no longer used, having been replaced by the combination emission control valve. This valve is energized through the transmission to increase idle speed under conditions of high gear deceleration and to provide full vacuum spark advance during high gear operation. The valve is de-energized at curb idle and in the lower gears to provide a retarded spark under these conditions, the result of which is lower hydrocarbon emissions.

The valve need not be adjusted unless the solenoid or throttle body is removed or the carburetor overhauled. Plastic idle limiter caps have been placed over the mixture screws to prevent tampering with the factory mixture setting. Changing this mixture setting could upset the emissions output. As a result, only idle setting procedures are given below.

L-6

1. Disconnect the fuel tank "EVAP" hose from the vapor storage canister.

2. Disconnect and plug the carburetor-to-vacuum (distributor vacuum) solenoid hose at the solenoid. Disconnect the throttle solenoid wire on 4 bbl manual transmission engines.

3. Set the dwell and timing (in that order) at the specified idle speed.

4. Adjust the carburetor speed screw to obtain the specified idle speed. Do this with the automatic transmission in Drive or the manual in Neutral.

5. On 4 bbl manual transmission models, reconnect the throttle solenoid wire, manually extend the solenoid screw and adjust to the specified idle rpm.

6. Place the automatic transmission in Park or the manual in Neutral and check the fast idle speed with the screw on the top step of the cam. Adjust the fast idle screw to obtain 1,700 rpm.

NOTE: *2 bbl carburetors are not adjustable for fast idle.*

7. Reconnect the distributor vacuum and vapor storage hoses.

C.E.C. Valve Adjustment

This valve is to be adjusted only after the solenoid has been replaced or after the carburetor has been overhauled.

1. With the engine running at the specified slow idle, manually extend the C.E.C. plunger to contact the throttle lever.

2. Adjust the plunger length to obtain 850 rpm for the L-6 (manual), 650 rpm for the L-6 and 307 automatic, 900 rpm for the 307 manual, or 1,000 rpm for the 400 4 bbl and 455 H.O. 4 bbl with manual transmission.

1972

NOTE: *Adjust with the air cleaner installed.*

Plastic idle limiter caps have been placed over the mixture screws to prevent tampering with the factory mixture setting. Changing this mixture setting could upset the emissions output. As a result, only idle setting procedures are given below.

1. Disconnect and plug the carburetor hose to the vapor canister.

2. The choke must be opened fully, the A/C must be turned off, and any disconnected vacuum hoses must be plugged. Automatic transmissions must be placed in Drive while those equipped with manual transmissions must be placed in Neutral.

3. With the engine running at normal operating temperature, adjust the carburetor speed screw to the specified idle speed.

4. On six cylinder models, DO NOT ADJUST the solenoid screw. On V8 4 bbl models, reconnect the throttle solenoid wire, manually extend the solenoid screw and adjust to the specified rpm. On V8 models, merely adjust the carburetor speed screw to the specified rpm.

C.E.C. Adjustment (6 cyl.)

This valve is to be adjusted only after the solenoid has been replaced or after the carburetor has been overhauled.

1. Adjust the slow idle to the specified rpm and manually extend the valve plunger so that it contacts the throttle lever.

2. Adjust the plunger length to get the specified rpm.

1973

NOTE: *Adjust with the air cleaner installed.*

Plastic idle limiter caps have been placed over the mixture screws to prevent tampering with the factory mixture setting. Changing this mixture setting could upset the emissions output. As a result, only idle setting procedures are given below. Idle adjustments must be made with the engine at normal operating temperature, the A/C off, the choke fully opened and any disconnected vacuum hoses plugged.

L-6

1. Disconnect and plug the fuel tank hose from the vapor canister.

2. Disconnect and plug the distributor vacuum hose from the distributor.

3. Set the dwell and then the timing at the rpm specified.

4. With the solenoid not energized, turn the hex screw to obtain the specified low idle.

5. With the solenoid energized, turn the assembly in or out to obtain the specified rpm.

C.E.C. Adjustment (6 cyl.)

This valve is to be adjusted only after the solenoid has been replaced or after the carburetor has been overhauled.

1. Disconnect and plug the distributor vacuum hose. Adjust the slow idle to the specified rpm and manually extend the valve plunger so that it contacts the throttle lever.

2. Adjust the plunger length to get the specified rpm.

3. Place automatic transmission in Park (manual transmission in Neutral) and check the fast idle speed with the fast idle speed screw on top of the fast idle cam. Bend the tang to adjust to the specific rpm.

V8

1. Disconnect and plug the carburetor hose from the vapor canister.

2. Disconnect and plug the distributor and EGR valve vacuum hoses and disconnect the throttle solenoid wire or the idle stop solenoid if so equipped.

3. Set the dwell and then the timing at the specified idle rpm.

4. Adjust the carburetor speed screw to the specified rpm.

5. Reconnect the solenoid wire (idle stop solenoid if so equipped), manually extend the solenoid screw and adjust to the specified rpm.

6. On those cars having automatic transmissions and a 4 bbl carburetor, place the transmission in Park (Neutral for manual transmission) and check the fast idle speed with the fast idle tang on the top step of the fast idle cam. Turn the fast idle speed screw to obtain the specified rpm.

7. Reconnect the hoses.

8. Fast idle speed cannot be adjusted on the 2 bbl carburetor.

Engine Tune-Up

Engine tune-up is a procedure performed to restore engine performance, deteriorated due to normal wear and loss of adjustment. The three major areas considered in a routine tune-up are compression, ignition, and carburetion, although valve adjustment may be included.

A tune-up is performed in three steps: *analysis*, in which it is determined whether normal wear is responsible for performance loss, and which parts require replacement or service; *parts replacement or service*; and *adjustment*, in which engine adjustments are returned to original specifications. Since the advent of emission control equipment, precision adjustment has become increasingly critical, in order to maintain pollutant emission levels.

Analysis

The procedures below are used to indicate where adjustments, parts service or replacement are necessary within the realm of a normal tune-up. If, following these tests, all systems appear to be functioning properly, proceed to the Troubleshooting Section for further diagnosis.

—Remove all spark plugs, noting the cylinder in which they were installed. Remove the air cleaner, and position the throttle and choke in the full open position. Disconnect the coil high tension lead from the coil and the distributor cap. Insert a compression gauge into the spark plug port of each cylinder, in succession, and crank the engine with

Maxi. Press. Lbs. Sq. In.	Min. Press. Lbs. Sq. In.	Max. Press. Lbs. Sq. In.	Min. Press. Lbs. Sq. In.
134	101	188	141
136	102	190	142
138	104	192	144
140	105	194	145
142	107	196	147
146	110	198	148
148	111	200	150
150	113	202	151
152	114	204	153
154	115	206	154
156	117	208	156
158	118	210	157
160	120	212	158
162	121	214	160
164	123	216	162
166	124	218	163
168	126	220	165
170	127	222	166
172	129	224	168
174	131	226	169
176	132	228	171
178	133	230	172
180	135	232	174
182	136	234	175
184	138	236	177
186	140	238	178

Compression pressure limits
© Buick Div. G.M. Corp.)

the starter to obtain the highest possible reading. Record the readings, and compare the highest to the lowest on the compression pressure limit chart. If the difference exceeds the limits on the chart, or if all readings are excessively low, proceed to a wet compression check (see Troubleshooting Section).

—Evaluate the spark plugs according to the spark plug chart in the Troubleshooting Section, and proceed as indicated in the chart.

—Remove the distributor cap, and inspect it inside and out for cracks and/or carbon tracks, and inside for excessive wear or burning of the rotor contacts. If any of these faults are evident, the cap must be replaced.

—Check the breaker points for burning, pitting or wear, and the contact heel resting on the distributor cam for excessive wear. If defects are noted, replace the entire breaker point set.

—Remove and inspect the rotor. If the contacts are burned or worn, or if the rotor is excessively loose on the distributor shaft (where applicable), the rotor must be replaced.

—Inspect the spark plug leads and the coil high tension lead for cracks or brittleness. If any of the wires appear defective, the entire set should be replaced.

—Check the air filter to ensure that it is functioning properly.

Parts Replacement and Service

The determination of whether to replace or service parts is at the mechanic's discretion; however, it is suggested that any parts in questionable condition be replaced rather than reused.

—Clean and regap, or replace, the spark plugs as needed. Lightly coat the threads with engine oil and install the plugs. CAUTION: *Do not over-torque taper-seat spark plugs, or plugs being installed in aluminum cylinder heads.*

—If the distributor cap is to be reused, clean the inside with a dry rag, and remove corrosion from the rotor contact points with fine emery cloth. Remove the spark plug wires one by one, and clean the wire ends and the inside of the towers. If the boots are loose, they should be replaced.

If the cap is to be replaced, transfer the wires one by one, cleaning the wire ends and replacing the boots if necessary.

—If the original points are to remain in service, clean them lightly with emery cloth, lubricate the contact heel with grease specifically designed for this purpose. Rotate the crankshaft until the heel rests on a high point of the distributor cam, and adjust the point gap to specifications.

When replacing the points, remove the original points and condenser, and wipe out the inside of the distributor housing with a clean, dry rag. Lightly lubricate the contact heel and pivot point, and install the points and condenser. Rotate the crankshaft until the heel rests on a high point of the distributor cam, and adjust the point gap to specifications. NOTE: *Always replace the condenser when changing the points.*

—If the rotor is to be reused, clean the contacts with solvent. Do not alter the spring tension of the rotor center contact. Install the rotor and the distributor cap.

—Replace the coil high tension lead and/or the spark plug leads as necessary.

—Clean the carburetor using a spray solvent (e.g., Gumout Spray). Remove the varnish from the throttle bores, and clean the linkage. Disconnect and plug the fuel line, and run the engine until it runs out of fuel. Partially fill the float chamber with solvent, and reconnect the fuel line. In extreme cases, the jets can be pressure flushed by inserting a rubber plug into the float vent, running the spray nozzle through it, and spraying the solvent until it squirts out of the venturi fuel dump.

—Clean and tighten all wiring connections in the primary electrical circuit.

Additional Services

The following services *should* be performed in conjunction with a routine tune-up to ensure efficient performance.

—Inspect the battery and fill to the proper level with distilled water. Remove the cable clamps, clean clamps and posts thoroughly, coat the posts lightly with petroleum jelly, reinstall and tighten.

—Inspect all belts, replace and/or adjust as necessary.

—Test the PCV valve (if so equipped), and clean or replace as indicated. Clean all crankcase ventilation hoses, or replace if cracked or hardened.

—Adjust the valves (if necessary) to manufacturer's specifications.

Adjustments

—Connect a dwell-tachometer between the distributor primary lead and ground. Remove the distributor cap and rotor (unless equipped with Delco externally adjustable distributor). With the ignition off, crank the engine with a remote starter switch and measure the point dwell angle. Adjust the dwell angle to specifications. NOTE: *Increasing the gap decreases the dwell angle and* vice-versa. Install the rotor and distributor cap.

—Connect a timing light according to the manufacturer's specifications. Identify the proper timing marks with chalk or paint. NOTE: *Luminescent (day-glo) paint is excellent for this purpose.* Start the engine, and run it until it reaches operating temperature. Disconnect and plug any distributor vacuum lines, and adjust idle to the speed required to adjust timing, according to specifications. Loosen the distributor clamp and adjust timing to specifications by rotating the distributor in the engine. NOTE: *To advance timing, rotate distributor opposite normal direction of rotor rotation, and vice-versa.*

—Synchronize the throttles and mixture of multiple carburetors (if so equipped) according to procedures given in the individual car sections.

—Adjust the idle speed, mixture, and idle quality, as specified in the car sections. Final idle adjustments should be made with the air cleaner installed. CAUTION: *Due to strict emission control requirements on 1969 and later models, special test equipment (CO meter, SUN Tester) may be necessary to properly adjust idle mixture to specifications.*

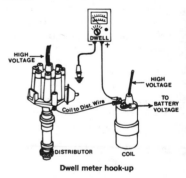

Dwell meter hook-up

Trouble-shooting

The following section is designed to aid in the rapid diagnosis of engine problems. The systematic format is used to diagnose problems ranging from engine starting difficulties to the need for engine overhaul. It is assumed that the user is equipped with basic hand tools and test equipment (tach-dwell meter, timing light, voltmeter, and ohmmeter).

Troubleshooting is divided into two sections. The first, *General Diagnosis*, is used to locate the problem area. In the second, *Specific Diagnosis*, the problem is systematically evaluated.

General Diagnosis

PROBLEM: Symptom	Begin diagnosis at Section Two, Number ————
Engine won't start:	
Starter doesn't turn	1.1, 2.1
Starter turns, engine doesn't	2.1
Starter turns engine very slowly	1.1, 2.4
Starter turns engine normally	3.1, 4.1
Starter turns engine very quickly	6.1
Engine fires intermittently	4.1
Engine fires consistently	5.1, 6.1
Engine runs poorly:	
Hard starting	3.1, 4.1, 5.1, 8.1
Rough idle	4.1, 5.1, 8.1
Stalling	3.1, 4.1, 5.1, 8.1
Engine dies at high speeds	4.1, 5.1
Hesitation (on acceleration from standing stop)	5.1, 8.1
Poor pickup	4.1, 5.1, 8.1
Lack of power	3.1, 4.1, 5.1, 8.1
Backfire through the carburetor	4.1, 8.1, 9.1
Backfire through the exhaust	4.1, 8.1, 9.1
Blue exhaust gases	6.1, 7.1
Black exhaust gases	5.1
Running on (after the ignition is shut off)	3.1, 8.1
Susceptible to moisture	4.1
Engine misfires under load	4.1, 7.1, 8.4, 9.1
Engine misfires at speed	4.1, 8.4
Engine misfires at idle	3.1, 4.1, 5.1, 7.1, 8.4

PROBLEM: Symptom	Probable Cause
Engine noises: ①	
Metallic grind while starting	Starter drive not engaging completely
Constant grind or rumble	*Starter drive not releasing, worn main bearings
Constant knock	Worn connecting rod bearings
Knock under load	Fuel octane too low, worn connecting rod bearings
Double knock	Loose piston pin
Metallic tap	*Collapsed or sticky valve lifter, excessive valve clearance, excessive end play in a rotating shaft
Scrape	*Fan belt contacting a stationary surface
Tick while starting	S.U. electric fuel pump (normal), starter brushes
Constant tick	*Generator brushes, shreaded fan belt
Squeal	*Improperly tensioned fan belt
Hiss or roar	*Steam escaping through a leak in the cooling system or the radiator overflow vent
Whistle	*Vacuum leak
Wheeze	Loose or cracked spark plug

①—It is extremely difficult to evaluate vehicle noises. While the above are general definitions of engine noises, those starred (*) should be considered as possibly originating elsewhere in the car. To aid diagnosis, the following list considers other potential sources of these sounds.

Metallic grind:
　Throwout bearing; transmission gears, bearings, or synchronizers; differential bearings, gears; something metallic in contact with brake drum or disc.

Metallic tap:
　U-joints; fan-to-radiator (or shroud) contact.

Scrape:
　Brake shoe or pad dragging; tire to body contact; suspension contacting undercarriage or exhaust; something non-metallic contacting brake shoe or drum.

Tick:
　Transmission gears; differential gears; lack of radio suppression; resonant vibration of body panels; windshield wiper motor or transmission; heater motor and blower.

Squeal:
　Brake shoe or pad not fully releasing; tires (excessive wear, uneven wear, improper inflation); front or rear wheel alignment (most commonly due to improper toe-in).

Hiss or whistle:
　Wind leaks (body or window); heater motor and blower fan.

Roar:
　Wheel bearings; wind leaks (body and window).

Specific Diagnosis

This section is arranged so that following each test, instructions are given to proceed to another, until a problem is diagnosed.

INDEX

*—The engine need not be running.
**—The engine must be running.

SAMPLE SECTION

Test and Procedure	Results and Indications	Proceed to
4.1—Check for spark: Hold each spark plug wire approximately ¼″ from ground with gloves or a heavy, dry rag. Crank the engine and observe the spark.	If no spark is evident: →	4.2
	If spark is good in some cases: →	4.3
	If spark is good in all cases: →	4.6

DIAGNOSIS

1.1—Inspect the battery visually for case condition (corrosion, cracks) and water level.	If case is cracked, replace battery:	1.4
	If the case is intact, remove corrosion with a solution of baking soda and water (CAUTION: *do not get the solution into the battery*), and fill with water:	1.2
1.2—Check the battery cable connections: Insert a screwdriver between the battery post and the cable clamp. Turn the headlights on high beam, and observe them as the screwdriver is gently twisted to ensure good metal to metal contact. 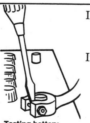 **Testing battery cable connections using a screwdriver**	If the lights brighten, remove and clean the clamp and post; coat the post with petroleum jelly, install and tighten the clamp:	1.4
	If no improvement is noted:	1.3

1.3—Test the state of charge of the battery using an individual cell tester or hydrometer.

Spec. Grav. Reading	Charged Condition
1.260-1.280	Fully Charged
1.230-1.250	Three Quarter Charged
1.200-1.220	One Half Charged
1.170-1.190	One Quarter Charged
1.140-1.160	Just About Flat
1.110-1.130	All The Way Down

State of battery charge

If indicated, charge the battery. NOTE: *If no obvious reason exists for the low state of charge (i.e., battery age, prolonged storage), the charging system should be tested:* 1.4

The effect of temperature on the specific gravity of battery electrolyte

Test and Procedure	*Results and Indications*	*Proceed to*
1.4—Visually inspect battery cables for cracking, bad connection to ground, or bad connection to starter.	If necessary, tighten connections or replace the cables:	2.1

Tests in Group 2 are performed with coil high tension lead disconnected to prevent accidental starting.

2.1—Test the starter motor and solenoid: Connect a jumper from the battery post of the solenoid (or relay) to the starter post of the solenoid (or relay).	If starter turns the engine normally:	2.2
	If the starter buzzes, or turns the engine very slowly:	2.4
	If no response, replace the solenoid (or relay).	3.1
	If the starter turns, but the engine doesn't, ensure that the flywheel ring gear is intact. If the gear is undamaged, replace the starter drive.	3.1
2.2—Determine whether ignition override switches are functioning properly (clutch start switch, neutral safety switch), by connecting a jumper across the switch(es), and turning the ignition switch to "start".	If starter operates, adjust or replace switch:	3.1
	If the starter doesn't operate:	2.3
2.3—Check the ignition switch "start" position: Connect a 12V test lamp between the starter post of the solenoid (or relay) and ground. Turn the ignition switch to the "start" position, and jiggle the key.	If the lamp doesn't light when the switch is turned, check the ignition switch for loose connections, cracked insulation, or broken wires. Repair or replace as necessary:	3.1
	If the lamp flickers when the key is jiggled, replace the ignition switch.	3.3

Checking the ignition switch "start" position

2.4—Remove and bench test the starter, according to specifications in the car section.	If the starter does not meet specifications, repair or replace as needed:	3.1
	If the starter is operating properly:	2.5
2.5—Determine whether the engine can turn freely: Remove the spark plugs, and check for water in the cylinders. Check for water on the dipstick, or oil in the radiator. Attempt to turn the engine using an 18" flex drive and socket on the crankshaft pulley nut or bolt.	If the engine will turn freely only with the spark plugs out, and hydrostatic lock (water in the cylinders) is ruled out, check valve timing:	9.2
	If engine will not turn freely, and it is known that the clutch and transmission are free, the engine must be disassembled for further evaluation:	Next Chapter

Tests and Procedures	*Results and Indications*	*Proceed to*
3.1—Check the ignition switch "on" position: Connect a jumper wire between the distributor side of the coil and ground, and a 12V test lamp between the switch side of the coil and ground. Remove the high tension lead from the coil. Turn the ignition switch on and jiggle the key.	If the lamp lights:	3.2
	If the lamp flickers when the key is jiggled, replace the ignition switch:	3.3
	If the lamp doesn't light, check for loose or open connections. If none are found, remove the ignition switch and check for continuity. If the switch is faulty, replace it:	3.3

Checking the ignition switch "on" position

3.2—Check the ballast resistor or resistance wire for an open circuit, using an ohmmeter.	Replace the resistor or the resistance wire if the resistance is zero.	3.3
3.3—Visually inspect the breaker points for burning, pitting, or excessive wear. Gray coloring of the point contact surfaces is normal. Rotate the crankshaft until the contact heel rests on a high point of the distributor cam, and adjust the point gap to specifications.	If the breaker points are intact, clean the contact surfaces with fine emery cloth, and adjust the point gap to specifications. If pitted or worn, replace the points and condenser, and adjust the gap to specifications: NOTE: *Always lubricate the distributor cam according to manufacturer's recommendations when servicing the breaker points.*	3.4
3.4—Connect a dwell meter between the distributor primary lead and ground. Crank the engine and observe the point dwell angle.	If necessary, adjust the point dwell angle: NOTE: *Increasing the point gap decreases the dwell angle, and vice-versa.*	3.6
	If dwell meter shows little or no reading:	3.5

Dwell meter hook-up

Dwell angle

3.5—Check the condenser for short: Connect an ohmmeter across the condenser body and the pigtail lead.	If any reading other than infinite resistance is noted, replace the condenser:	3.6

Checking the condenser for short

Test and Procedure	Results and Indications	Proceed to
3.6—Test the coil primary resistance: Connect an ohmmeter across the coil primary terminals, and read the resistance on the low scale. Note whether an external ballast resistor or resistance wire is utilized. 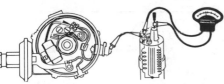 **Testing the coil primary resistance**	Coils utilizing ballast resistors or resistance wires should have approximately 1.0Ω resistance; coils with internal resistors should have approximately 4.0Ω resistance. If values far from the above are noted, replace the coil:	4.1
4.1—Check for spark: Hold each spark plug wire approximately $\frac{1}{4}$" from ground with gloves or a heavy, dry rag. Crank the engine, and observe the spark.	If no spark is evident:	4.2
	If spark is good in some cylinders:	4.3
	If spark is good in all cylinders:	4.6
4.2—Check for spark at the coil high tension lead: Remove the coil high tension lead from the distributor and position it approximately $\frac{1}{4}$" from ground. Crank the engine and observe spark. CAUTION: *This test should not be performed on cars equipped with transistorized ignition.*	If the spark is good and consistent:	4.3
	If the spark is good but intermittent, test the primary electrical system starting at 3.3:	3.3
	If the spark is weak or non-existent, replace the coil high tension lead, clean and tighten all connections and retest. If no improvement is noted:	4.4
4.3—Visually inspect the distributor cap and rotor for burned or corroded contacts, cracks, carbon tracks, or moisture. Also check the fit of the rotor on the distributor shaft (where applicable).	If moisture is present, dry thoroughly, and retest per 4.1:	4.1
	If burned or excessively corroded contacts, cracks, or carbon tracks are noted, replace the defective part(s) and retest per 4.1:	4.1
	If the rotor and cap appear intact, or are only slightly corroded, clean the contacts thoroughly (including the cap towers and spark plug wire ends) and retest per 4.1: If the spark is good in all cases: If the spark is poor in all cases:	4.6 4.5
4.4—Check the coil secondary resistance: Connect an ohmmeter across the distributor side of the coil and the coil tower. Read the resistance on the high scale of the ohmmeter.	The resistance of a satisfactory coil should be between $4K\Omega$ and $10K\Omega$. If the resistance is considerably higher (i.e., $40K\Omega$) replace the coil, and retest per 4.1: NOTE: *This does not apply to high performance coils.*	4.1

Testing the coil secondary resistance

Test and Procedure	Results and Indications	Proceed to
4.5—Visually inspect the spark plug wires for cracking or brittleness. Ensure that no two wires are positioned so as to cause induction firing (adjacent and parallel). Remove each wire, one by one, and check resistance with an ohmmeter.	Replace any cracked or brittle wires. If any of the wires are defective, replace the entire set. Replace any wires with excessive resistance (over 8000Ω per foot for suppression wire), and separate any wires that might cause induction firing.	4.6
4.6—Remove the spark plugs, noting the cylinders from which they were removed, and evaluate according to the chart below.	See below.	See below.

	Condition	Cause	Remedy	Proceed to
	Electrodes eroded, light brown deposits.	Normal wear. Normal wear is indicated by approximately .001″ wear per 1000 miles.	Clean and regap the spark plug if wear is not excessive: Replace the spark plug if excessively worn:	4.7
	Carbon fouling (black, dry, fluffy deposits).	If present on one or two plugs:		
		Faulty high tension lead(s).	Test the high tension leads:	4.5
		Burnt or sticking valve(s).	Check the valve train: (Clean and regap the plugs in either case.)	9.1
		If present on most or all plugs: Overly rich fuel mixture, due to restricted air filter, improper carburetor adjustment, improper choke or heat riser adjustment or operation.	Check the fuel system:	5.1
	Oil fouling (wet black deposits).	Worn engine components. NOTE: *Oil fouling may occur in new or recently rebuilt engines until broken in.*	Check engine vacuum and compression: Replace with new spark plug	6.1
	Lead fouling (gray, black, tan, or yellow deposits, which appear glazed or cinderlike).	Combustion by-products.	Clean and regap the plugs: (Use plugs of a different heat range if the problem recurs.)	4.7

	Condition	Cause	Remedy	Proceed to
	Gap bridging (deposits lodged between the electrodes).	Incomplete combustion, or transfer of deposits from the combustion chamber.	Replace the spark plugs:	4.7
	Overheating (burnt electrodes, and extremely white insulator with small black spots).	Ignition timing advanced too far.	Adjust timing to specifications:	8.2
		Overly lean fuel mixture.	Check the fuel system:	5.1
		Spark plugs not seated properly.	Clean spark plug seat and install a new gasket washer: (Replace the spark plugs in all cases.)	4.7
	Fused spot deposits on the insulator.	Combustion chamber blow-by.	Clean and regap the spark plugs:	4.7
	Pre-ignition (melted or severely burned electrodes, blistered or cracked insulators, or metallic deposits on the insulator).	Incorrect spark plug heat range.	Replace with plugs of the proper heat range:	4.7
		Ignition timing advanced too far.	Adjust timing to specifications:	8.2
		Spark plugs not being cooled efficiently.	Clean the spark plug seat, and check the cooling system:	11.1
		Fuel mixture too lean.	Check the fuel system:	5.1
		Poor compression.	Check compression:	6.1
		Fuel grade too low.	Use higher octane fuel:	4.7

Test and Procedure		Results and Indications	Proceed to
4.7—Determine the static ignition timing: Using the flywheel or crankshaft pulley timing marks as a guide, locate top dead center on the *compression* stroke of the No. 1 cylinder. Remove the distributor cap.		Adjust the distributor so that the rotor points toward the No. 1 tower in the distributor cap, and the points are just opening:	4.8
4.8—Check coil polarity: Connect a voltmeter negative lead to the coil high tension lead, and the positive lead to ground (NOTE: *reverse the hook-up for positive ground cars*). Crank the engine momentarily.		If the voltmeter reads up-scale, the polarity is correct:	5.1
		If the voltmeter reads down-scale, reverse the coil polarity (switch the primary leads):	5.1

Checking coil polarity

Test and Procedure	*Results and Indications*	*Proceed to*
5.1—Determine that the air filter is functioning efficiently: Hold paper elements up to a strong light, and attempt to see light through the filter.	Clean permanent air filters in gasoline (or manufacturer's recommendation), and allow to dry. Replace paper elements through which light cannot be seen:	5.2
5.2—Determine whether a flooding condition exists: Flooding is identified by a strong gasoline odor, and excessive gasoline present in the throttle bore(s) of the carburetor.	If flooding is not evident:	5.3
	If flooding is evident, permit the gasoline to dry for a few moments and restart.	
	If flooding doesn't recur:	5.6
	If flooding is persistant:	5.5
5.3—Check that fuel is reaching the carburetor: Detach the fuel line at the carburetor inlet. Hold the end of the line in a cup (not styrofoam), and crank the engine.	If fuel flows smoothly:	5.6
	If fuel doesn't flow (NOTE: *Make sure that there is fuel in the tank*), or flows erratically:	5.4
5.4—Test the fuel pump: Disconnect all fuel lines from the fuel pump. Hold a finger over the input fitting, crank the engine (with electric pump, turn the ignition or pump on); and feel for suction.	If suction is evident, blow out the fuel line to the tank with low pressure compressed air until bubbling is heard from the fuel filler neck. Also blow out the carburetor fuel line (both ends disconnected):	5.6
	If no suction is evident, replace or repair the fuel pump:	5.6
	NOTE: *Repeated oil fouling of the spark plugs, or a no-start condition, could be the result of a ruptured vacuum booster pump diaphragm, through which oil or gasoline is being drawn into the intake manifold (where applicable).*	
5.5—Check the needle and seat: Tap the carburetor in the area of the needle and seat.	If flooding stops, a gasoline additive (e.g., Gumout) will often cure the problem:	5.6
	If flooding continues, check the fuel pump for excessive pressure at the carburetor (according to specifications). If the pressure is normal, the needle and seat must be removed and checked, and/or the float level adjusted:	5.6
5.6—Test the accelerator pump by looking into the throttle bores while operating the throttle.	If the accelerator pump appears to be operating normally:	5.7
	If the accelerator pump is not operating, the pump must be reconditioned. Where possible, service the pump with the carburetor(s) installed on the engine. If necessary, remove the carburetor. Prior to removal:	5.7
5.7—Determine whether the carburetor main fuel system is functioning: Spray a commercial starting fluid into the carburetor while attempting to start the engine.	If the engine starts, runs for a few seconds, and dies:	5.8
	If the engine doesn't start:	6.1

Test and Procedures	Results and Indications	Proceed to
5.8—Uncommon fuel system malfunctions: See below:	If the problem is solved: If the problem remains, remove and recondition the carburetor.	6.1

Condition	Indication	Test	Usual Weather Conditions	Remedy
Vapor lock	Car will not restart shortly after running.	Cool the components of the fuel system until the engine starts.	Hot to very hot	Ensure that the exhaust manifold heat control valve is operating. Check with the vehicle manufacturer for the recommended solution to vapor lock on the model in question.
Carburetor icing	Car will not idle, stalls at low speeds.	Visually inspect the throttle plate area of the throttle bores for frost.	High humidity, 32-40° F.	Ensure that the exhaust manifold heat control valve is operating, and that the intake manifold heat riser is not blocked.
Water in the fuel	Engine sputters and stalls; may not start.	Pump a small amount of fuel into a glass jar. Allow to stand, and inspect for droplets or a layer of water.	High humidity, extreme temperature changes.	For droplets, use one or two cans of commercial gas dryer (Dry Gas) For a layer of water, the tank must be drained, and the fuel lines blown out with compressed air.

Test and Procedure	Results and Indications	Proceed to
6.1—Test engine compression: Remove all spark plugs. Insert a compression gauge into a spark plug port, crank the engine to obtain the maximum reading, and record.	If compression is within limits on all cylinders:	7.1
	If gauge reading is extremely low on all cylinders:	6.2
	If gauge reading is low on one or two cylinders: (If gauge readings are identical and low on two or more adjacent cylinders, the head gasket must be replaced.)	6.2

Testing compression
(© Chevrolet Div. G.M. Corp.)

Compression pressure limits
(© Buick Div. G.M. Corp.)

Maxi. Press. Lbs. Sq. In.	Min. Press. Lbs. Sq. In.	Maxi. Press. Lbs. Sq. In.	Min. Press. Lbs. Sq. In.	Max. Press. Lbs. Sq. In.	Min. Press. Lbs. Sq. In.	Max. Press. Lbs. Sq. In.	Min. Press. Lbs. Sq. In.
134	101	162	121	188	141	214	160
136	102	164	123	190	142	216	162
138	104	166	124	192	144	218	163
140	105	168	126	194	145	220	165
142	107	170	127	196	147	222	166
146	110	172	129	198	148	224	168
148	111	174	131	200	150	226	169
150	113	176	132	202	151	228	171
152	114	178	133	204	153	230	172
154	115	180	135	206	154	232	174
156	117	182	136	208	156	234	175
158	118	184	138	210	157	236	177
160	120	186	140	212	158	238	178

Test and Procedure	*Results and Indications*	*Proceed to*
6.2—Test engine compression (wet): Squirt approximately 30 cc. of engine oil into each cylinder, and retest per 6.1.	If the readings improve, worn or cracked rings or broken pistons are indicated:	Next Chapter
	If the readings do not improve, burned or excessively carboned valves or a jumped timing chain are indicated:	
	NOTE: *A jumped timing chain is often indicated by difficult cranking.*	7.1
7.1—Perform a vacuum check of the engine: Attach a vacuum gauge to the intake manifold beyond the throttle plate. Start the engine, and observe the action of the needle over the range of engine speeds.	See below.	See below

	Reading	*Indications*	*Proceed to*
	Steady, from 17-22 in. Hg.	Normal.	8.1
	Low and steady.	Late ignition or valve timing, or low compression:	6.1
	Very low	Vacuum leak:	7.2
	Needle fluctuates as engine speed increases.	Ignition miss, blown cylinder head gasket, leaking valve or weak valve spring:	6.1, 8.3
	Gradual drop in reading at idle.	Excessive back pressure in the exhaust system:	10.1
	Intermittent fluctuation at idle.	Ignition miss, sticking valve:	8.3, 9.1
	Drifting needle.	Improper idle mixture adjustment, carburetors not synchronized (where applicable), or minor intake leak. Synchronize the carburetors, adjust the idle, and retest. If the condition persists:	7.2
	High and steady.	Early ignition timing:	8.2

Test and Procedure	Results and Indications	Proceed to
7.2—Attach a vacuum gauge per 7.1, and test for an intake manifold leak. Squirt a small amount of oil around the intake manifold gaskets, carburetor gaskets, plugs and fittings. Observe the action of the vacuum gauge.	If the reading improves, replace the indicated gasket, or seal the indicated fitting or plug: If the reading remains low:	8.1 7.3
7.3—Test all vacuum hoses and accessories for leaks as described in 7.2. Also check the carburetor body (dashpots, automatic choke mechanism, throttle shafts) for leaks in the same manner.	If the reading improves, service or replace the offending part(s): If the reading remains low:	8.1 6.1
8.1—Check the point dwell angle: Connect a dwell meter between the distributor primary wire and ground. Start the engine, and observe the dwell angle from idle to 3000 rpm.	If necessary, adjust the dwell angle. NOTE: *Increasing the point gap reduces the dwell angle and vice-versa.* If the dwell angle moves outside specifications as engine speed increases, the distributor should be removed and checked for cam accuracy, shaft endplay and concentricity, bushing wear, and adequate point arm tension (NOTE: *Most of these items may be checked with the distributor installed in the engine, using an oscilloscope*):	8.2
8.2—Connect a timing light (per manufacturer's recommendation) and check the dynamic ignition timing. Disconnect and plug the vacuum hose(s) to the distributor if specified, start the engine, and observe the timing marks at the specified engine speed.	If the timing is not correct, adjust to specifications by rotating the distributor in the engine: (Advance timing by rotating distributor opposite normal direction of rotor rotation, retard timing by rotating distributor in same direction as rotor rotation.)	8.3
8.3—Check the operation of the distributor advance mechanism(s): To test the mechanical advance, disconnect all but the mechanical advance, and observe the timing marks with a timing light as the engine speed is increased from idle. If the mark moves smoothly, without hesitation, it may be assumed that the mechanical advance is functioning properly. To test vacuum advance and/or retard systems, alternately crimp and release the vacuum line, and observe the timing mark for movement. If movement is noted, the system is operating.	If the systems are functioning: If the systems are not functioning, remove the distributor, and test on a distributor tester:	8.4 8.4
8.4—Locate an ignition miss: With the engine running, remove each spark plug wire, one by one, until one is found that doesn't cause the engine to roughen and slow down.	When the missing cylinder is identified:	4.1

Test and Procedure	Results and Indications	Proceed to
9.1—Evaluate the valve train: Remove the valve cover, and ensure that the valves are adjusted to specifications. A mechanic's stethoscope may be used to aid in the diagnosis of the valve train. By pushing the probe on or near push rods or rockers, valve noise often can be isolated. A timing light also may be used to diagnose valve problems. Connect the light according to manufacturer's recommendations, and start the engine. Vary the firing moment of the light by increasing the engine speed (and therefore the ignition advance), and moving the trigger from cylinder to cylinder. Observe the movement of each valve.	See below	See below

Observation	Probable Cause	Remedy	Proceed to
Metallic tap heard through the stethoscope.	Sticking hydraulic lifter or excessive valve clearance.	Adjust valve. If tap persists, remove and replace the lifter:	10.1
Metallic tap through the stethoscope, able to push the rocker arm (lifter side) down by hand.	Collapsed valve lifter.	Remove and replace the lifter:	10.1
Erratic, irregular motion of the valve stem.*	Sticking valve, burned valve.	Recondition the valve and/or valve guide:	Next Chapter
Eccentric motion of the pushrod at the rocker arm.*	Bent pushrod.	Replace the pushrod:	10.1
Valve retainer bounces as the valve closes.*	Weak valve spring or damper.	Remove and test the spring and damper. Replace if necessary:	10.1

*—When observed with a timing light.

Test and Procedure	Results and Indications	Proceed to
9.2—Check the valve timing: Locate top dead center of the No. 1 piston, and install a degree wheel or tape on the crankshaft pulley or damper with zero corresponding to an index mark on the engine. Rotate the crankshaft in its direction of rotation, and observe the opening of the No. 1 cylinder intake valve. The opening should correspond with the correct mark on the degree wheel according to specifications.	If the timing is not correct, the timing cover must be removed for further investigation:	

Test and Procedure	Results and Indications	Proceed to
10.1—Determine whether the exhaust manifold heat control valve is operating: Operate the valve by hand to determine whether it is free to move. If the valve is free, run the engine to operating temperature and observe the action of the valve, to ensure that it is opening.	If the valve sticks, spray it with a suitable solvent, open and close the valve to free it, and retest. If the valve functions properly: If the valve does not free, or does not operate, replace the valve:	 10.2 10.2
10.2—Ensure that there are no exhaust restrictions: Visually inspect the exhaust system for kinks, dents, or crushing. Also note that gasses are flowing freely from the tailpipe at all engine speeds, indicating no restriction in the muffler or resonator.	Replace any damaged portion of the system:	11.1
11.1—Visually inspect the fan belt for glazing, cracks, and fraying, and replace if necessary. Tighten the belt so that the longest span has approximately ½″ play at its midpoint under thumb pressure. **Checking the fan belt tension** (© Nissan Motor Co. Ltd.)	Replace or tighten the fan belt as necessary:	11.2
11.2—Check the fluid level of the cooling system.	If full or slightly low, fill as necessary: If extremely low:	11.5 11.3
11.3—Visually inspect the external portions of the cooling system (radiator, radiator hoses, thermostat elbow, water pump seals, heater hoses, etc.) for leaks. If none are found, pressurize the cooling system to 14-15 psi.	If cooling system holds the pressure: If cooling system loses pressure rapidly, re-inspect external parts of the system for leaks under pressure. If none are found, check dipstick for coolant in crankcase. If no coolant is present, but pressure loss continues: If coolant is evident in crankcase, remove cylinder head(s), and check gasket(s). If gaskets are intact, block and cylinder head(s) should be checked for cracks or holes. If the gasket(s) is blown, replace, and purge the crankcase of coolant: NOTE: *Occasionally, due to atmospheric and driving conditions, condensation of water can occur in the crankcase. This causes the oil to appear milky white. To remedy, run the engine until hot, and change the oil and oil filter.*	11.5 11.4 12.6

Test and Procedure	*Results and Indication*	*Proceed to*
11.4—Check for combustion leaks into the cooling system: Pressurize the cooling system as above. Start the engine, and observe the pressure gauge. If the needle fluctuates, remove each spark plug wire, one by one, noting which cylinder(s) reduce or eliminate the fluctuation. **Radiator pressure tester** (© American Motors Corp.)	Cylinders which reduce or eliminate the fluctuation, when the spark plug wire is removed, are leaking into the cooling system. Replace the head gasket on the affected cylinder bank(s).	
11.5—Check the radiator pressure cap: Attach a radiator pressure tester to the radiator cap (wet the seal prior to installation). Quickly pump up the pressure, noting the point at which the cap releases. **Testing the radiator pressure cap** (© American Motors Corp.)	If the cap releases within ± 1 psi of the specified rating, it is operating properly: If the cap releases at more than ± 1 psi of the specified rating, it should be replaced:	11.6 11.6
11.6—Test the thermostat: Start the engine cold, remove the radiator cap, and insert a thermometer into the radiator. Allow the engine to idle. After a short while, there will be a sudden, rapid increase in coolant temperature. The temperature at which this sharp rise stops is the thermostat opening temperature.	If the thermostat opens at or about the specified temperature: If the temperature doesn't increase: (If the temperature increases slowly and gradually, replace the thermostat.)	11.7 11.7
11.7—Check the water pump: Remove the thermostat elbow and the thermostat, disconnect the coil high tension lead (to prevent starting), and crank the engine momentarily.	If coolant flows, replace the thermostat and retest per 11.6: If coolant doesn't flow, reverse flush the cooling system to alleviate any blockage that might exist. If system is not blocked, and coolant will not flow, recondition the water pump.	11.6 —
12.1—Check the oil pressure gauge or warning light: If the gauge shows low pressure, or the light is on, for no obvious reason, remove the oil pressure sender. Install an accurate oil pressure gauge and run the engine momentarily.	If oil pressure builds normally, run engine for a few moments to determine that it is functioning normally, and replace the sender. If the pressure remains low: If the pressure surges: If the oil pressure is zero:	— 12.2 12.3 12.3

Test and Procedure	*Results and Indications*	*Proceed to*
12.2—Visually inspect the oil: If the oil is watery or very thin, milky, or foamy, replace the oil and oil filter.	If the oil is normal:	12.3
	If after replacing oil the pressure remains low:	12.3
	If after replacing oil the pressure becomes normal:	—
12.3—Inspect the oil pressure relief valve and spring, to ensure that it is not sticking or stuck. Remove and thoroughly clean the valve, spring, and the valve body.	If the oil pressure improves:	—
	If no improvement is noted:	12.4

Oil pressure relief valve
((© British Leyland Motors)

12.4—Check to ensure that the oil pump is not cavitating (sucking air instead of oil): See that the crankcase is neither over nor underfull, and that the pickup in the sump is in the proper position and free from sludge.	Fill or drain the crankcase to the proper capacity, and clean the pickup screen in solvent if necessary. If no improvement is noted:	12.5
12.5—Inspect the oil pump drive and the oil pump:	If the pump drive or the oil pump appear to be defective, service as necessary and retest per 12.1:	12.1
	If the pump drive and pump appear to be operating normally, the engine should be disassembled to determine where blockage exists:	Next Chapter
12.6—Purge the engine of ethylene glycol coolant: Completely drain the crankcase and the oil filter. Obtain a commercial butyl cellosolve base solvent, designated for this purpose, and follow the instructions precisely. Following this, install a new oil filter and refill the crankcase with the proper weight oil. The next oil and filter change should follow shortly thereafter (1000 miles).		

3 · Engine and Engine Rebuilding

Engine Electrical

DISTRIBUTOR

Three types of distributors are used: An aluminum internal adjustment on the 6-cylinder engines, an aluminum external adjustment on the 8 cylinder engines, and an aluminum unitized ignition distributor.

All distributors include centrifugal and

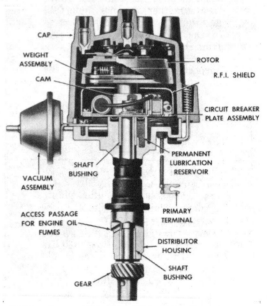

V8 Distributor (© Pontiac Div., G.M. Corp.)

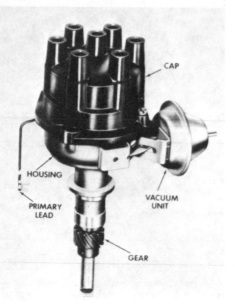

6 Cylinder Distributor (© Pontiac Div., G.M. Corp.)

vacuum advance mechanisms. The centrifugal advance mechanisms are located directly beneath the rotor (V8) or beneath the breaker plate assembly (6-cylinder). It consists of a centrifugal advance cam actuated by two centrifugal weights controlled by small springs. When the engine speed increases, so does the distributor shaft speed causing the weights to be thrown outward against the pull of the springs. This advances the breaker cam and causes the points to open earlier resulting in a spark advance.

Removal and Installation

1. Disconnect the battery ground cable.
2. Remove the distributor cap.
3. Make a reference mark on the distributor housing that aligns with the tip of the rotor. Matchmark the distributor and the engine block. Do not crank the engine after these marks have been made.
4. Disconnect the vacuum line at the distributor.

5. Remove the hold-down clamp.
6. Lift out the distributor.
7. Insert the gasket and then the distributor into the block; the rotor should be moved slightly to one side. This is necessary because of the cut of the gears. As the distributor seats in its bore, the rotor will rotate slightly so that the reference marks will once again be in line.
8. Install the hold-down clamp, the vacuum line, and the distributor cap.
9. Connect the battery cable.

If for some reason, the engine crankshaft

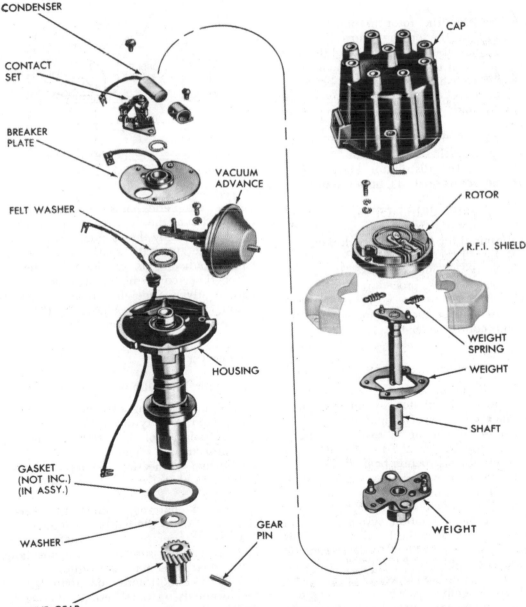

CONDENSER

CONTACT SET

BREAKER PLATE

FELT WASHER

VACUUM ADVANCE

HOUSING

GASKET (NOT INC.) (IN ASSY.)

WASHER

GEAR PIN

DRIVE GEAR

CAP

ROTOR

R.F.I. SHIELD

WEIGHT SPRING

WEIGHT

SHAFT

WEIGHT

Exploded View of V8 Distributor (© Pontiac Div., G.M. Corp.)

was turned during distributor removal, install the distributor as follows:

1. Remove the No. 1 spark plug and hold your finger over the plug hole while an assistant slowly cranks the engine. When the No. 1 piston is at TDC on its compression stroke the pressure will force your finger out of the hole.

2. Replace the distributor-to-block gasket.

3. Install the distributor in the block so that the vacuum diaphragm faces the left side of the engine on V8 engines, and to the front of the engine on 6 cylinder engines.

4. Position the rotor to point toward the front of the engine. Turn the rotor counterclockwise about one-eighth of a turn and push the distributor down to engage the camshaft drive. It may be necessary to move the rotor one way or the other to mesh the drive and driven gears properly.

5. Install the hold-down clamp and snug up the bolt.

6. Turn the distributor body slightly until the points open. Tighten the distributor hold-down bolt.

7. Place the distributor cap in position and see that the rotor lines up with the cap terminal for the No. 1 spark plug.

8. Install the cap.

9. Start the engine and set the timing according to the procedure in Chapter Two.

10. Reconnect the vacuum hose to the vacuum control assembly.

Unitized Ignition System

First offered in 1971, this system consists of a special distributor, an ignition pulse amplifier, and a special ignition coil. The distributor is similar in external appearance to the standard V8 distributor, but the internal construction bears little resemblance to the contact point unit. The ignition coil and control module are attached to the distributor body, making for a compact, one-piece ignition system. An iron timer core replaces the breaker cam. This eight-lobed timer rotates inside a magnetic pick-up assembly, which replaces the contact points and condenser. The magnetic pick-up assembly consists of a ceramic permanent magnet, a steel pole piece, and a pick-up coil.

Firing Order

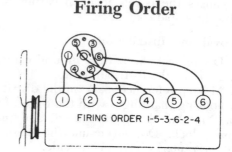

6 Cylinder (© Pontiac Div., G.M. Corp.)

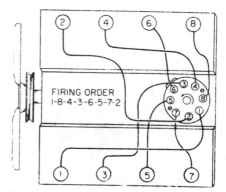

V8 (© Pontiac Div., G.M. Corp.)

The magnetic pick-up assembly is mounted over the distributor shaft bearing and is rotated by the vacuum advance unit to provide automatic spark advance. Centrifugal advance is provided by the rotating timer core which is attached to the normal advance weights. Removal, installation, and timing procedures are the same as the standard distributor.

ALTERNATOR

Alternator Precautions

1. When installing a battery, ensure that the ground polarity of the battery and the ground polarity of the alternator and the regulator are the same.

2. When connecting a jumper battery, be certain that the correct terminals are connected.

3. When charging, connect the correct charger leads to the battery terminals.

4. Never operate the alternator on an open circuit. Be sure that all connections in the charging circuit are tight.

5. Do not short across or ground any of the terminals on the alternator or regulator.

6. Never polarize an AC system.

Removal and Installation

1. Disconnect the negative battery cable.

2. Remove the alternator wires or the connector.

3. Loosen the adjusting bolt.

4. Remove the V-belt. Remove or loosen power steering, A.I.R., and A.C. belts as necessary. On power steering equipped six-cylinder models, loosen the A.I.R. pump.

5. Remove the alternator retaining bolts or through bolt.

6. Remove the alternator.

7. To install, reverse the removal procedure. Tighten the bracket bolt on non-A/C cars to 10–25 ft lbs, all other bolts to 25–35 ft lbs.

Belt Tension Adjustment

See "Drive Belts" under "Routine Maintenance" in Chapter One.

REGULATOR

From 1968 through 1970, all A body cars (Tempest, LeMans, T-37, GTO) used a mechanical regulator mounted on the fire-wall. Beginning with the 1971 models, the regulator is a solid state unit contained

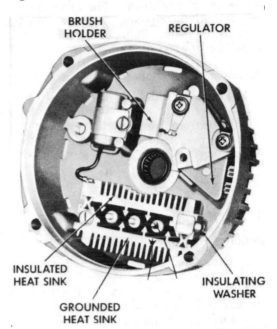

Regulator Posistron, 1971–73 (© Pontiac Div., G.M. Corp.)

Alternator and Regulator Specification Chart

Year	Alternator Part No. or Manufacturer	Field Current @ 12 V	Output (amps)	Regulator Part No. or Manufacturer	Field Relay Air Gap (in.)	Point Gap (in.)	Volts to Close	Regulator Air Gap (in.)	Point Gap (in.)	Volts @ 75°
1968–69	1100761	2.2–2.6	37	1119515	0.015	0.030	1.5–3.2	0.067	0.014	13.5–16.0
	1100704	2.2–2.6	37	1119515	0.015	0.030	1.5–3.2	0.067	0.014	13.5–16.0
	1100832③	4.0–4.5	37	1119515	0.015	0.030	1.5–3.2	0.067	0.014	13.5–16.0
	1100830③	4.0–4.5	37	1119515	0.015	0.030	1.5–3.2	0.067	0.014	13.5–16.0
	1100700	2.2–2.6	55	1119515	0.015	0.030	1.5–3.2	0.067	0.014	13.5–16.0
	1100760	2.2–2.6	55	1119515	0.015	0.030	1.5–3.2	0.007	0.014	13.5–16.0
1970	1100704	2.2–2.6	37	1119515②	0.015	0.030	1.5–3.2	0.067	0.014	13.5–16.0
	1100888	2.2–2.6	37	1119515	0.015	0.030	1.5–3.2	0.067	0.014	13.5–16.0
	1100950	2.2–2.6	37	1119515	0.015	0.030	1.5–3.2	0.067	0.014	13.5–16.0
	1100700	2.2–2.6	55	1119515	0.015	0.030	1.5–3.2	0.067	0.014	13.5–16.0
	1100891	2.2–2.6	55	1119515	0.015	0.030	1.5–3.2	0.067	0.014	13.5–16.0
	1100906	2.2–2.6	55	1119515	0.015	0.030	1.5–3.2	0.067	0.014	13.5–16.0
	1100906	2.2–2.6	55	1119515	0.015	0.030	1.5–3.2	0.067	0.014	13.5–16.0
	1100895	2.2–2.6	61	1119515	0.015	0.030	1.5–3.2	0.067	0.014	13.5–16.0
1971–73	1100927	4.0–4.5	37	——	Integral with Alternator			Integral with Alternator		
	1100920	4.0–4.5	55	——	Integral with Alternator			Integral with Alternator		
	1100928	4.0–4.5	55	——	Integral with Alternator			Integral with Alternator		
	11001015	4.0–4.5	80	——	Integral with Alternator			Integral with Alternator		

② Transistor regulator 1116368 optional equipment until 1970

③ Integrated Circuit Generator (C.S.I.—no external regulator)

within the alternator. Unlike the earlier externally mounted unit, this regulator has no means of adjustment. The following removal and installation procedure applies only to the externally mounted mechanical regulator of 1968 through 1970.

Removal and Installation

1. Disconnect the battery ground cable.
2. Disconnect the wiring harness connector from the regulator.
3. Remove the regulator mounting screws.
4. Remove the regulator.
5. Reverse the procedure to install.

STARTER

Removal and Installation

1. Disconnect the negative battery cable.
2. On V8 models, jack up the front of the car and place jackstands under the car.
3. Disconnect the solenoid wires.
4. Disconnect the starter brace, if so equipped.
5. Remove the mounting bolts and remove the starter.
6. Reverse the procedures to install.

Starter Drive

REMOVAL AND INSTALLATION

1. Disconnect the field straps from the solenoid terminal.
2. Remove the through bolts.
3. Remove the commutator end frame, the field frame, and armature from the drive housing.
4. Remove the starter drive from the armature shaft in the following manner:
    a. Slide the thrust collar from the end of the armature shaft.
    b. Slide a ½ in. piece of pipe coupling or other spacer onto the shaft so that the end of the coupling hits against the edge of the retainer.

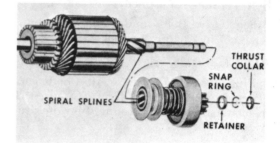

Starter Drive Assembly (© Pontiac Div., G.M. Corp.)

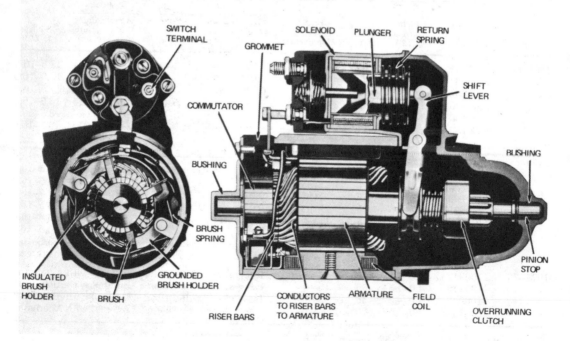

. Starter Motor, Cross Section (© Pontiac Div., G.M. Corp.)

c. Tap the end of the coupling with a hammer so that the retainer moves toward the armature end of the snap-ring.

d. Remove the snap-ring from its groove in the shaft. Slide the assembly from the shaft.

5. To install, assemble the starter drive to the shaft in the following manner:

a. Lubricate the drive end of the shaft with silicone lubricant.

b. Slide the clutch assembly onto the shaft with the pinion outward.

c. Slide the retainer onto the shaft with the cupped surface facing away from the pinion.

d. Stand the armature up on a wooden surface with the commutator facing down. Position the snap-ring on the upper end of the shaft and drive it onto the shaft with a small block of wood and a hammer. Slide the snap-ring into its groove.

e. Install the thrust collar onto the shaft with the shoulder next to the snap-ring.

f. With the retainer on one side of the snap-ring and the thrust collar on the other side, squeeze together with two sets of pliers until the ring seats in the retainer. On those models without the thrust collar, use a washer. Remember to remove the washer before continuing.

6. Lubricate the drive end bushing with lubricant, then slide the armature and clutch assembly into place, at the same time engaging the shift lever with the clutch.

7. Position the field frame over the armature and apply sealer between the frame and the solenoid case. Position the frame against the drive housing, making sure that you don't damage the brushes.

8. Lubricate the commutator end bushing with silicone lubricant. Place a leather brake washer on the armature shaft and slide the commutator end frame onto the shaft. Install the through bolts and tighten them to 65 in lbs.

9. Reconnect the field coil connector(s) to the solenoid motor terminal.

BATTERY

Removal and Installation

1. Remove both battery cables from the battery.

2. Remove the battery clamp.

3. Lift out the battery being careful not to spill any electrolyte.

4. To install, reverse the removal procedure. Be sure to install the cables correctly.

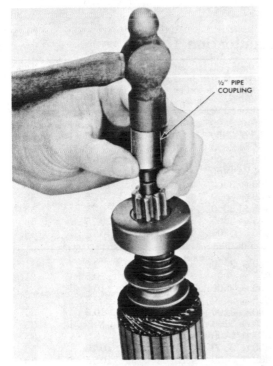

Removing Snap-Ring (© Pontiac Div., G.M. Corp.)

½" PIPE COUPLING

Engine Mechanical

DESIGN

Both six and eight cylinder engines are available in the Tempest and the LeMans, but the V8 is standard equipment in the GTO. The six cylinder engine of 1968 and 1969 is an inline overhead camshaft design. The camshaft is mounted above the valve assembly and, as the cam turns, its lobes push down on the rocker arms below it. The rocker arm contacts the valve stem and pushes the valve downward. It has no valve lifters but stationary hydraulic lash adjusters instead which are located in the cylinder head. A timing belt located outside of the crankcase connects the cam sprocket with the crankshaft sprocket and accessory drive sprocket. The timing belt and its mechanism is contained within an aluminum cover. An aluminum accessory

Battery and Starter Specification Chart

Year	Engine Cu In. Displacement	Battery			Starter				Brush Spring Tension (oz)
		Ampere Hour Capacity	Volts	Terminal Grounded	No-Load Test				
					Amps	Volts	RPM		
68–69	6	44①	12	Neg	49–76	10.6	6,200–9,600		35
	8-350	53①	12	Neg	65–100	10.6	3,600–5,100		35
	8-400	61	12	Neg	Not Recommended				35
70–73	6	45①	12	Neg	Not Recommended				35
	8-350	53	12	Neg	Not Recommended				35
	80400, 455	61①	12	Neg	Not Recommended				35

① 61 amp. battery used w/AC or H.D. battery option

drive housing assembly is mounted to the side of the block. This housing contains the accessory drive sprocket which is attached to a shaft. The timing belt rides on this sprocket and turns it along with the shaft. Mounted on the shaft is a gear that operates the fuel pump, the oil pump, and the distributor. Attached to this drive housing assembly is the distributor, the fuel pump, the oil pump, and the oil filter assembly.

1969 was the last year for the OHC six cylinder. In 1970, it was replaced with the conventional overhead valve (OHV) six cylinder engine (L6). The camshaft is supported by four bearings and is driven at one half crankshaft speed. The crankshaft is supported by seven main bearings. This engine is basically the same as the Chevrolet 250 cu in. engine.

In 1968, an all new 350 cu in. engine of Pontiac design was introduced. This engine is used as the standard base engine up to the present. Optional engines are 400 and, beginning in 1970, 455 cu in. versions of the Pontiac V8. All of these engines are similar and, in fact, the basic design is much like that of the 370 cu in. version introduced in 1958.

General Engine Specification Chart

Year	Engine Cu In. Displacement	Carburetor Type	Horsepower @ rpm	Torque @ rpm (ft lbs)	Bore x Stroke (in.)	Compression Ratio	Oil Pressure (psi) @ rpm
1968	6-250 OHC	1 bbl	175 @ 4800	240 @ 2600	3.8762 x 3.530	9.0 : 1	31①
	6-250 OHC	4 bbl	215 @ 5200	255 @ 3800	3.8762 x 3.530	10.5 : 1	31①
	8-350	2 bbl	265 @ 4600	355 @ 2800	3.8762 x 3.750	9.2 : 1	35
	8-350 HO	4 bbl	320 @ 5100	380 @ 3200	3.8762 x 3.750	10.5 : 1	35
	8-400	2 bbl	265 @ 4600	397 @ 2400	4.1212 x 3.750	8.6 : 1	58
	8-400	4 bbl	330 @ 4800	430 @ 3300	4.1212 x 3.750	10.75 : 1	58
	8-400 Ram Air	4 bbl	335 @ 5300	430 @ 3600	4.1212 x 3.750	10.75 : 1	58
	8-400	4 bbl	350 @ 5000	445 @ 3000	4.1212 x 3.750	10.75 : 1	58
	8-400 HO	4 bbl	360 @ 5100	445 @ 3600	4.1212 x 3.750	10.75 : 1	58
	8-400 Ram Air	4 bbl	360 @ 5400	445 @ 3800	4.1212 x 3.750	10.75 : 1	58
1969	6-250 OHC	1 bbl	175 @ 4800	240 @ 2600	3.8762 x 3.530	9.0 : 1	31①
	6-250 OHC	4 bbl	215 @ 5200	255 @ 3000	3.8762 x 3.530	10.5 : 1	31①
	6-250 OHC	4 bbl	230 @ 5400	260 @ 3600	3.8762 x 3.530	10.5 : 1	31①
	8-350	2 bbl	265 @ 4600	325 @ 2800	3.8762 x 3.750	9.2 : 1	35
	8-350	4 bbl	325 @ 5100	380 @ 3200	3.8762 x 3.750	10.5 : 1	35
	8-350	4 bbl	330 @ 5100	380 @ 3200	3.8762 x 3.750	10.5 : 1	35
	8-400	2 bbl	265 @ 4600	397 @ 2400	4.1212 x 3.750	8.6 : 1	35
	8-400	4 bbl	330 @ 4800	430 @ 3300	4.1212 x 3.750	10.75 : 1	58
	8-400 HO	4 bbl	335 @ 5000	430 @ 3400	4.1212 x 3.750	10.75 : 1	58
	8-400 Ram Air	4 bbl	345 @ 5400	430 @ 3700	4.1212 x 3.750	10.75 : 1	58

General Engine Specification Chart (cont.)

Year	Engine Cu In. Displacement	Carburetor Type	Horsepower @ rpm	Torque @ rpm (ft lbs)	Bore x Stroke (in.)	Compression Ratio	Oil Pressure (psi) @ rpm
1969	8-400 Ram Air	4 bbl	366 @ 5100	445 @ 3600	4.1212 x 3.750	10.75 : 1	58
	8-400 Ram Air IV	4 bbl	370 @ 5500	445 @ 3900	4.1212 x 3.750	10.75 : 1	58
1970	6-250	1 bbl	155 @ 4200	235 @ 1600	3.8762 x 3.530	8.5 : 1	53②
	8-350	2 bbl	255 @ 4600	355 @ 2800	3.8762 x 3.750	8.8 : 1	35
	8-400	2 bbl	265 @ 4600	397 @ 2400	4.1212 x 3.750	8.8 : 1	35
	8-400	4 bbl	330 @ 4800	430 @ 3000	4.1212 x 3.750	10.25 : 1③	35
	8-400 Ram Air	4 bbl	345 @ 5000	430 @ 3400	4.1212 x 3.750	10.5 : 1	35
	8-400	4 bbl	350 @ 4800	445 @ 2900	4.1212 x 3.750	10.0 : 1	35
	8-400	4 bbl	366 @ 5100	445 @ 3600	4.1212 x 3.750	10.5 : 1	35
	8-400	4 bbl	370 @ 5500	445 @ 3900	4.1212 x 3.750	10.5 : 1	35
	8-455	4 bbl	360 @ 4600	500 @ 3100	4.1522 x 4.210	10.25 : 1	35
1971	6-250	1 bbl	145 @ 4200	230 @ 1600	3.8750 x 3.530	8.5 : 1	38④
	8-350	2 bbl	250 @ 4400	350 @ 2400	3.8762 x 3.750	8.0 : 1	35
	8-400	2 bbl	265 @ 4400	400 @ 2400	4.1212 x 3.750	8.2 : 1	58
	8-400	4 bbl	300 @ 4800	400 @ 3600	4.1212 x 3.750	8.2 : 1	58
	8-455	4 bbl	325 @ 4400	455 @ 3200	4.1522 x 4.210	8.2 : 1	35
	8-455 HO	4 bbl	335 @ 4800	480 @ 3600	4.1522 x 4.210	8.4 : 1	35
1972	6-250	1 bbl	110 @ 3800	185 @ 1600	3.8750 x 3.530	8.5 : 1	40②
	8-350	2 bbl	160 @ 4400	270 @ 2000	3.8762 x 3.750	8.2 : 1	35
	8-400	2 bbl	175 @ 4000	310 @ 2400	4.1212 x 3.750	8.2 : 1	35
	8-400	4 bbl	200 @ 4000	295 @ 2800	4.1212 x 3.750	8.2 : 1	35
	8-400	4 bbl	250 @ 4400	325 @ 3200	4.1212 x 3.750	8.2 : 1	35
	8-455	4 bbl	250 @ 3600	375 @ 2400	4.1522 x 4.210	8.2 : 1	35
	8-455	4 bbl	300 @ 4000	415 @ 3200	4.1522 x 4.210	8.4 : 1	35
1973	6-250	1 bbl	110 @ 3800	185 @ 1600	3.8750 x 3.530	8.5 : 1	40
	8-350 SE	2 bbl	150 @ 4000	270 @ 2000	3.8762 x 3.750	7.6 : 1	35
	8-350 DE	2 bbl	175 @ 4400	280 @ 2400	3.8762 x 3.750	7.6 : 1	35
	8-400 SE	2 bbl	170 @ 3600	320 @ 2000	4.1212 x 3.750	8.0 : 1	35
	8-400 DE	2 bbl	185 @ 4000	320 @ 2400	4.1212 x 3.750	8.0 : 1	35
	8-400 SE	4 bbl	200 @ 4000	310 @ 2400	4.1212 x 3.750	8.0 : 1	35
	8-400 DE	4 bbl	230 @ 4400	325 @ 3200	4.1212 x 3.750	8.0 : 1	35
	8-455 SE	4 bbl	215 @ 3600	350 @ 2400	4.1522 x 4.210	8.0 : 1	35
	8-455 DE	4 bbl	250 @ 4000	370 @ 2800	4.1522 x 4.210	8.0 : 1	35
	8-455 S.D. DE	4 bbl	310 @ 4000	390 @ 3600	4.1522 x 4.210	8.4 : 1	35

① Oil Pressure at 2800 rpm
② Oil Pressure at 2000 rpm
③ For vehicles equipped with automatic transmissions, advertised compression ratio is 10.0 :1
④ Oil Pressure at 1500 rpm

HO High Output
OHC Overhead Cam
SE Single Exhaust
DE Dual Exhaust

Valve Specification Chart

Year	Engine Cu In. Displacement	Seat Angle (deg)	Face Angle (deg)	Spring Test Pressure (lbs @ in.)	Spring Installed Height (in.)	Stem to Guide Clearance (in.)		Stem Diameter (in.)	
						Intake	Exhaust	Intake	Exhaust
1968	6-250 1 bbl	30	29	98 @ 1.63	1⅝	0.0016–0.0033	0.0021–0.0038	0.3416	0.3416
	6-250 4 bbl	30	29	65 @ 1.63	1⅝	0.0016–0.0033	0.0021–0.0038	0.3416	0.3411
	8-350	30	29	63 @ 1.58	1³⁷⁄₆₄	0.0016–0.0033	0.0021–0.0038	0.3416	0.3411
	8-400 2 bbl	30	29	63 @ 1.58	1³⁷⁄₆₄	0.0016–0.0033	0.0021–0.0038	0.3416	0.3411
	8-400 4 bbl①	30	29	66 @ 1.56	1⁹⁄₁₆	0.0016–0.0033	0.0021–0.0038	0.3416	0.3411
	8-400 R.A.	30	29	76 @ 1.71	1²³⁄₃₆	0.0016–0.0033	0.0021–0.0038	0.3416	0.3411

Valve Specification Chart (cont.)

Year	Engine Cu In. Displacement	Seat Angle (deg)	Face Angle (deg)	Spring Test Pressure (lbs @ in.)	Spring Installed Height (in.)	Stem to Guide Clearance (in.)		Stem Diameter (in.)	
						Intake	Exhaust	Intake	Exhaust
1969	6-250 1 bbl	45	44	98 @ 1.63	$1\frac{5}{8}$	0.0016–0.0033	0.0021–0.0038	0.3416	0.3411
	6-250 4 bbl	45	44	65 @ 1.63	$1\frac{5}{8}$	0.0016–0.0033	0.0021–0.0038	0.3416	0.3411
	8-350 2 bbl	45	44	63 @ 1.58	$1\frac{37}{64}$	0.0016–0.0033	0.0021–0.0038	0.3416	0.3411
	8-350 4 bbl	45	44	83 @ 1.59	$1\frac{19}{32}$	0.0016–0.0033	0.0021–0.0038	0.3416	0.3411
	8-400 2 bbl	30	29	63 @ 1.58	$1\frac{37}{64}$	0.0016–0.0033	0.0021–0.0038	0.3416	0.3411
	8-400 4 bbl	30	29	66 @ 1.56	$1\frac{5}{8}$	0.0016–0.0033	0.0021–0.0038	0.3416	0.3411
	8-400 R.A.	30	29	83 @ 1.59	$1\frac{19}{32}$	0.0016–0.0032	0.0021–0.0038	0.3416	0.3411
	8-400 R.A. IV	30	29	75 @ 1.82	$1\frac{53}{64}$	0.0016–0.0033	0.0021–0.0038	0.3416	0.3411
1970	6-250 1 bbl	46④	45⑤	60 @ 1.66	$1\frac{21}{32}$	0.0010–0.0027	0.0021–0.0027	0.3414	0.3414
	8-350 2 bbl	45	44	63 @ 1.58	$1\frac{37}{64}$	0.0010–0.0033	0.0021–0.0038	0.3416	0.3416
	8-400 2 bbl	45	44	63 @ 1.58	$1\frac{37}{64}$	0.0016–0.0033	0.0021–0.0038	0.3416	0.3411
	8-400 4 bbl②	30	29	61 @ 1.59	$1\frac{19}{32}$	0.0016–0.0033	0.0021–0.0038	0.3416	0.3411
	8-400 4 bbl③	30	29	66 @ 1.56	$1\frac{9}{16}$	0.0016–0.0033	0.0021–0.0038	0.3416	0.3416
	8-400 R.A. IV	30	29	76 @ 1.82	$1\frac{13}{16}$	0.0016–0.0033	0.0021–0.0038	0.3416	0.3411
	8-455	30	29 –	66 @ 1.56	$1\frac{9}{16}$	0.0016–0.0033	0.0021–0.0038	0.3416	0.3411
1971	6-250 1 bbl	46②	45②	61 @ 1.66	$1\frac{21}{32}$	0.0010–0.0027	0.0021–0.0027	0.3414	0.3414
	8-350 2 bbl	45	44	61 @ 1.59	$1\frac{19}{32}$	0.0016–0.0033	0.0021–0.0038	0.3416	0.3411
	8-400⑥	30	29	60 @ 1.60	$1\frac{19}{32}$	0.0016–0.0033	0.0021–0.0038	0.3416	0.3411
	8-400 2 bbl	45	44	61 @ 1.59	$1\frac{19}{32}$	0.0016–0.0033	0.0021–0.0038	0.3416	0.3411
	8-400 4 bbl	30	29	65 @ 1.57	$1\frac{9}{16}$	0.0016–0.0033	0.0021–0.0038	0.3416	0.3411
	8-455	30	29	65 @ 1.57	$1\frac{9}{16}$	0.0016–0.0033	0.0021–0.0038	0.3416	0.3416
	8-455 H.O.	30	29	66 @ 1.56	$1\frac{9}{16}$	0.0016–0.0033	0.0021–0.0038	0.3416	0.3416
1972	6-250	46②	45②	60 @ 1.66	$1\frac{21}{32}$	0.0010–0.0027	0.0010–0.0027	0.3414	0.3414
	8-350	45	44	61 @ 1.59	$1\frac{19}{32}$	0.0016–0.0033	0.0021–0.0038	0.3416	0.3411
	8-400⑥	30	29	60 @ 1.60	$1\frac{19}{32}$	0.0016–0.0033	0.0021–0.0038	0.3416	0.3411
	8-400 2 bbl	45	44	61 @ 1.59	$1\frac{19}{32}$	0.0016–0.0033	0.0021–0.0038	0.3416	0.3411
	8-400 4 bbl	30	29	65 @ 1.57	$1\frac{9}{16}$	0.0016–0.0033	0.0021–0.0038	0.3416	0.3411
	8-455	30	29	64 @ 1.57	$1\frac{9}{16}$	0.0016–0.0033	0.0021–0.0038	0.3416	0.3416
	8-455 H.O.	30	29	66 @ 1.56	$1\frac{9}{16}$	0.0016–0.0033	0.0021–0.0038	0.3416	0.3416
1973	6-250	46	45	60 @ 1.66	$1\frac{21}{32}$	0.0010–0.0027	0.0010–0.0027	0.3414	0.3414
	8-350	45	44	61 @ 1.59	$1\frac{19}{32}$	0.0016–0.0033	0.0021–0.0038	0.3416	0.3411
	8-400	30	29	60 @ 1.60	$1\frac{19}{32}$	0.0016–0.0033	0.0021–0.0038	0.3416	0.3411
	8-400 2 bbl	45	44	61 @ 1.59	$1\frac{19}{32}$	0.0016–0.0033	0.0021–0.0038	0.3416	0.3411
	8-400 4 bbl	30	29	65 @ 1.57	$1\frac{9}{16}$	0.0016–0.0033	0.0021–0.0038	0.3416	0.3411
	8-455	30	29	64 @ 1.57	$1\frac{9}{16}$	0.0016–0.0033	0.0021–0.0038	0.3416	0.3416
	8-455 H.O.	30	29	66 @ 1.56	$1\frac{9}{16}$	0.0016–0.0033	0.0021–0.0038	0.3416	0.3416

① Applies to HO also
② Standard and Ram Air GTO with manual transmission
③ Standard GTO with automatic transmission
④ Exhaust valve seat angle 46°
⑤ Exhaust valve face angle 45°
⑥ All 400 cu in. engines with manual transmission
R.A. Ram Air
H.O. High Output

Crankshaft and Connecting Rod Specification Chart

(All measurements are given in inches)

Year	Engine Cu In. Displacement	Crankshaft				Connecting Rod		
		Main Brg Journal Dia	Main Brg Oil Clearance	Shaft End-Play	Thrust on No.	Journal Diameter	Oil Clearance	Side Clearance
1968	6	2.30	0.0003–0.0019	0.002–0.006	7	2.000	0.0007–0.0027 [8]	0.0085–0.0135 [1]
	8-350	3.00	0.0002–0.0017	0.0035–0.0085	4	2.250	0.0005–0.0025	0.006–0.011 [1]
1969	8-400	3.00	0.0002–0.0017	0.0035–0.0085	4	2.250	0.0005–0.0026	0.006–0.011 [1]
	6	2.30	0.0003–0.0019	0.002–0.006	7	2.000	0.0007–0.0027 [8]	0.0085–0.0135 [1]
	8-350	3.00	0.0002–0.0017 [4]	0.0035–0.0085	4	2.250	0.0005–0.0025	0.006–0.011 [1]
	8-400	3.00	0.0002–0.0017 [4]	0.0035–0.0085	4	2.250	0.0005–0.0026 [5]	0.006–0.011 [1]
1970	6	2.30	0.0003–0.0029	0.002–0.006	7	2.000	0.0007–0.0027	0.009–0.013
	8-350	3.00	0.0002–0.0017	0.0035–0.0085	4	2.250	0.0005–0.0025	0.012–0.017 [1]
	8-400	3.00	0.0002–0.0017 [6]	0.0035–0.0085	4	2.250	0.0005–0.0026 [6]	0.012–0.017 [1]
	8-455	3.25	0.0005–0.0021 [8]	0.0035–0.0085	4	2.250	0.0010–0.0031	0.012–0.017 [1]
1971-73	6	2.2983–2.2993	0.0003–0.0029	0.002–0.006	7	2.000	0.0007–0.0027	0.009–0.014
	8-350	3.00	0.0002–0.0017	0.003–0.009	4	2.250	0.0005–0.0025	0.012–0.017 [1]
	8-400	3.00	0.0002–0.0017	0.003–0.009	4	2.250	0.0005–0.0025	0.012–0.017 [1]
	8-455	3.25	[7]	0.003–0.009	4	2.250	0.0025–0.0025	0.012–0.017 [1]

[1] Total for 2 connecting rods
[8] 0.0007–0.0028 on 6 cyl. 4-bbl engine option
[4] 0.0012–0.0028 on Ram Air IV engine option
[5] 0.0015–0.0031 on Ram Air IV engine option
[6] No.'s 1, 2, 3, 4, on Ram Air IV option—0.007–0.0023

No.'s 1, 2, 3, 4 on Ram Air IV option—0.0012–0.0028
No. 5 on Ram Air IV option—0.007–0.0022
[7] w/small valve—0.0003–0.0019
w/small valve—0.0005–0.0021

Piston and Ring Specifications Chart

(All measurements in inches)

Year	Engine Cu In. Displacement	Ring Gap			Ring Side Clearance		
		Top Compression	Bottom Compression	Oil Control	Top Compression	Bottom Compression	Oil Control
1968–69	250	0.005–0.025	0.005–0.025	0.015–0.055	0.0015–0.0050	0.0015–0.0050	0.0015–0.0050
1968–69	All 8 cyl	0.010–0.030	0.010–0.030	0.015–0.055	0.0015–0.0050	0.0015–0.0050	0.0015–0.0050
1970–73	350, 400	0.009–0.029	0.005–0.025	0.015–0.055	0.0015–0.0050	0.0015–0.0050	0.0015–0.0050
1970–73	455	0.011–0.031	0.005–0.025	0.015–0.055	0.0015–0.0050	0.0015–0.0050	0.0015–0.0050

Piston Clearance Chart

Year	Engine	Piston-to-Bore Clearance (in.)
1968	6-250 OHC	0.0022–0.0028
	8-350 & 400	0.0025–0.0031
1969	6-250 OHC	0.0022–0.0028
	8-350 & 400	0.0025–0.0031
	8-400 Ram Air	0.0055–0.0061
1970	6-250 OHV	0.0005–0.0015
	8-350, 400, 455	0.0025–0.0033
	8-400 Ram Air	0.0055–0.0061
1971	6-250 OHV	0.0005–0.0015
	8-350, 400, 455	0.0025–0.0033
1972	6-250 OHV	0.0005–0.0015
	8-350, 400, 455	0.0025–0.0033
1973	6-250 OHV	0.0005–0.0015
	8-350, 400	0.0029–0.0037
	8-455	0.0025–0.0033
	8-455 S.D.	0.0060–0.0068

Torque Specification Chart

(All readings in ft lbs)

Year	Engine	Cylinder Head Bolts	Rod Bearing Bolts	Main Bearing Bolts	Crankshaft Pulley Bolt	Flywheel to Crankshaft Bolts	Manifold	
							Intake	Exhaust
1968–69	6	85–100	30–35	60–70	Pressed on	60–70	25–40	15–25
	V8	85–100	40–46	90–110 ▲	130–190	85–100	20–35	30–45
1970–73	6	95	35	65	Pressed on	60	25–30	25
	V8	95	43①	90–110 ▲	160	95	40	30

▲ Rear main—120 ft lbs   ① S.D. 455—63 ft lbs

ENGINE

Removal and Installation

ALL MODELS

1. Remove the battery cables.
2. Drain the cooling system.
3. Scribe marks around the hood hinges and then remove the hood from the hinges.
4. Disconnect the engine wiring harness and the engine ground straps.
5. Remove the air cleaner and the fan shield.
6. Disconnect all cooling system hoses from the engine.
7. If equipped with a manual transmission, it may be necessary to remove the radiator.
8. If the car has power steering or air conditioning, remove the power steering and/or compressor from their mounting brackets.

CAUTION: *Do not disconnect any of the hoses.*

9. Remove the engine fan and the front pulley.
10. Disconnect the accelerator linkage and remove the linkage support bracket.
11. Disconnect the transmission modulator and power brake vacuum lines.
12. Raise the car and drain the oil pan.
13. Disconnect the fuel lines from the fuel pump.
14. Disconnect the exhaust pipes from the engine.
15. Tag and disconnect the wires from the starter motor.
16. If the car has an automatic transmission, remove the converter bolts and slide the converter to the rear.
17. If the car is equipped with a manual transmission, disconnect the clutch linkage, remove the cross shaft, the starter, and the lower flywheel cover.
18. Remove the four bolts from the lower bell housing.
19. Remove the transmission filler tube support and the starter wire harness shield.
20. Remove the two front motor mount bolts.
21. Lower the car and support the transmission with a jack and a block of wood.
22. Remove the remaining bellhousing bolts.
23. Raise the transmission and hook up a block and tackle and remove the engine.

24. To install, lower the engine into the car, making sure that the engine aligns with the bellhousing, and install the two upper bellhousing bolts.
25. Remove the jack from under the transmission.
26. Lower the engine, raise the car and install the remaining bellhousing bolts.
27. Install the front motor mount bolts.
28. To complete the installation reverse the remaining removal procedures.

CYLINDER HEAD

Removal and Installation

SIX CYLINDER 1968–69 OHC

1. Remove the air cleaner and drain the cooling system.
2. Disconnect the accelerator pedal cable and the fuel and vacuum lines from the carburetor.
3. Disconnect the exhaust pipe from the carburetor.
4. Disconnect the exhaust pipe from the manifold then remove the manifold and carburetor as an assembly.
5. Remove the rocker arm cover assembly.
6. Remove the timing belt rear lower cover and the support bracket for the upper front cover.
7. Disconnect the spark plug wires.
8. Remove the rocker arms and the valve lash adjusters and tag them so that they can be returned to exactly the same location.
9. Remove the cylinder head bolts, the cylinder head, and its gasket. The head should be placed on two blocks of wood to prevent any damage.
10. Before installing the cylinder head, the gasket surfaces on the head and on the block must be clean.
11. Apply sealer and place a new gasket over the dowel pins on the block.

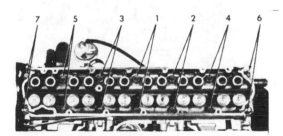

Cylinder head tightening sequence—OHC 6 cylinder (© Pontiac Div., G.M. Corp.)

12. Carefully lower the head into place on the block.

13. Install the bolts.

IMPORTANT: *The head bolts are of two different lengths and must be placed in the proper holes. When placed in the proper holes they will all rise an equal length from the head. Sealer must not be used on the bolts.*

14. The head bolts should be tightened in the proper sequence a little at a time with a torque wrench. Tighten the center bolts first and then the end bolts. All bolts should be tightened to 95 ft lbs. To complete installation, reverse the applicable steps of the removal procedures.

1970–73 (6 Cylinder)

1. Remove the air cleaner and drain the cooling system.

2. Disconnect the gas pedal rod from its connection on the manifold and detach the fuel and vacuum lines from the carburetor.

3. Disconnect the exhaust pipe from the manifold and then remove the manifolds and carburetor as an assembly.

4. Disconnect the wiring harness from the temperature sending unit and the coil.

5. Disconnect the radiator hose from the water outlet and detach the battery ground strap from the head.

6. Remove the spark plugs and the coil.

7. Remove the valve cover, loosen the rocker arm nuts and remove the pushrods.

8. Remove the cylinder head bolts and then remove the head and its gasket. To prevent any damage, place the head on two blocks of wood.

9. Install a new head gasket over the dowel pins in the block.

Installing Cylinder Head (© Pontiac Div., G.M. Corp.)

10. Carefully lower the head into position over the dowel pins.

11. Coat the head bolt threads with a sealing compound and install them.

12. Using a torque wrench, tighten the bolts a little at a time. The bolts should be tightened in the proper sequence. Their final torque must be 95 ft lbs.

13. Install the pushrods through the head and seat them into the lifters.

14. Install the rocker arms, the balls and nuts, and tighten the nuts until pushrod play is eliminated.

15. Connect the radiator hose.

16. Install the coil, connect the temperature sending unit, and attach the battery ground cable to the head.

17. Clean the manifold gasket surfaces and install the manifold and carburetor using a new gasket. Torque the bolts as shown in the picture.

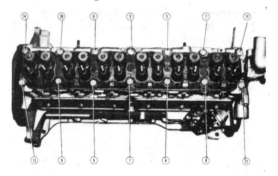

Cylinder Head Tightening Sequence—6 Cylinder (© Pontiac Div., G.M. Corp.)

18. Connect the throttle linkage and the fuel and vacuum lines.

19. Fill the cooling system.

20. Position the rocker arms and torque the rocker arm nuts to 20 ft lbs and further tighten until any valve train play is removed. Adjust the valve lash as outlined in Chapter Two.

21. Install the spark plugs.

22. Install the valve cover being careful not to overtighten the bolts.

23. Install the spark plug wires and the air cleaner.

1968–72 (V8)

NOTE: *Drain the cooling system including the block.*

1. Remove the intake manifold, the valley cover, and the valve covers.

2. Loosen the rocker arm retaining nuts and pivot the rockers off of the pushrods.

3. Remove the pushrods and tag them as to location so they may be returned to the same position.

4. Remove the exhaust pipe flange bolts.

5. Remove the battery ground strap and the engine ground strap from the left head. Remove the engine ground strap and the automatic transmission oil filler tube bracket from the right head.

6. Remove the head bolts and lift off the head with the exhaust manifold attached.

7. Check the head surface for straightness and install a new head gasket onto the block.

NOTE: *The head bolts are of three different lengths on all V8's. When the bolts are properly installed, they will project an equal distance from the head.*

8. Install all head bolts and tighten them evenly to 95 ft lbs in the sequence shown.

Cylinder Head Tightening Sequence—V8 (© Pontiac Div., G.M. Corp.)

9. Install the pushrods in their original position.

10. Position the rocker arms over the pushrods and tighten the ball retaining nuts to 20 ft lbs and adjust the valve lash as outlined in Chapter Two.

11. Install the valve covers.

12. Replace the valley cover.

13. Replace the ground straps, the oil filler tube bracket, and the intake manifold.

14. Install the exhaust pipe flange nuts.

Overhaul

For cylinder head overhaul, see the "Engine Rebuilding" section.

ROCKER ARM AND HYDRAULIC VALVE LASH ADJUSTER

Removal

OHC SIX CYLINDER

1. Remove the valve cover from the engine.

2. Remove the rocker arm and the hydraulic lash adjuster and tag them as to location so that they can be returned to their original positions.

3. If the lash adjuster becomes stuck in its cylinder, proceed as follows:

4. Remove the rocker arm and fill the hole next to the lifter with engine oil.

5. Insert a rod into the vent hole and hit the end of it with a hammer. The hydraulic effect of the oil should free the adjuster from its cylinder.

6. Place the adjuster in its cylinder and install the rocker arms and the cover assembly.

INTAKE MANIFOLD

Removal and Installation

V8

1. Drain the cooling system.

2. Remove the air cleaner assembly.

3. Remove the water outlet fitting allowing the radiator hose to remain attached.

4. If necessary, disconnect the heater hose from its fitting.

5. Disconnect the wire from the thermogauge unit.

6. Remove the spark plug wire brackets.

7. If equipped with power brakes, remove the vacuum pipe from the carburetor.

8. Disconnect the fuel line and the vacuum hoses.

9. Disconnect the crankcase vent hose from the manifold.

10. Disconnect the throttle linkage from the carburetor.

11. Remove the screws from the throttle control bracket.

12. Remove the manifold bolts and lift off the manifold.

INSTALLATION

1. Install new gaskets on the heads keeping them in position with plastic gasket retainers.

2. Lower the intake manifold onto the engine and install the O-ring seal.

3. Loosely install the bolts and nuts.

4. Install the throttle control bracket assembly.

5. Install a new O-ring seal (use the old one if undamaged) between the timing

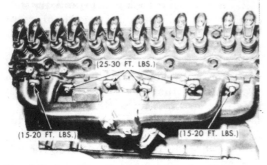

Manifold Attaching Points—6 Cylinder (© Pontiac Div., G.M. Corp.)

chain cover and the intake manifold and tighten the bolt to 15 ft lbs.

6. Tighten all bolts and nuts evenly to 40 ft lbs, starting from the center and working out.

7. To complete the installation, reverse the removal procedure.

EXHAUST MANIFOLD

Removal and Installation

V8

1. Remove the alternator and bracket as an assembly.

2. Disconnect the exhaust pipe from the manifold.

3. Remove the carburetor air preheater shroud from the manifold.

4. Straighten the tabs on the manifold bolt locks, remove the bolts and the manifold.

5. To install, clean the gasket surfaces and position the manifold on the engine, holding it in place with the two end bolts.

6. Insert the gasket between the manifold and the head.

7. Install the remaining bolts with new bolt locks and torque them evenly to 30 ft lbs. Bolt locks go only on the front and rear bolts.

8. Install the carburetor air preheater shroud.

9. Connect the exhaust pipe to the manifold and torque to 30 ft lbs.

COMBINATION MANIFOLD

Removal and Installation

SIX CYLINDER

1. Remove the air cleaner.

2. Disconnect the throttle linkage or cable and the return spring.

3. Disconnect the fuel and vacuum

lines and the choke coil rod if so equipped.

4. If the manifold is to be replaced, remove the carburetor and, if so equipped, the heat shield.

5. Disconnect the exhaust pipe from the manifold.

Cutting Tabs on Oil Pan Front Seal (© Pontiac Div., G.M. Corp.)

6. Remove the manifold bolts and then the manifolds as an assembly.

7. To install, clean the gasket surfaces.

8. If one manifold must be separated from the other, remove the one bolt and two nuts at the center of the assembly. When reassembling, use a new gasket and torque to 25 ft lbs.

9. Using new gaskets, carefully install the manifold.

Applying Sealant (© Pontiac Div., G.M. Corp.)

10. Hold the manifold in place and install the clamp and bolts.

11. Tighten the center clamp bolts to 30 ft lbs and the end bolts to 20 ft lbs.

12. Connect the exhaust pipe to the manifold using a new packing seal.

13. To complete installation, reverse the remaining removal steps.

TIMING GEAR COVER AND OIL SEAL

Replacement

Six Cylinder—OHV

1. Drain the cooling system and disconnect the radiator hoses at the radiator.

2. Remove the fan and the water pump pulley.

3. Remove the radiator.

4. Using a puller, remove the harmonic balancer.

5. Loosen the oil pan bolts and allow the pan to rest against the front crossmember.

6. Remove the timing gear cover bolts and remove the cover and its gasket.

7. Using a screwdriver, remove the oil seal.

Installing Oil Seal—6 Cylinder (© Pontiac Div., G.M. Corp.)

NOTE: *The seal can be replaced with the cover installed.*

8. Install the new seal with the lip toward the inside of the cover. Drive it into place using a proper seal installer or an old wheel bearing outer race.

9. Inspect the oil nozzle for any damage and replace if necessary; clean all gasket surfaces.

10. Install the cover and its gasket making sure that the cover is properly centered on the crankshaft end.

11. Tighten the cover bolts to 7 ft lbs.

V8

1. Drain the radiator and the block.

2. Remove the fan belt and the accessory belt.

3. Remove the fan and the pulley from the water pump.

4. If necessary, remove the water pump.

5. Disconnect the lower radiator hose.

6. Remove the fuel pump.

NOTE: *It is not necessary to remove the fuel pump if only the seal is to be replaced.*

7. Remove the harmonic balancer.

NOTE: *Do not pry on the rubber mounted balancers. The seal can be removed at this time with a screwdriver. Install the new seal with the lip inward.*

8. Remove the cover bolts and remove the cover.

9. Remove the O-ring from its recess in the intake manifold and then clean all gasket surfaces.

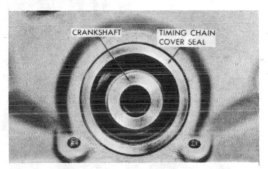

Timing Cover Oil Seal—V8 (© Pontiac Div., G.M Corp.)

10. If damaged, replace the front oil pan gasket using gasket cement.

11. To replace the seal, pry it out of the cover with a screwdriver. Install the new seal with the lip inward.

12. To install, reverse the removal procedure, making sure all gaskets are replaced. Tighten the four oil pan bolts to 12 ft lbs, the harmonic balancer bolt to 160 ft lbs and the fan pulley bolts to 20 ft lbs.

TIMING BELT, CRANKSHAFT SPROCKET, OR LOWER CRANKCASE COVER SEAL

Removal and Installation

OHC 6 Cylinder

Radiator removal, at this point, is a distinct advantage for this operation.

1. Remove upper front timing cover.
2. Align timing marks.

NOTE: *There are three sets of timing marks that must be aligned. One set is located on the harmonic balancer and the lower front belt cover. A second set is located on the accessory drive housing pulley and the lower front belt cover. The third set is the camshaft pulley set.*

The mark on the harmonic balancer must be aligned with zero (0°) on the cover with the no. 1 cylinder on TDC of the compression stroke. The mark on the drive pulley should point toward the water pump and align with its mark on the belt cover. The mark on the camshaft pulley, in 1968, aligns with a mark on the cover behind the pulley. In 1969, the camshaft pul-

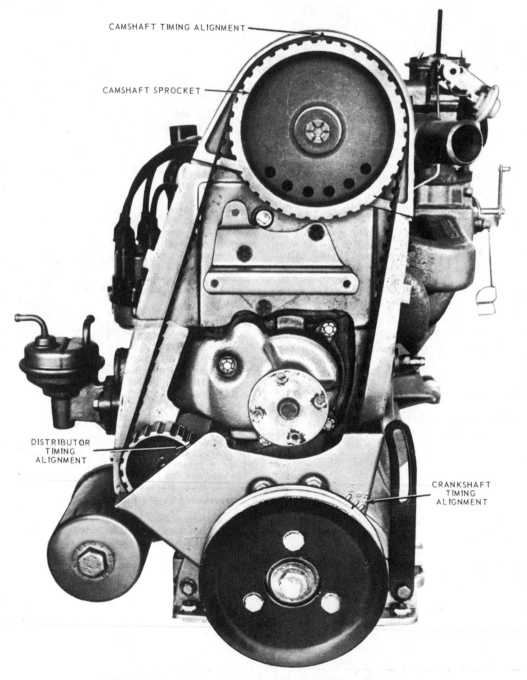

1968 OHC 6 cylinder timing marks (© Pontiac Div., G.M. Corp.)

ley mark aligns with a mark on a bolt head located directly below the camshaft pulley.

All three sets of marks must be aligned at the same time when replacing the camshaft drive belt.

3. Remove fan and water pump pulley.
4. Remove harmonic balancer.

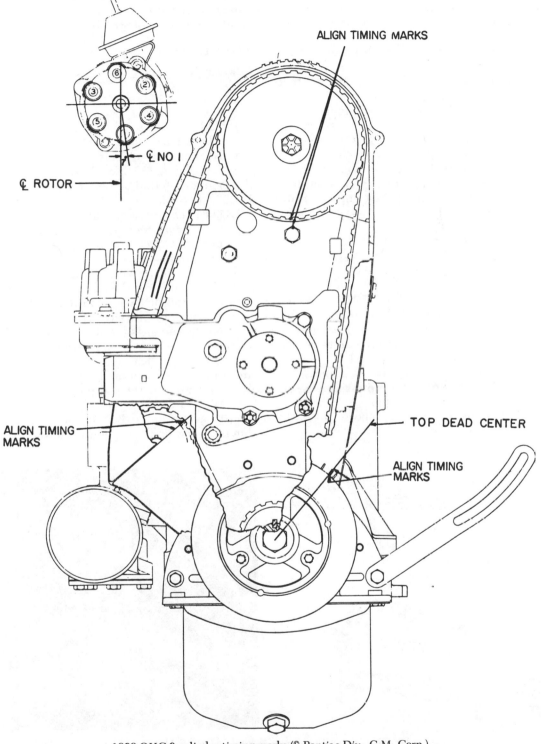

ALIGN TIMING MARKS

℄ NO I

℄ ROTOR

ALIGN TIMING MARKS

TOP DEAD CENTER

ALIGN TIMING MARKS

1969 OHC 6 cylinder timing marks (© Pontiac Div., G.M. Corp.)

5. Remove timing belt lower front cover.

6. Loosen accessory drive mounting bolts to provide slack in timing belt.

7. Remove timing belt.

8. Remove crankshaft timing belt flange and sprocket.

9. Carefully remove seal from crankcase cover.

10. Install new seal, with lip of seal inward.

11. Replace crankshaft timing belt sprocket and flange.

12. Align timing marks and replace timing belt.

13. Replace timing belt lower cover and harmonic balancer.

14. Adjust timing belt tension.

15. Replace water pump pulley and fan.

16. Replace timing belt upper front cover.

FRONT CRANKCASE COVER AND GASKET

Removal and Installation

OHC 6 CYLINDER

1. Remove timing belt sprocket, as described above.

2. Remove four front oil pan-to-crankcase cover retaining bolts.

3. Loosen remaining oil pan bolts, as necessary, to provide clearance between crankcase cover and oil pan.

4. Remove five front crankcase cover attaching bolts.

5. Remove front crankcase cover and gasket, clean off the old gasket.

6. Inspect cover seal for wear or distortion.

7. Using new gasket installed over dowels and, if necessary, new seal, reverse removal procedures, torque oil pan and crankcase cover bolts to 10–15 ft lbs.

TIMING BELT

Adjustment

OHC 6 CYLINDER

NOTE: *Pontiac special tools, numbers J-22232-1 and J-22232-1, are necessary for this adjustment.*

1. Remove timing belt top front cover.

2. Using J-22232-2 calibration bar, set the pointer of timing belt tension fixture J-22232-1 to zero.

NOTE: *This calibration must be performed before each use of J-22232 fixture to insure an accurate timing belt adjustment.*

3. Remove camshaft sprocket to camshaft bolt and install J-22232-1 (tension fixture) on the belt with the rollers on the outside (smooth) surface of belt. Thread the fixture mounting bolt into camshaft sprocket bolt location, finger-tight.

4. Squeeze indicator end (upper) of fixture and quickly release so the fixture assumes released or relaxed position.

5. With J-22232-1 installed, as above, adjust accessory drive housing up or down, as required, to obtain a tension ad-

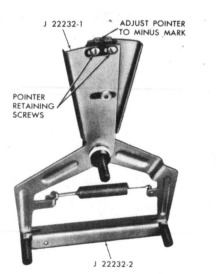

Timing belt adjustment tools (© Pontiac Div., G.M. Corp.)

justment indicator reading centered in the green range, with drive housing mounting bolts torqued to 15 ± 3 ft. lbs.

6. Remove tension fixture and install sprocket retaining bolt, making sure bolt threads and washers are free of dirt.

7. Install upper front timing belt cover.

ACCESSORY DRIVE HOUSING ASSEMBLY, OIL PUMP, DISTRIBUTOR AND FUEL PUMP —OHC 6 CYLINDER

The housing is unique, and consists of the oil pump, distributor and the fuel pump. The oil filter is also attached to this housing. The housing carries the drive sprocket for the above units and is used as a tensioner for the timing belt.

Oil Pressure Regulator and Removal and Installation

1. Remove cap washer and spring from housing assembly.

2. Using magnet, remove valve from housing assembly.

3. Install valve on spring and install as an assembly.

4. Install cap washer.

Oil Pump Removal and Installation

1. Remove oil pump cover and gasket.
2. Remove drive gear and driven gear.
3. Install gears.
4. Replace cover using new gasket. Torque attaching bolts to 20 ft lbs.

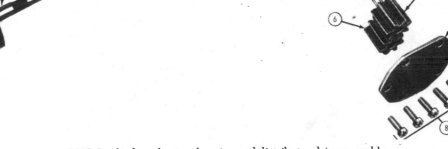

OHC 6 cylinder oil pump housing and distributor drive assembly

1. Housing
2. Shaft and Sprocket Assembly
3. Seal, Distributor Drive Shaft
4. Bearing, Distributor Drive
5. Gear and Shaft Assembly Oil Pump Drive
6. Gear, Oil Pump Driven
7. Cover, Oil Pump
8. Bolt, Oil Pump Cover to Housing
9. Valve, Oil Pressure Regulator
10. Spring, Oil Pressure Regulator
11. Gasket, Oil Pressure Regulator Valve Cap
12. Cap, Oil Pressure Regulator Valve
13. Seat, Oil Filter By-Pass Valve
14. Spring, Oil Filter By-Pass Valve
15. Retainer, Oil Filter By-Pass Valve
16. Screw, Oil Filter By-Pass Valve Retainer
17. Gear and Eccentric
18. Pin, Distributor Oil and Fuel Pump Gear and Eccentric

Housing Assembly Removal and Installation

1. Remove timing belt top front cover.
2. Align timing marks.
3. Loosen six housing assembly from cylinder block retaining bolts.
4. Remove timing belt from camshaft sprocket and distributor drive.
5. Disconnect fuel lines from fuel pump.
6. Remove distributor cap, vacuum lines and wires from distributor.
7. Remove housing by removing six retaining bolts.
8. Install, using a new gasket, and loosely install housing assembly to cylinder block with six retaining bolts.
9. Align timing marks and install timing belt.
10. Connect fuel lines to fuel pump.
11. Replace distributor cap, vacuum lines and wires.
12. Adjust timing belt tension. See timing belt adjustment.
13. Replace timing belt top front cover.

CAMSHAFT

Removal and Installation

OHC 6 Cylinder

1. Remove camshaft sprocket and seal.
2. Remove rocker cover assembly.
3. Using an adapter and a slide hammer, drive camshaft to the rear. Make sure bearing surfaces are not damaged during this operation.

Camshaft removal—OHC 6 cylinder (© Pontiac Div., G.M. Corp.)

4. Disconnect slide hammer and remove camshaft from rear of rocker cover.
5. Remove thrust washer, retaining washer, and bolt from rear of camshaft.
6. Clean and inspect all parts for wear

or damage, then inspect bearing surfaces for wear or scoring.
7. Clean camshaft oil passages.
8. To install, reverse removal procedure making sure thrust washer is installed as illustrated. Tighten retaining bolt to 40 ft. lbs.

INDEX THRUST WASHER
TANG IN HOLE IN ROCKER
ARM COVER

Thrust washer positioning (© Pontiac Div., G.M. Corp.)

9. Check camshaft end-play, using a dial indicator on the front sprocket; end-play should be 0.003–0.009 in. and is controlled by the camshaft bore plug.
NOTE: *Lubricate camshaft lobes and rockers with special lubricant or gear oil. Tighten rocker cover bolts and nuts to 15 ft lbs. from center outward.*

1970–73 (OHV) 6 Cylinder

1. Drain the cooling system.
2. Remove the radiator, fan, and water pump pulley.
3. Remove the grill.
4. Remove the valve cover and gasket. Loosen the rocker arm nuts and move the rocker arms out of the way.
5. Remove the pushrods.
6. Remove the distributor, fuel pump, and spark plugs.
7. Remove the ignition coil, pushrod covers, and gasket. Remove the valve lifters making sure to note their positions for reinstalling.
8. Remove the harmonic balancer, then loosen the oil pan bolts and allow the pan to drop.
9. Remove the timing gear cover.
10. Remove the two camshaft thrust plate bolts.

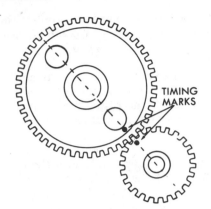

1970–73 OHV 6 cylinder timing marks

Removing Camshaft Thrust Plate Screws (© Pontiac Div., G.M. Corp.)

11. Remove the camshaft by pulling it out straight forward. If the cam gear is to be replaced, press it off using an arbor press.

CAUTION: *The thrust plate must be positioned so the woodruff key does not damage it during removal.*

14. Install the camshaft into the engine, turn it so that the timing marks align, and tighten the thrust plate bolts to 5–8 ft lbs.

15. Reverse the remaining procedures to complete installation.

V8 ENGINE

1. Drain the cooling system and remove the air cleaner.

2. Disconnect all water hoses, vacuum lines, and spark plug wires. Remove the radiator.

3. Disconnect the accelerator linkage, temperature gauge wire, and fuel lines.

4. Remove the hood latch brace.

5. Remove the PCV hose, then remove the rocker covers.

NOTE: *On air-conditioned models, remove the alternator and bracket.*

6. Remove the distributor, then remove the intake manifold.

7. Remove the valley cover.

8. Loosen the rocker arm nuts and pivot the rockers out of the way.

9. Remove the pushrods and lifters, keeping them in proper order.

10. Remove the harmonic balancer, fuel pump, and four oil pan-to-timing cover bolts.

11. Remove the timing cover and gasket, then remove the fuel pump eccentric and the bushing.

12. Align the timing marks, then remove the timing chain and sprockets.

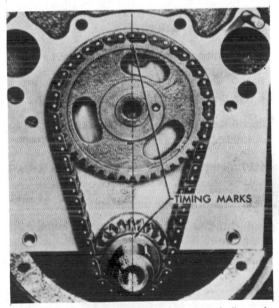

1969–73 V8 timing marks, rotate camshaft mark 180° for 1968 V8 (© Pontiac Div., G.M. Corp.)

13. Remove the camshaft thrust plate.

14. Remove the camshaft by pulling it straight forward, being careful not to damage the cam bearings in the process.

15. Install the new camshaft (with the lobes and journals coated with heavy (SAE 50-60) oil) into the engine, being careful not to damage the cam bearings.

16. Install the camshaft thrust plate and tighten the bolts to 20 ft lbs.

17. To install, reverse Steps 1–12, tightening the sprocket bolts to 40 ft lbs, timing cover bolts and nuts to 30 ft lbs, oil pan bolts to 12 ft lbs, and harmonic balancer bolt to 160 ft lbs.

PISTON AND CONNECTING RODS

Removal and Installation

OHC 6 CYLINDER

1. Remove the rocker arm cover.
2. Disconnect the fuel and vacuum lines from the carburetor.
3. Remove the cylinder head and the intake and exhaust manifold as an assembly.
4. Remove the ring ridge, using an appropriate cutter.

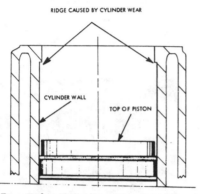

Piston Ring Ridge (© Pontiac Div., G.M. Corp.)

5. Remove the oil pan.
6. Mark the connecting rod and piston assembly to make sure they go into the same cylinder and that the same piston face is pointing toward the front of the engine upon reassembly. Do not reverse the bearing caps on the end of the connecting rods.

7. Remove the bearing cap and carefully push the piston and rod from its bore. Do not allow the piston and rod assembly to be scratched, nicked, or struck against a hard surface.

8. Using a ring compressor, insert the rod and piston assembly into the cylinder.

9. Pull the assembly into place against the crankpin, install the bearing cap and torque it to 33 ft lbs.

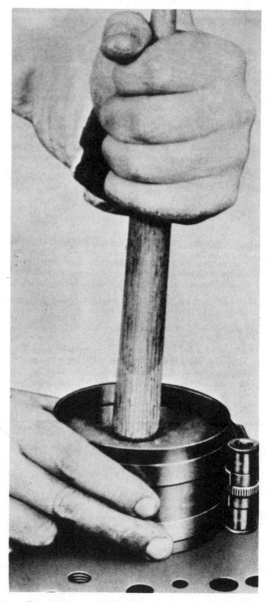

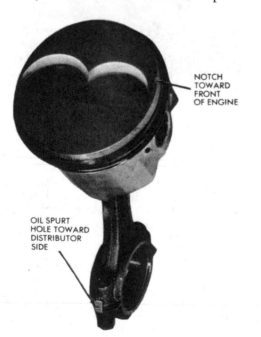

Piston and Rod Assembly, 6 Cylinder (© Pontiac Div., G.M. Corp.)

Installing Piston in Cylinder (© Pontiac Div., G.M. Corp.)

10. Install the oil pan.

11. Install the cylinder head assembly.

12. Connect the fuel and vacuum lines and install the rocker arm cover.

OHV 6 Cylinder

Piston and piston ring removal and installation are the same as for the OHC six-cylinder engine. However, ring clearances are different. These are 0.010–0.020 in. end clearance for the upper and lower compressing rings and 0.015–0.055 in. for the oil ring. Side clearance is: 0.0012–0.0027 in. for the upper compression ring; 0.0012–0.0032 in. for the lower compression ring; 0.001–0.005 in. for the oil ring.

Checking Ring Clearance (© Pontiac Div., G.M. Corp.)

V8 Engine

1. Remove the oil pan, oil baffle, and oil pump.

2. Remove the intake manifold, exhaust manifolds, and cylinder heads.

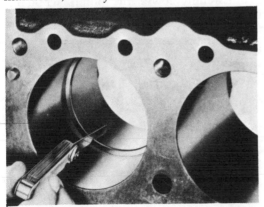

Checking Ring Gap (© Pontiac Div., G.M. Corp.)

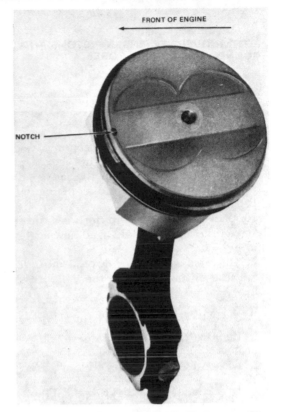

FRONT OF ENGINE

NOTCH

Piston and Rod Assembly—V8 (© Pontiac Div., G.M. Corp.)

3. Rotate the crankshaft to allow access to the rods being removed.

4. Remove the ring ridge, using a reamer.

5. Remove the bearing cap.

6. Push the assembly from the cylinder.

7. To install, reverse the removal procedures. Torque the bearing caps to specifications.

Engine Lubrication

OIL PAN

Removal and Installation

1968–70 V8 AND 1971 WITH MANUAL TRANSMISSION

1. Remove the engine from the car.

2. Remove the oil pan bolts.

3. Remove the oil pan.

1971–73 V8

1. Rotate the engine until the timing mark is at the two o'clock position.

2. Disconnect the battery cables.

3. Remove the fan.

4. Move all water hoses and electrical wiring out of the way.

5. Raise the car and drain the engine oil.

6. Disconnect the exhaust pipe(s) at the manifold.

7. Remove the starter and its bracket, then remove the flywheel inspection cover.

8. Support the engine with a jack. Use a wooden board to cushion the jack pad.

9. Remove both frame-to-motor mount bolts.

10. Jack the engine up for clearance. Remove the oil pan bolts and lower the pan.

11. Reverse the removal procedure to install the oil pan. Tighten the bolts to 12 ft lbs.

1970–73 OHV 6 CYLINDER

1. Remove the upper radiator shield assembly.

2. Disconnect the negative battery cable.

3. Jack up the front of the car and drain the engine oil.

4. Remove the starter motor and flywheel cover.

5. Raise the engine slightly, using a chain hoist, then remove both front motor mount-to-frame bolts and the right motor mount.

6. Remove the oil pan bolts, then raise the engine and remove the oil pan.

7. To install, reverse the removal procedure.

OHC ENGINE

1. Disconnect the battery.

2. Remove the air cleaner assembly.

3. On air conditioned cars, remove the compressor from the mounting brackets and position it to one side.

4. Raise the car and drain the crankcase.

5. Remove the starter assembly and flywheel cover.

6. Reroute or disconnect any wiring between the bellhousing and the floor pan to ensure against damage when the bellhousing contacts the pan.

7. Loosen the transmission insulator-to-crossmember retaining bolts.

8. Remove the right and left engine insulator-to-frame bracket through bolts.

9. Rotate the harmonic balancer until the timing mark is at the bottom. (This properly positions the crankshaft counterweights.)

10. With suitable equipment, raise the engine until the insulators clear the frame brackets.

11. Remove the oil pan bolts.

12. Raise the engine. Apply a rearward force on the engine-transmission assembly until the oil pan clears the flywheel housing. Remove the oil pan.

13. Reverse the procedure to install.

OIL PUMP

Removal and Installation

1. Remove the engine oil pan. (See the previous procedure.)

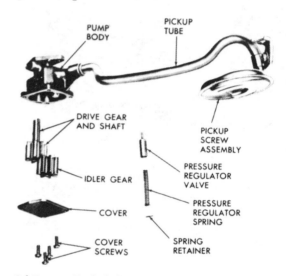

Oil Pump—Exploded View—6 Cylinder (© Pontiac Div., G.M. Corp.)

2. Remove the pump attaching screws and carefully lower the pump, while removing the pump drive shaft.

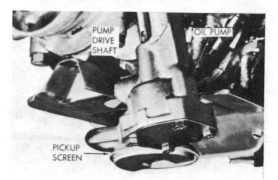

Oil Pump Installed—V8 (© Pontiac Div., G.M. Corp.)

3. Reinstall in the reverse order of removal.

REAR MAIN OIL SEAL

Removal and Installation

6 CYLINDER

1. Remove the engine oil pan.
2. Remove the rear main bearing cap.
3. Remove the oil seal from the groove in the cap by prying from the bottom with a small screwdriver.

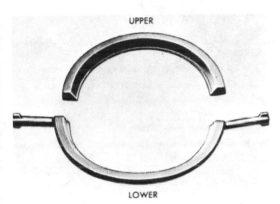

Rear Main Oil Seal—6 Cylinder (© Pontiac Div., G.M. Corp.)

Removing Rear Main Oil Seal—6 Cylinder (© Pontiac Div., G.M. Corp.)

4. Insert a new seal, well lubricated with engine oil, into the bearing cap groove.
5. Remove the upper half of the seal. Use a small hammer and brass pin and tap one end of the oil seal until it protrudes far enough to be removed with pliers.
6. Install a new seal with the lip toward the front of the engine.
7. Install the bearing cap and torque it to specifications.

V8 ENGINE

1. Remove the oil pan, baffle, and oil pump.
2. Remove the rear main bearing cap.
3. Make a seal tool as illustrated.
4. Insert the tool against one end of the oil seal in the block and drive the seal gently into the groove a distance of ¾ in. Repeat on the other end of the seal.
5. Form a new seal in the cap. Cut four ⅜ in. long pieces from this seal.
6. Work two of the pieces into each of the gaps which have been made at the end of the seal in the block. Do not cut off any material to make them fit.
7. Form a new seal in the bearing cap.
8. Apply a ¹⁄₁₆ in. bead of sealer from the center of the seal across to the external cork groove.
9. Reassemble the cap and torque to specifications.

Engine Cooling

RADIATOR

Removal and Installation

1. Drain the cooling system.
2. Remove the fan shield assembly.
3. Disconnect the radiator hoses.
4. Disconnect and plug the transmission cooler lines.
5. Remove the fan shroud.
6. Remove the radiator.
7. Reverse the procedures to install.

WATER PUMP

Removal and Installation

1. Disconnect the negative battery cable and drain the cooling system.

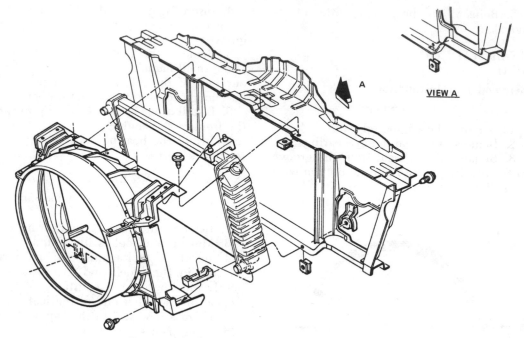

VIEW A

Removing Radiator—V8 (© Pontiac Div., G.M. Corp.)

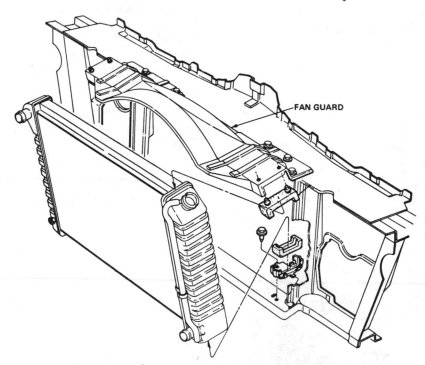

FAN GUARD

Removing Radiator—6 Cylinder (© Pontiac Div., G.M. Corp.)

2. Loosen the generator and remove the fan belt.

3. Remove the power steering and air conditioning belts, if so equipped.

4. Remove the fan and water pump pulley.

5. Remove the front generator bracket.

6. Remove the heater hose and radiator hose at the pump.

NOTE: *Remove the upper front timing cover and the two accessory drive housing bolts on OHC six engines.*

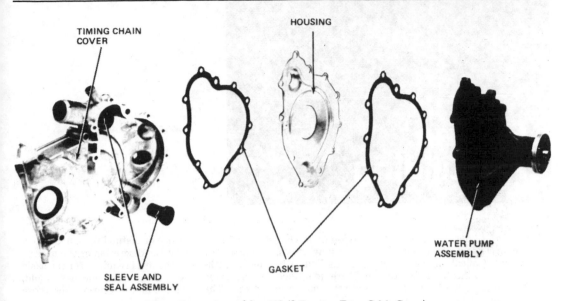

Water Pump Assembly—V8 (© Pontiac Div., G.M. Corp.)

7. Remove the water pump retaining bolts and the pump.

8. Install the pump by reversing the above steps. Make sure that all gasket surfaces are clean and smooth. Always use a gasket sealer on both sides of the gasket. Torque the retaining bolts to 20 ft lbs on six-cylinder engines, 30 ft lbs on the 307, and 15 ft lbs on all other V8 engines.

THERMOSTAT

Removal and Installation

1. Drain the cooling system.

2. Disconnect the upper radiator hose and remove the water outlet.

3. Reverse the order to replace. Torque the attaching bolts to 20–30 ft lbs. Clean the gasket surfaces and use sealer on a new gasket.

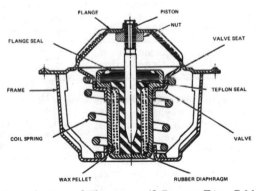

Cross Section of Thermostat (© Pontiac Div., G.M. Corp.)

Engine Rebuilding

This section describes, in detail, the procedures involved in rebuilding a typical engine. The procedures specifically refer to an inline engine, however, they are basically identical to those used in rebuilding engines of nearly all design and configurations. Procedures for servicing atypical engines (i.e., horizontally opposed) are described in the appropriate section, although in most cases, cylinder head reconditioning procedures described in this chapter will apply.

The section is divided into two sections. The first, Cylinder Head Reconditioning, assumes that the cylinder head is removed from the engine, all manifolds are removed, and the cylinder head is on a workbench. The camshaft should be removed from overhead cam cylinder heads. The second section, Cylinder Block Reconditioning, covers the block, pistons, connecting rods and crankshaft. It is assumed that the engine is mounted on a work stand, and the cylinder head and all accessories are removed.

Procedures are identified as follows:

Unmarked—Basic procedures that must be performed in order to successfully complete the rebuilding process.

Starred (*)—Procedures that should be performed to ensure maximum performance and engine life.

Double starred (**)—Procedures that may be performed to increase engine performance and reliability. These procedures are usually reserved for extremely heavy-duty or competition usage.

In many cases, a choice of methods is also provided. Methods are identified in the same manner as procedures. The choice of method for a procedure is at the discretion of the user.

The tools required for the basic rebuilding procedure should, with minor exceptions, be those

TORQUE (ft. lbs.)*

U.S.

Bolt Diameter (inches)	Bolt Grade (SAE)				Wrench Size (inches)	
	1 and 2	5	6	8	Bolt	Nut
1/4	5	7	10	10.5	3/8	7/16
5/16	9	14	19	22	1/2	9/16
3/8	15	25	34	37	9/16	5/8
7/16	24	40	55	60	5/8	3/4
1/2	37	60	85	92	3/4	13/16
9/16	53	88	120	132	7/8	7/8
5/8	74	120	167	180	15/16	1
3/4	120	200	280	296	1-1/8	1-1/8
7/8	190	302	440	473	1-5/16	1-5/16
1	282	466	660	714	1-1/2	1-1/2

Metric

Bolt Diameter (mm)	Bolt Grade				Wrench Size (mm) Bolt and Nut
	5D	8G	10K	12K	
6	5	6	8	10	10
8	10	16	22	27	14
10	19	31	40	49	17
12	34	54	70	86	19
14	55	89	117	137	22
16	83	132	175	208	24
18	111	182	236	283	27
22	182	284	394	464	32
24	261	419	570	689	36

*—Torque values are for lightly oiled bolts. CAUTION: Bolts threaded into aluminum require much less torque.

General Torque Specifications

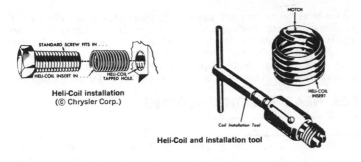

Heli-Coil installation
(© Chrysler Corp.)

Heli-Coil and installation tool

Heli-Coil Insert			Drill	Tap	Insert. Tool	Extract- ing Tool
Thread Size	Part No.	Insert Length (In.)	Size	Part No.	Part No.	Part No.
1/2 -20	1185-4	3/8	17/64(.266)	4 CPB	528-4N	1227-6
5/16-18	1185-5	15/32	Q(.332)	5 CPB	528-5N	1227-6
3/8 -16	1185-6	9/16	X(.397)	6 CPB	528-6N	1227-6
7/16-14	1185-7	21/32	29/64(.453)	7 CPB	528-7N	1227-16
1/2 -13	1185-8	3/4	33/64(.516)	8 CPB	528-8N	1227-16

Heli-Coil Specifications

included in a mechanic's tool kit. An accurate torque wrench, and a dial indicator (reading in thousandths) mounted on a universal base should be available. Bolts and nuts with no torque specification should be tightened according to size (see chart). Special tools, where required, all are readily available from the major tool suppliers (i.e., Craftsman, Snap-On, K-D). The services of a competent automotive machine shop must also be readily available.

When assembling the engine, any parts that will be in frictional contact must be pre-lubricated, to provide protection on initial start-up. Vortex Pre-Lube, STP, or any product specifically formulated for this purpose may be used. NOTE: *Do not use engine oil.* Where semi-permanent (locked but removable) installation of bolts or nuts is desired, threads should be cleaned and coated with Loctite. Studs may be permanently installed using Loctite Stud and Bearing Mount.

Aluminum has become increasingly popular for use in engines, due to its low weight and excellent heat transfer characteristics. The following precautions

must be observed when handling aluminum engine parts:
—Never hot-tank aluminum parts.
—Remove all aluminum parts (identification tags, etc.) from engine parts before hot-tanking (otherwise they will be removed during the process).
—Always coat threads lightly with engine oil or anti-seize compounds before installation, to prevent seizure.
—Never over-torque bolts or spark plugs in aluminum threads. Should stripping occur, threads can be restored according to the following procedure, using Heli-Coil thread inserts:

Tap drill the hole with the stripped threads to the specified size (see chart). Using the specified tap (NOTE: *Heli-Coil tap sizes refer to the size thread being replaced, rather than the actual tap size*), tap the hole for the Heli-Coil. Place the insert on the proper installation tool (see chart). Apply pressure on the insert while winding it clockwise into the hole, until the top of the insert is one turn below the surface. Remove the installation tool, and break the installation tang from the bottom of the in-

sert by moving it up and down. If the Heli-Coil must be removed, tap the removal tool firmly into the hole, so that it engages the top thread, and turn the tool counter-clockwise to extract the insert.

Snapped bolts or studs may be removed, using a stud extractor (unthreaded) or Vise-Grip pliers (threaded). Penetrating oil (e.g., Liquid Wrench) will often aid in breaking frozen threads. In cases where the stud or bolt is flush with, or below the surface, proceed as follows:

Drill a hole in the broken stud or bolt, approximately ½ its diameter. Select a screw extractor (e.g., Easy-Out) of the proper size, and tap it into the stud or bolt. Turn the extractor counterclockwise to remove the stud or bolt.

Magnaflux and Zyglo are inspection techniques used to locate material flaws, such as stress cracks. Magnafluxing coats the part with fine magnetic particles, and subjects the part to a magnetic field. Cracks cause breaks

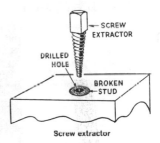

Screw extractor

in the magnetic field, which are outlined by the particles. Since Magnaflux is a magnetic process, it is applicable only to ferrous materials. The Zyglo process coats the material with a fluorescent dye penetrant, and then subjects it to blacklight inspection, under which cracks glow bright-

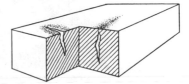

Magnaflux indication of cracks

ly. Parts made of any material may be tested using Zyglo. While Magnaflux and Zyglo are excellent for general inspection, and locating hidden defects, specific checks of suspected cracks may be made at lower cost and more readily using spot check dye. The dye is sprayed onto the suspected area, wiped off, and the area is then sprayed with a developer. Cracks then will show up brightly. Spot check dyes will only indicate surface cracks; therefore, structural cracks below the surface may escape detection. When questionable, the part should be tested using Magnaflux or Zyglo.

CYLINDER HEAD RECONDITIONING

Procedure	Method
Identify the valves: **Valve identification** (© SAAB)	Invert the cylinder head, and number the valve faces front to rear, using a permanent felt-tip marker.
Remove the rocker arms:	Remove the rocker arms with shaft(s) or balls and nuts. Wire the sets of rockers, balls and nuts together, and identify according to the corresponding valve.
Remove the valves and springs:	Using an appropriate valve spring compressor (depending on the configuration of the cylinder head), compress the valve springs. Lift out the keepers with needlenose pliers, release the compressor, and remove the valve, spring, and spring retainer.
Check the valve stem-to-guide clearance: **Checking the valve stem-to-guide clearance** (© American Motors Corp.)	Clean the valve stem with lacquer thinner or a similar solvent to remove all gum and varnish. Clean the valve guides using solvent and an expanding wire-type valve guide cleaner. Mount a dial indicator so that the stem is at 90° to the valve stem, as close to the valve guide as possible. Move the valve off its seat, and measure the valve guide-to-stem clearance by moving the stem back and forth to actuate the dial indicator. Measure the valve stems using a micrometer, and compare to specifications, to determine whether stem or guide wear is responsible for excessive clearance.
De-carbon the cylinder head and valves: **Removing carbon from the cylinder head** (© Chevrolet Div. G.M. Corp.)	Chip carbon away from the valve heads, combustion chambers, and ports, using a chisel made of hardwood. Remove the remaining deposits with a stiff wire brush. NOTE: *Ensure that the deposits are actually removed, rather than burnished.*

Procedure	Method
Hot-tank the cylinder head:	Have the cylinder head hot-tanked to remove grease, corrosion, and scale from the water passages. NOTE: *In the case of overhead cam cylinder heads, consult the operator to determine whether the camshaft bearings will be damaged by the caustic solution.*
Degrease the remaining cylinder head parts:	Using solvent (i.e., Gunk), clean the rockers, rocker shaft(s) (where applicable), rocker balls and nuts, springs, spring retainers, and keepers. Do not remove the protective coating from the springs.
Check the cylinder head for warpage:  ① ③ CHECK DIAGONALLY ② CHECK ACROSS CENTER A 2895-A **Checking the cylinder head for warpage** (© Ford Motor Co.)	Place a straight-edge across the gasket surface of the cylinder head. Using feeler gauges, determine the clearance at the center of the straight-edge. Measure across both diagonals, along the longitudinal centerline, and across the cylinder head at several points. If warpage exceeds .003″ in a 6″ span, or .006″ over the total length, the cylinder head must be resurfaced. NOTE: *If warpage exceeds the manufacturers maximum tolerance for material removal, the cylinder head must be replaced.* When milling the cylinder heads of V-type engines, the intake manifold mounting position is altered, and must be corrected by milling the manifold flange a proportionate amount.
** Porting and gasket matching:  **Marking the cylinder head for gasket matching** (© Petersen Publishing Co.) **Port configuration before and after gasket matching** (© Petersen Publishing Co.)	** Coat the manifold flanges of the cylinder head with Prussian blue dye. Glue intake and exhaust gaskets to the cylinder head in their installed position using rubber cement and scribe the outline of the ports on the manifold flanges. Remove the gaskets. Using a small cutter in a hand-held power tool (i.e., Dremel Moto-Tool), gradually taper the walls of the port out to the scribed outline of the gasket. Further enlargement of the ports should include the removal of sharp edges and radiusing of sharp corners. Do not alter the valve guides. NOTE: *The most efficient port configuration is determined only by extensive testing. Therefore, it is best to consult someone experienced with the head in question to determine the optimum alterations.*

Procedure	*Method*

** Polish the ports:

Relieved and polished ports
(© Petersen Publishing Co.)

Polished combustion chamber
(© Petersen Publishing Co.)

** Using a grinding stone with the above mentioned tool, polish the walls of the intake and exhaust ports, and combustion chamber. Use progressively finer stones until all surface imperfections are removed. NOTE: *Through testing, it has been determined that a smooth surface is more effective than a mirror polished surface in intake ports, and vice-versa in exhaust ports.*

* Knurling the valve guides:

Cut-away view of a knurled valve guide
(© Petersen Publishing Co.)

* Valve guides which are not excessively worn or distorted may, in some cases, be knurled rather than replaced. Knurling is a process in which metal is displaced and raised, thereby reducing clearance. Knurling also provides excellent oil control. The possibility of knurling rather than replacing valve guides should be discussed with a machinist.

Replacing the valve guides: NOTE: *Valve guides should only be replaced if damaged or if an oversize valve stem is not available.*

A-VALVE GUIDE I.D.
B-SLIGHTLY SMALLER THAN VALVE GUIDE O.D.
Valve guide removal tool

WASHERS

A-VALVE GUIDE I.D.
B-LARGER THAN THE VALVE GUIDE O.D.
Valve guide installation tool (with washers used during installation)

Depending on the type of cylinder head, valve guides may be pressed, hammered, or shrunk in. In cases where the guides are shrunk into the head, replacement should be left to an equipped machine shop. In other cases, the guides are replaced as follows: Press or tap the valve guides out of the head using a stepped drift (see illustration). Determine the height above the boss that the guide must extend, and obtain a stack of washers, their I.D. similar to the guide's O.D., of that height. Place the stack of washers on the guide, and insert the guide into the boss. NOTE: *Valve guides are often tapered or beveled for installation.* Using the stepped installation tool (see illustration), press or tap the guides into position. Ream the guides according to the size of the valve stem.

Procedure	*Method*
Replacing valve seat inserts:	Replacement of valve seat inserts which are worn beyond resurfacing or broken, if feasible, must be done by a machine shop.

Resurfacing (grinding) the valve face:

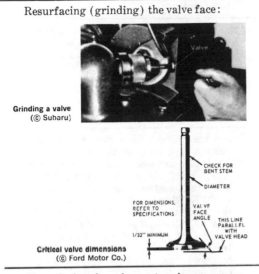

Grinding a valve
(© Subaru)

Using a valve grinder, resurface the valves according to specifications. CAUTION: *Valve face angle is not always identical to valve seat angle.* A minimum margin of 1/32″ should remain after grinding the valve. The valve stem tip should also be squared and resurfaced, by placing the stem in the V-block of the grinder, and turning it while pressing lightly against the grinding wheel.

CHECK FOR BENT STEM

DIAMETER

FOR DIMENSIONS, REFER TO SPECIFICATIONS

VALVE FACE ANGLE

THIS LINE PARALLEL WITH VALVE HEAD

1/32″ MINIMUM

Critical valve dimensions
(© Ford Motor Co.)

Resurfacing the valve seats using reamers:

Reaming the valve seat
(© S.p.A. Fiat)

Valve seat width and centering
(© Ford Motor Co.)

VALVE SEAT WIDTH

A 2897-A

Select a reamer of the correct seat angle, slightly larger than the diameter of the valve seat, and assemble it with a pilot of the correct size. Install the pilot into the valve guide, and using steady pressure, turn the reamer clockwise. CAUTION: *Do not turn the reamer counter-clockwise.* Remove only as much material as necessary to clean the seat. Check the concentricity of the seat (see below). If the dye method is not used, coat the valve face with Prussian blue dye, install and rotate it on the valve seat. Using the dye marked area as a centering guide, center and narrow the valve seat to specifications with correction cutters. NOTE: *When no specifications are available, minimum seat width for exhaust valves should be 5/64″, intake valves 1/16″.* After making correction cuts, check the position of the valve seat on the valve face using Prussian blue dye.

* Resurfacing the valve seats using a grinder:

Grinding a valve seat
(© Subaru)

Select a pilot of the correct size, and a coarse stone of the correct seat angle. Lubricate the pilot if necessary, and install the tool in the valve guide. Move the stone on and off the seat at approximately two cycles per second, until all flaws are removed from the seat. Install a fine stone, and finish the seat. Center and narrow the seat using correction stones, as described above.

Procedure	Method
Checking the valve seat concentricity:  **Checking the valve seat concentricity using a dial gauge** (© American Motors Corp.)	Coat the valve face with Prussian blue dye, install the valve, and rotate it on the valve seat. If the entire seat becomes coated, and the valve is known to be concentric, the seat is concentric.
	* Install the dial gauge pilot into the guide, and rest the arm on the valve seat. Zero the gauge, and rotate the arm around the seat. Run-out should not exceed .002″.
* Lapping the valves: NOTE: *Valve lapping is done to ensure efficient sealing of resurfaced valves and seats. Valve lapping alone is not recommended for use as a resurfacing procedure.* 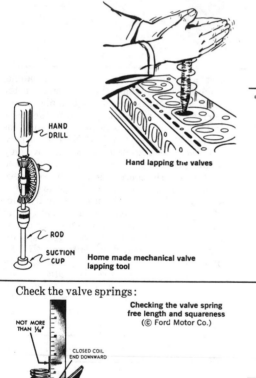 **Hand lapping the valves** **Home made mechanical valve lapping tool**	* Invert the cylinder head, lightly lubricate the valve stems, and install the valves in the head as numbered. Coat valve seats with fine grinding compound, and attach the lapping tool suction cup to a valve head (NOTE: *Moisten the suction cup*). Rotate the tool between the palms, changing position and lifting the tool often to prevent grooving. Lap the valve until a smooth, polished seat is evident. Remove the valve and tool, and rinse away all traces of grinding compound.
	** Fasten a suction cup to a piece of drill rod, and mount the rod in a hand drill. Proceed as above, using the hand drill as a lapping tool. CAUTION: *Due to the higher speeds involved when using the hand drill, care must be exercised to avoid grooving the seat.* Lift the tool and change direction of rotation often.
Check the valve springs: **Checking the valve spring free length and squareness** (© Ford Motor Co.) **Checking the valve spring tension** (© Chrysler Corp.)	Place the spring on a flat surface next to a square. Measure the height of the spring, and rotate it against the edge of the square to measure distortion. If spring height varies (by comparison) by more than 1/16″ or if distortion exceeds 1/16″, replace the spring.
	** In addition to evaluating the spring as above, test the spring pressure at the installed and compressed (installed height minus valve lift) height using a valve spring tester. Springs used on small displacement engines (up to 3 liters) should be ± 1 lb. of all other springs in either position. A tolerance of ± 5 lbs. is permissible on larger engines.

Procedure	Method
* Install valve stem seals: **Valve stem seal installation** (© Ford Motor Co.) SEAL	* Due to the pressure differential that exists at the ends of the intake valve guides (atmospheric pressure above, manifold vacuum below), oil is drawn through the valve guides into the intake port. This has been alleviated somewhat since the addition of positive crankcase ventilation, which lowers the pressure above the guides. Several types of valve stem seals are available to reduce blow-by. Certain seals simply slip over the stem and guide boss, while others require that the boss be machined. Recently, Teflon guide seals have become popular. Consult a parts supplier or machinist concerning availability and suggested usages. NOTE: *When installing seals, ensure that a small amount of oil is able to pass the seal to lubricate the valve guides; otherwise, excessive wear may result.*
Install the valves:	Lubricate the valve stems, and install the valves in the cylinder head as numbered. Lubricate and position the seals (if used, see above) and the valve springs. Install the spring retainers, compress the springs, and insert the keys using needlenose pliers or a tool designed for this purpose. NOTE: *Retain the keys with wheel bearing grease during installation.*
Checking valve spring installed height: **Valve spring installed height dimension** (© Porsche) **Measuring valve spring installed height** (© Petersen Publishing Co.)	Measure the distance between the spring pad and the lower edge of the spring retainer, and compare to specifications. If the installed height is incorrect, add shim washers between the spring pad and the spring. CAUTION: *Use only washers designed for this purpose.*
** CC'ing the combustion chambers:	** Invert the cylinder head and place a bead of sealer around a combustion chamber. Install an apparatus designed for this purpose (burette mounted on a clear plate; see illustration) over the combustion chamber, and fill with the specified fluid to an even mark on the burette. Record the burette reading, and fill the combustion chamber with fluid. (NOTE: *A hole drilled in the plate will permit air to escape*). Subtract the burette reading, with the combustion chamber filled, from the previous reading, to determine combustion chamber volume in cc's. Duplicate this procedure in all combustion

Procedure	*Method*

CC'ing the combustion chamber
(© Petersen Publishing Co.)

chambers on the cylinder head, and compare the readings. The volume of all combustion chambers should be made equal to that of the largest. Combustion chamber volume may be increased in two ways. When only a small change is required (usually), a small cutter or coarse stone may be used to remove material from the combustion chamber. NOTE: *Check volume frequently.* Remove material over a wide area, so as not to change the configuration of the combustion chamber. When a larger change is required, the valve seat may be sunk (lowered into the head). NOTE: *When altering valve seat, remember to compensate for the change in spring installed height.*

Inspect the rocker arms, balls, studs, and nuts (where applicable):

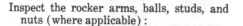

Stress cracks in rocker nuts
(© Ford Motor Co.)

SMALL FRACTURES

Visually inspect the rocker arms, balls, studs, and nuts for cracks, galling, burning, scoring, or wear. If all parts are intact, liberally lubricate the rocker arms and balls, and install them on the cylinder head. If wear is noted on a rocker arm at the point of valve contact, grind it smooth and square, removing as little material as possible. Replace the rocker arm if excessively worn. If a rocker stud shows signs of wear, it must be replaced (see below). If a rocker nut shows stress cracks, replace it. If an exhaust ball is galled or burned, substitute the intake ball from the same cylinder (if it is intact), and install a new intake ball. NOTE: *Avoid using new rocker balls on exhaust valves.*

Replacing rocker studs:

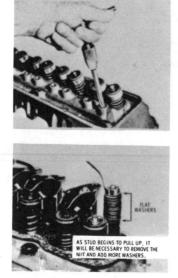

Reaming the stud bore for oversize rocker studs
(© Buick Div. G.M. Corp.)

Extracting a pressed in rocker stud
(© Buick Div. G.M. Corp.)

FLAT WASHERS

AS STUD BEGINS TO PULL UP, IT WILL BE NECESSARY TO REMOVE THE NUT AND ADD MORE WASHERS.

In order to remove a threaded stud, lock two nuts on the stud, and unscrew the stud using the lower nut. Coat the lower threads of the new stud with Loctite, and install.

Two alternative methods are available for replacing pressed in studs. Remove the damaged stud using a stack of washers and a nut (see illustration). In the first, the boss is reamed .005-.006″ oversize, and an oversize stud pressed in. Control the stud extension over the boss using washers, in the same manner as valve guides. Before installing the stud, coat it with white lead and grease. To retain the stud more positively, drill a hole through the stud and boss, and install a roll pin. In the second method, the boss is tapped, and a threaded stud installed. Retain the stud using Loctite Stud and Bearing Mount.

Procedure	*Method*
Inspect the rocker shaft(s) and rocker arms (where applicable): 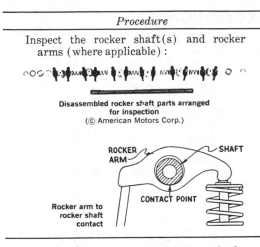 **Disassembled rocker shaft parts arranged for inspection** (© American Motors Corp.) ROCKER ARM — SHAFT Rocker arm to rocker shaft contact CONTACT POINT	Remove rocker arms, springs and washers from rocker shaft. NOTE: *Lay out parts in the order they are removed.* Inspect rocker arms for pitting or wear on the valve contact point, or excessive bushing wear. Bushings need only be replaced if wear is excessive, because the rocker arm normally contacts the shaft at one point only. Grind the valve contact point of rocker arm smooth if necessary, removing as little material as possible. If excessive material must be removed to smooth and square the arm, it should be replaced. Clean out all oil holes and passages in rocker shaft. If shaft is grooved or worn, replace it. Lubricate and assemble the rocker shaft.
Inspect the camshaft bushings and the camshaft (overhead cam engines):	See next section.
Inspect the pushrods:	Remove the pushrods, and, if hollow, clean out the oil passages using fine wire. Roll each pushrod over a piece of clean glass. If a distinct clicking sound is heard as the pushrod rolls, the rod is bent, and must be replaced.
	* The length of all pushrods must be equal. Measure the length of the pushrods, compare to specifications, and replace as necessary.
Inspect the valve lifters:  Check for Concave Wear on Face of Tappet Using Tappet for Straight Edge **Checking the lifter face** (© American Motors Corp.)	Remove lifters from their bores, and remove gum and varnish, using solvent. Clean walls of lifter bores. Check lifters for concave wear as illustrated. If face is worn concave, replace lifter, and carefully inspect the camshaft. Lightly lubricate lifter and insert it into its bore. If play is excessive, an oversize lifter must be installed (where possible). Consult a machinist concerning feasibility. If play is satisfactory, remove, lubricate, and reinstall the lifter.
* Testing hydraulic lifter leak down: Lock Ring Plunger Cap Push Rod Socket Metering Disc Plunger Valve Seat Valve Valve Spring Valve Retainer Plunger Return Spring Tappet Body **Exploded view of a typical hydraulic lifter** (© American Motors Corp.)	Submerge lifter in a container of kerosene. Chuck a used pushrod or its equivalent into a drill press. Position container of kerosene so pushrod acts on the lifter plunger. Pump lifter with the drill press, until resistance increases. Pump several more times to bleed any air out of lifter. Apply very firm, constant pressure to the lifter, and observe rate at which fluid bleeds out of lifter. If the fluid bleeds very quickly (less than 15 seconds), lifter is defective. If the time exceeds 60 seconds, lifter is sticking. In either case, recondition or replace lifter. If lifter is operating properly (leak down time 15-60 seconds), lubricate and install it.

CYLINDER BLOCK RECONDITIONING

Procedure	Method

Checking the main bearing clearance:

Plastigage installed on main bearing journal
(© Chevrolet Div. G.M. Corp.)

Measuring Plastigage to determine
main bearing clearance
(© Chevrolet Div. G.M. Corp.)

Causes of bearing failure
(© Ford Motor Co.)

Invert engine, and remove cap from the bearing to be checked. Using a clean, dry rag, thoroughly clean all oil from crankshaft journal and bearing insert. NOTE: *Plastigage is soluble in oil; therefore, oil on the journal or bearing could result in erroneous readings.* Place a piece of Plastigage along the full length of journal, reinstall cap, and torque to specifications. Remove bearing cap, and determine bearing clearance by comparing width of Plastigage to the scale on Plastigage envelope. Journal taper is determined by comparing width of the Plastigage strip near its ends. Rotate crankshaft 90° and retest, to determine journal eccentricity. NOTE: *Do not rotate crankshaft with Plastigage installed.* If bearing insert and journal appear intact, and are within tolerances, no further main bearing service is required. If bearing or journal appear defective, cause of failure should be determined before replacement.

* Remove crankshaft from block (see below). Measure the main bearing journals at each end twice (90° apart) using a micrometer, to determine diameter, journal taper and eccentricity. If journals are within tolerances, reinstall bearing caps at their specified torque. Using a telescope gauge and micrometer, measure bearing I.D. parallel to piston axis and at 30° on each side of piston axis. Subtract journal O.D. from bearing I.D. to determine oil clearance. If crankshaft journals appear defective, or do not meet tolerances, there is no need to measure bearings; for the crankshaft will require grinding and/or undersize bearings will be required. If bearing appears defective, cause for failure should be determined prior to replacement.

Checking the connecting rod bearing clearance:

Plastigage installed on connecting rod
bearing journal
(© Chevrolet Div. G.M. Corp.)

Connecting rod bearing clearance is checked in the same manner as main bearing clearance, using Plastigage. Before removing the crankshaft, connecting rod side clearance also should be measured and recorded.

* Checking connecting rod bearing clearance, using a micrometer, is identical to checking main bearing clearance. If no other service

Procedure	Method

Measuring Plastigage to determine connecting rod bearing clearance
(© Chevrolet Div. G.M. Corp.)

is required, the piston and rod assemblies need not be removed.

Removing the crankshaft:

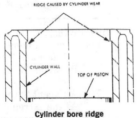

Connecting rod matching marks
(© Ford Motor Co.)

Using a punch, mark the corresponding main bearing caps and saddles according to position (i.e., one punch on the front main cap and saddle, two on the second, three on the third, etc.). Using number stamps, identify the corresponding connecting rods and caps, according to cylinder (if no numbers are present). Remove the main and connecting rod caps, and place sleeves of plastic tubing over the connecting rod bolts, to protect the journals as the crankshaft is removed. Lift the crankshaft out of the block.

Remove the ridge from the top of the cylinder:

Cylinder bore ridge
(© Pontiac Div. G.M. Corp.)

In order to facilitate removal of the piston and connecting rod, the ridge at the top of the cylinder (unworn area; see illustration) must be removed. Place the piston at the bottom of the bore, and cover it with a rag. Cut the ridge away using a ridge reamer, exercising extreme care to avoid cutting too deeply. Remove the rag, and remove cuttings that remain on the piston. CAUTION: *If the ridge is not removed, and new rings are installed, damage to rings will result.*

Removing the piston and connecting rod:

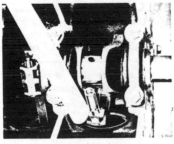

Removing the piston
(© SAAB)

Invert the engine, and push the pistons and connecting rods out of the cylinders. If necessary, tap the connecting rod boss with a wooden hammer handle, to force the piston out. CAUTION: *Do not attempt to force the piston past the cylinder ridge* (see above).

Procedure	Method
Service the crankshaft:	Ensure that all oil holes and passages in the crankshaft are open and free of sludge. If necessary, have the crankshaft ground to the largest possible undersize.
	** Have the crankshaft Magnafluxed, to locate stress cracks. Consult a machinist concerning additional service procedures, such as surface hardening (e.g., nitriding, Tuftriding) to improve wear characteristics, cross drilling and chamfering the oil holes to improve lubrication, and balancing.
Removing freeze plugs:	Drill a small hole in the center of the freeze plugs. Thread a large sheet metal screw into the hole and remove the plug with a slide hammer.
Remove the oil gallery plugs:	Threaded plugs should be removed using an appropriate (usually square) wrench. To remove soft, pressed in plugs, drill a hole in the plug, and thread in a sheet metal screw. Pull the plug out by the screw using a slide hammer.
Hot-tank the block:	Have the block hot-tanked to remove grease, corrosion, and scale from the water jackets. NOTE: *Consult the operator to determine whether the camshaft bearings will be damaged during the hot-tank process.*
Check the block for cracks:	Visually inspect the block for cracks or chips. The most common locations are as follows: Adjacent to freeze plugs. Between the cylinders and water jackets. Adjacent to the main bearing saddles. At the extreme bottom of the cylinders. Check only suspected cracks using spot check dye (see introduction). If a crack is located, consult a machinist concerning possible repairs.
	** Magnaflux the block to locate hidden cracks. If cracks are located, consult a machinist about feasibility of repair.
Install the oil gallery plugs and freeze plugs:	Coat freeze plugs with sealer and tap into position using a piece of pipe, slightly smaller than the plug, as a driver. To ensure retention, stake the edges of the plugs. Coat threaded oil gallery plugs with sealer and install. Drive replacement soft plugs into block using a large drift as a driver.
	* Rather than reinstalling lead plugs, drill and tap the holes, and install threaded plugs.

Procedure	Method
Check the bore diameter and surface:	Visually inspect the cylinder bores for roughness, scoring, or scuffing. If evident, the cylinder bore must be bored or honed oversize to eliminate imperfections, and the smallest possible oversize piston used. The new pistons should be given to the machinist with the block, so that the cylinders can be bored or honed exactly to the piston size (plus clearance). If no flaws are evident, measure the bore diameter using a telescope gauge and micrometer, or dial gauge, parallel and perpendicular to the engine centerline, at the top (below the ridge) and bottom of the bore. Subtract the bottom measurements from the top to determine taper, and the parallel to the centerline measurements from the perpendicular measurements to determine eccentricity. If the measurements are not within specifications, the cylinder must be bored or honed, and an oversize piston installed. If the measurements are within specifications the cylinder may be used as is, with only finish honing (see below). NOTE: *Prior to submitting the block for boring, perform the following operation(s).*

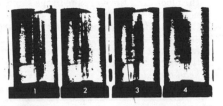

1, 2, 3 Piston skirt seizure resulted in this pattern. Engine must be rebored

4. Piston skirt and oil ring seizure caused this damage. Engine must be rebored

5, 6 Score marks caused by a split piston skirt. Damage is not serious enough to warrant reboring

7 Ring seized longitudinally, causing a score mark 1 3/16" wide, on the land side of the piston groove. The honing pattern is destroyed and the cylinder must be rebored

8. Result of oil ring seizure. Engine must be rebored

9. Oil ring seizure here was not serious enough to warrant reboring. The honing marks are still visible

Cylinder wall damage
(© Daimler-Benz A.G.)

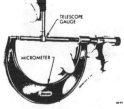

Cylinder bore measuring positions
(© Ford Motor Co.)

Measuring the cylinder bore with a telescope gauge
(© Buick Div. G.M. Corp.)

Determining the cylinder bore by measuring the telescope gauge with a micrometer
(© Buick Div. G.M. Corp.)

Measuring the cylinder bore with a dial gauge
(© Chevrolet Div. G.M. Corp.)

Procedure	Method
Check the block deck for warpage:	Using a straightedge and feeler gauges, check the block deck for warpage in the same manner that the cylinder head is checked (see Cylinder Head Reconditioning). If warpage exceeds specifications, have the deck resurfaced. NOTE: *In certain cases a specification for total material removal (Cylinder head and block deck) is provided. This specification must not be exceeded.*
* Check the deck height:	The deck height is the distance from the crankshaft centerline to the block deck. To measure, invert the engine, and install the crankshaft, retaining it with the center main cap. Measure the distance from the crankshaft journal to the block deck, parallel to the cylinder centerline. Measure the diameter of the end (front and rear) main journals, parallel to the centerline of the cylinders, divide the diameter in half, and subtract it from the previous measurement. The results of the front and rear measurements should be identical. If the difference exceeds .005″, the deck height should be corrected. NOTE: *Block deck height and warpage should be corrected concurrently.*
Check the cylinder block bearing alignment: Checking main bearing saddle alignment (© Petersen Publishing Co.)	Remove the upper bearing inserts. Place a straightedge in the bearing saddles along the centerline of the crankshaft. If clearance exists between the straightedge and the center saddle, the block must be align-bored.
Clean and inspect the pistons and connecting rods: Removing the piston rings (© Subaru)	Using a ring expander, remove the rings from the piston. Remove the retaining rings (if so equipped) and remove piston pin. NOTE: *If the piston pin must be pressed out, determine the proper method and use the proper tools; otherwise the piston will distort.* Clean the ring grooves using an appropriate tool, exercising care to avoid cutting too deeply. Thoroughly clean all carbon and varnish from the piston with solvent. CAUTION: *Do not use a wire brush or caustic solvent on pistons.* Inspect the pistons for scuffing, scoring, cracks, pitting, or excessive ring groove wear. If wear is evident, the piston must be replaced. Check the connecting rod length by measuring the rod from the inside of the large end to the inside of the small end using calipers (see

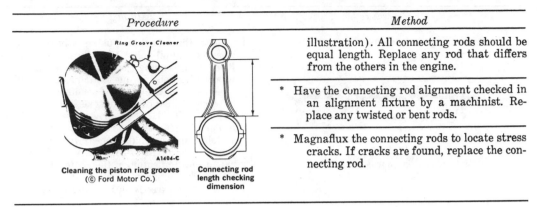

Procedure	Method

illustration). All connecting rods should be equal length. Replace any rod that differs from the others in the engine.

* Have the connecting rod alignment checked in an alignment fixture by a machinist. Replace any twisted or bent rods.

* Magnaflux the connecting rods to locate stress cracks. If cracks are found, replace the connecting rod.

Cleaning the piston ring grooves
(© Ford Motor Co.)

Connecting rod length checking dimension

Fit the pistons to the cylinders:

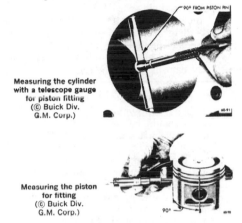

Measuring the cylinder with a telescope gauge for piston fitting
(© Buick Div. G.M. Corp.)

Measuring the piston for fitting
(© Buick Div. G.M. Corp.)

Using a telescope gauge and micrometer, or a dial gauge, measure the cylinder bore diameter perpendicular to the piston pin, $2\frac{1}{2}''$ below the deck. Measure the piston perpendicular to its pin on the skirt. The difference between the two measurements is the piston clearance. If the clearance is within specifications or slightly below (after boring or honing), finish honing is all that is required. If the clearance is excessive, try to obtain a slightly larger piston to bring clearance within specifications. Where this is not possible, obtain the first oversize piston, and hone (or if necessary, bore) the cylinder to size.

Assemble the pistons and connecting rods:

Installing piston pin lock rings
(© Nissan Motor Co., Ltd.)

Inspect piston pin, connecting rod small end bushing, and piston bore for galling, scoring, or excessive wear. If evident, replace defective part(s). Measure the I.D. of the piston boss and connecting rod small end, and the O.D. of the piston pin. If within specifications, assemble piston pin and rod. CAUTION: *If piston pin must be pressed in, determine the proper method and use the proper tools; otherwise the piston will distort.* Install the lock rings; ensure that they seat properly. If the parts are not within specifications, determine the service method for the type of engine. In some cases, piston and pin are serviced as an assembly when either is defective. Others specify reaming the piston and connecting rods for an oversize pin. If the connecting rod bushing is worn, it may in many cases be replaced. Reaming the piston and replacing the rod bushing are machine shop operations.

Procedure	Method

Clean and inspect the camshaft:

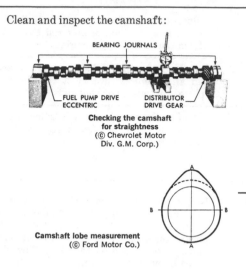

BEARING JOURNALS

FUEL PUMP DRIVE ECCENTRIC   DISTRIBUTOR DRIVE GEAR

Checking the camshaft for straightness
(© Chevrolet Motor Div. G.M. Corp.)

Camshaft lobe measurement
(© Ford Motor Co.)

Degrease the camshaft, using solvent, and clean out all oil holes. Visually inspect cam lobes and bearing journals for excessive wear. If a lobe is questionable, check all lobes as indicated below. If a journal or lobe is worn, the camshaft must be reground or replaced. NOTE: *If a journal is worn, there is a good chance that the bushings are worn.* If lobes and journals appear intact, place the front and rear journals in V-blocks, and rest a dial indicator on the center journal. Rotate the camshaft to check straightness. If deviation exceeds .001″, replace the camshaft.

* Check the camshaft lobes with a micrometer, by measuring the lobes from the nose to base and again at 90° (see illustration). The lift is determined by subtracting the second measurement from the first. If all exhaust lobes and all intake lobes are not identical, the camshaft must be reground or replaced.

Replace the camshaft bearings:

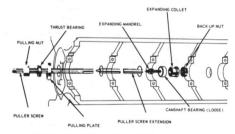

EXPANDING COLLET

THRUST BEARING   EXPANDING MANDREL   BACK-UP NUT

PULLING NUT

PULLER SCREW   CAMSHAFT BEARING (LOOSE)

PULLING PLATE   PULLER SCREW EXTENSION

Camshaft removal and installation tool (typical)
(© Ford Motor Co.)

If excessive wear is indicated, or if the engine is being completely rebuilt, camshaft bearings should be replaced as follows: Drive the camshaft rear plug from the block. Assemble the removal puller with its shoulder on the bearing to be removed. Gradually tighten the puller nut until bearing is removed. Remove remaining bearings, leaving the front and rear for last. To remove front and rear bearings, reverse position of the tool, so as to pull the bearings in toward the center of the block. Leave the tool in this position, pilot the new front and rear bearings on the installer, and pull them into position. Return the tool to its original position and pull remaining bearings into position. NOTE: *Ensure that oil holes align when installing bearings.* Replace camshaft rear plug, and stake it into position to aid retention.

Finish hone the cylinders:

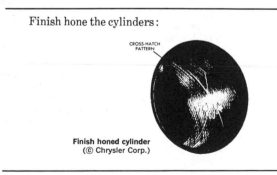

CROSS-HATCH PATTERN

Finish honed cylinder
(© Chrysler Corp.)

Chuck a flexible drive hone into a power drill, and insert it into the cylinder. Start the hone, and move it up and down in the cylinder at a rate which will produce approximately a 60° cross-hatch pattern (see illustration). NOTE: *Do not extend the hone below the cylinder bore.* After developing the pattern, remove the hone and recheck piston fit. Wash the cylinders with a detergent and water solution to remove abrasive dust, dry, and wipe several times with a rag soaked in engine oil.

Procedure	Method
Check piston ring end-gap:	Compress the piston rings to be used in a cylinder, one at a time, into that cylinder, and press them approximately 1″ below the deck with an inverted piston. Using feeler gauges, measure the ring end-gap, and compare to specifications. Pull the ring out of the cylinder and file the ends with a fine file to obtain proper clearance. CAUTION: *If inadequate ring end-gap is utilized, ring breakage will result.*

Checking ring end-gap
(© Chevrolet Motor Div. G.M. Corp.)

Procedure	Method
Install the piston rings:	Inspect the ring grooves in the piston for excessive wear or taper. If necessary, recut the groove(s) for use with an overwidth ring or a standard ring and spacer. If the groove is worn uniformly, overwidth rings, or standard rings and spacers may be installed without recutting. Roll the outside of the ring around the groove to check for burrs or deposits. If any are found, remove with a fine file. Hold the ring in the groove, and measure side clearance. If necessary, correct as indicated above. NOTE: *Always install any additional spacers above the piston ring.* The ring groove must be deep enough to allow the ring to seat below the lands (see illustration). In many cases, a "go-no-go" depth gauge will be provided with the piston rings. Shallow grooves may be corrected by recutting, while deep grooves require some type of filler or expander behind the piston. Consult the piston ring supplier concerning the suggested method. Install the rings on the piston, lowest ring first, using a ring expander. NOTE: *Position the ring markings as specified by the manufacturer (see car section).*

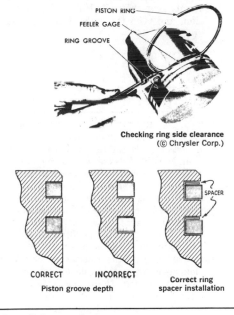

PISTON RING
FEELER GAGE
RING GROOVE

Checking ring side clearance
(© Chrysler Corp.)

SPACER

CORRECT   INCORRECT
Piston groove depth

Correct ring spacer installation

Procedure	Method
Install the camshaft:	Liberally lubricate the camshaft lobes and journals, and slide the camshaft into the block. CAUTION: *Exercise extreme care to avoid damaging the bearings when inserting the camshaft.* Install and tighten the camshaft thrust plate retaining bolts.
Check camshaft end-play:	Using feeler gauges, determine whether the clearance between the camshaft boss (or gear) and backing plate is within specifications. Install shims behind the thrust plate, or reposition the camshaft gear and retest end-play.

Checking camshaft end-play with a feeler gauge
(© Ford Motor Co.)

Procedure	Method

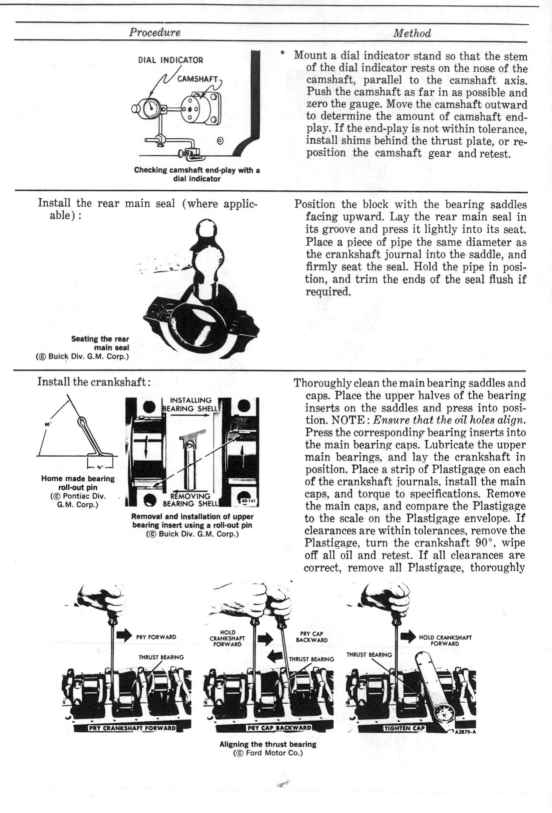

DIAL INDICATOR
CAMSHAFT

Checking camshaft end-play with a dial indicator

* Mount a dial indicator stand so that the stem of the dial indicator rests on the nose of the camshaft, parallel to the camshaft axis. Push the camshaft as far in as possible and zero the gauge. Move the camshaft outward to determine the amount of camshaft end-play. If the end-play is not within tolerance, install shims behind the thrust plate, or reposition the camshaft gear and retest.

Install the rear main seal (where applicable):

Seating the rear main seal
(© Buick Div. G.M. Corp.)

Position the block with the bearing saddles facing upward. Lay the rear main seal in its groove and press it lightly into its seat. Place a piece of pipe the same diameter as the crankshaft journal into the saddle, and firmly seat the seal. Hold the pipe in position, and trim the ends of the seal flush if required.

Install the crankshaft:

INSTALLING BEARING SHELL

Home made bearing roll-out pin
(© Pontiac Div. G.M. Corp.)

REMOVING BEARING SHELL

Removal and installation of upper bearing insert using a roll-out pin
(© Buick Div. G.M. Corp.)

Thoroughly clean the main bearing saddles and caps. Place the upper halves of the bearing inserts on the saddles and press into position. NOTE: *Ensure that the oil holes align.* Press the corresponding bearing inserts into the main bearing caps. Lubricate the upper main bearings, and lay the crankshaft in position. Place a strip of Plastigage on each of the crankshaft journals, install the main caps, and torque to specifications. Remove the main caps, and compare the Plastigage to the scale on the Plastigage envelope. If clearances are within tolerances, remove the Plastigage, turn the crankshaft 90°, wipe off all oil and retest. If all clearances are correct, remove all Plastigage, thoroughly

PRY FORWARD
THRUST BEARING
PRY CRANKSHAFT FORWARD

HOLD CRANKSHAFT FORWARD
PRY CAP BACKWARD
THRUST BEARING
PRY CAP BACKWARD

HOLD CRANKSHAFT FORWARD
THRUST BEARING
TIGHTEN CAP
A2879-A

Aligning the thrust bearing
(© Ford Motor Co.)

Procedure	Method
	lubricate the main caps and bearing journals, and install the main caps. If clearances are not within tolerance, the upper bearing inserts may be removed, without removing the crankshaft, using a bearing roll out pin (see illustration). Roll in a bearing that will provide proper clearance, and retest. Torque all main caps, excluding the thrust bearing cap, to specifications. Tighten the thrust bearing cap finger tight. To properly align the thrust bearing, pry the crankshaft the extent of its axial travel several times, the last movement held toward the front of the engine, and torque the thrust bearing cap to specifications. Determine the crankshaft end-play (see below), and bring within tolerance with thrust washers.
Measure crankshaft end-play: Checking crankshaft end-play with a dial indicator (ⓒ Ford Motor Co.) Checking crankshaft end-play with a feeler gauge (ⓒ Chevrolet Div. (G.M. Corp.)	Mount a dial indicator stand on the front of the block, with the dial indicator stem resting on the nose of the crankshaft, parallel to the crankshaft axis. Pry the crankshaft the extent of its travel rearward, and zero the indicator. Pry the crankshaft forward and record crankshaft end-play. NOTE: *Crankshaft end-play also may be measured at the thrust bearing, using feeler gauges* (see illustration).
Install the pistons:	Press the upper connecting rod bearing halves into the connecting rods, and the lower halves into the connecting rod caps. Position the piston ring gaps according to specifications (see car section), and lubricate the pistons. Install a ring compresser on a piston, and press two long (8") pieces of plastic tubing over the rod bolts. Using the plastic tubes as a guide, press the pistons into the bores and onto the crankshaft with a wooden hammer handle. After seating the rod on the crankshaft journal, remove the tubes and install the cap finger tight. Install the remaining pistons in the same man-

Procedure	Method

Tubing used as guide when installing a piston
(© Oldsmobile Div. G.M. Corp.)

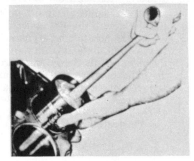

Installing a piston
(© Chevrolet Div. G.M. Corp.)

ner. Invert the engine and check the bearing clearance at two points (90° apart) on each journal with Plastigage. NOTE: *Do not turn the crankshaft with Plastigage installed.* If clearance is within tolerances, remove *all* Plastigage, thoroughly lubricate the journals, and torque the rod caps to specifications. If clearance is not within specifications, install different thickness bearing inserts and recheck. CAUTION: *Never shim or file the connecting rods or caps.* Always install plastic tube sleeves over the rod bolts when the caps are not installed, to protect the crankshaft journals.

Check connecting rod side clearance:

Checking connecting rod side clearance
(© Chevrolet Div. G.M. Corp.)

Determine the clearance between the sides of the connecting rods and the crankshaft, using feeler gauges. If clearance is below the minimum tolerance, the rod may be machined to provide adequate clearance. If clearance is excessive, substitute an unworn rod, and recheck. If clearance is still outside specifications, the crankshaft must be welded and reground, or replaced.

Inspect the timing chain:

Visually inspect the timing chain for broken or loose links, and replace the chain if any are found. If the chain will flex sideways, it must be replaced. Install the timing chain as specified. NOTE: *If the original timing chain is to be reused, install it in its original position.*

CHILTON'S
FUEL ECONOMY
& TUNE-UP TIPS

Tune-Up • Spark Plug Diagnosis • Emission Controls

Fuel System • Cooling System • Tires and Wheels

General Maintenance

CHILTON'S FUEL ECONOMY & TUNE-UP TIPS

Fuel economy is important to everyone, no matter what kind of vehicle you drive. The maintenance-minded motorist can save both money and fuel using these tips and the periodic maintenance and tune-up procedures in this Repair and Tune-Up Guide.

There are more than 130,000,000 cars and trucks registered for private use in the United States. Each travels an average of 10-12,000 miles per year, and, in total they consume close to 70 billion gallons of fuel each year. This represents nearly ⅔ of the oil imported by the United States each year. The Federal government's goal is to reduce consumption 10% by 1985. A variety of methods are either already in use or under serious consideration, and they all affect your driving and the cars you will drive. In addition to "down-sizing", the auto industry is using or investigating the use of electronic fuel delivery, electronic engine controls and alternative engines for use in smaller and lighter vehicles, among other alternatives to meet the federally mandated Corporate Average Fuel Economy (CAFE) of 27.5 mpg by 1985. The government, for its part, is considering rationing, mandatory driving curtailments and tax increases on motor vehicle fuel in an effort to reduce consumption. The government's goal of a 10% reduction could be realized — and further government regulation avoided — if every private vehicle could use just 1 less gallon of fuel per week.

How Much Can You Save?

Tests have proven that almost anyone can make at least a 10% reduction in fuel consumption through regular maintenance and tune-ups. When a major manufacturer of spark plugs sur-

TUNE-UP

1. Check the cylinder compression to be sure the engine will really benefit from a tune-up and that it is capable of producing good fuel economy. A tune-up will be wasted on an engine in poor mechanical condition.

2. Replace spark plugs regularly. New spark plugs alone can increase fuel economy 3%.

3. Be sure the spark plugs are the correct type (heat range) for your vehicle. See the Tune-Up Specifications.

Heat range refers to the spark plug's ability to conduct heat away from the firing end. It must conduct the heat away in an even pattern to avoid becoming a source of pre-ignition, yet it must also operate hot enough to burn off conductive deposits that could cause misfiring.

The heat range is usually indicated by a number on the spark plug, part of the manufacturer's designation for each individual spark plug. The numbers in bold-face indicate the heat range in each manufacturer's identification system.

Manufacturer	Typical Designation
AC	R **45** TS
Bosch (old)	WA **145** T30
Bosch (new)	HR **8** Y
Champion	RBL **15** Y
Fram/Autolite	**415**
Mopar	P-**62** PR
Motorcraft	BRF-**42**
NGK	BP **5** ES-15
Nippondenso	W **16** EP
Prestolite	14GR **5** 2A

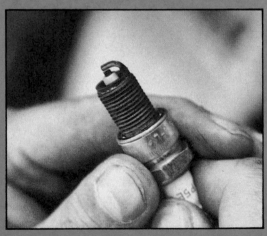

Periodically, check the spark plugs to be sure they are firing efficiently. They are excellent indicators of the internal condition of your engine.

On AC, Bosch (new), Champion, Fram/Autolite, Mopar, Motorcraft and Prestolite, a higher number indicates a hotter plug. On Bosch (old), NGK and Nippondenso, a higher number indicates a colder plug.

4. Make sure the spark plugs are properly gapped. See the Tune-Up Specifications in this book.

5. Be sure the spark plugs are firing efficiently. The illustrations on the next 2 pages show you how to "read" the firing end of the spark plug.

6. Check the ignition timing and set it to specifications. Tests show that almost all cars

veyed over 6,000 cars nationwide, they found that a tune-up, on cars that needed one, increased fuel economy over 11%. Replacing worn plugs alone, accounted for a 3% increase. The same test also revealed that 8 out of every 10 vehicles will have some maintenance deficiency that will directly affect fuel economy, emissions or performance. Most of this mileage-robbing neglect could be prevented with regular maintenance.

Modern engines require that all of the functioning systems operate properly for maximum efficiency. A malfunction anywhere wastes fuel. You can keep your vehicle running as efficiently and economically as possible, by being aware of your vehicles operating and performance characteristics. If your vehicle suddenly develops performance or fuel economy problems it could be due to one or more of the following:

PROBLEM	POSSIBLE CAUSE
Engine Idles Rough	Ignition timing, idle mixture, vacuum leak or something amiss in the emission control system.
Hesitates on Acceleration	Dirty carburetor or fuel filter, improper accelerator pump setting, ignition timing or fouled spark plugs.
Starts Hard or Fails to Start	Worn spark plugs, improperly set automatic choke, ice (or water) in fuel system.
Stalls Frequently	Automatic choke improperly adjusted and possible dirty air filter or fuel filter.
Performs Sluggishly	Worn spark plugs, dirty fuel or air filter, ignition timing or automatic choke out of adjustment.

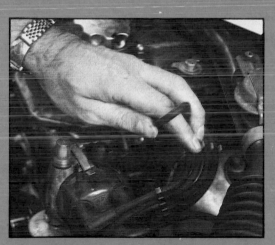

Check spark plug wires on conventional point type ignition for cracks by bending them in a loop around your finger.

Be sure that spark plug wires leading to adjacent cylinders do not run too close together. (Photo courtesy Champion Spark Plug Co.)

have incorrect ignition timing by more than 2°.

7. If your vehicle does not have electronic ignition, check the points, rotor and cap as specified.

8. Check the spark plug wires (used with conventional point-type ignitions) for cracks and burned or broken insulation by bending them in a loop around your finger. Cracked wires decrease fuel efficiency by failing to deliver full voltage to the spark plugs. One misfiring spark plug can cost you as much as 2 mpg.

9. Check the routing of the plug wires. Misfiring can be the result of spark plug leads to adjacent cylinders running parallel to each

other and too close together. One wire tends to pick up voltage from the other causing it to fire "out of time".

10. Check all electrical and ignition circuits for voltage drop and resistance.

11. Check the distributor mechanical and/or vacuum advance mechanisms for proper functioning. The vacuum advance can be checked by twisting the distributor plate in the opposite direction of rotation. It should spring back when released.

12. Check and adjust the valve clearance on engines with mechanical lifters. The clearance should be slightly loose rather than too tight.

SPARK PLUG DIAGNOSIS

Normal

APPEARANCE: This plug is typical of one operating normally. The insulator nose varies from a light tan to grayish color with slight electrode wear. The presence of slight deposits is normal on used plugs and will have no adverse effect on engine performance. The spark plug heat range is correct for the engine and the engine is running normally.

CAUSE: Properly running engine.

RECOMMENDATION: Before reinstalling this plug, the electrodes should be cleaned and filed square. Set the gap to specifications. If the plug has been in service for more than 10-12,000 miles, the entire set should probably be replaced with a fresh set of the same heat range.

Oil Deposits

APPEARANCE: The firing end of the plug is covered with a wet, oily coating.

CAUSE: The problem is poor oil control. On high mileage engines, oil is leaking past the rings or valve guides into the combustion chamber. A common cause is also a plugged PCV valve, and a ruptured fuel pump diaphragm can also cause this condition. Oil fouled plugs such as these are often found in new or recently overhauled engines, before normal oil control is achieved, and can be cleaned and reinstalled.

RECOMMENDATION: A hotter spark plug may temporarily relieve the problem, but the engine is probably in need of work.

Incorrect Heat Range

APPEARANCE: The effects of high temperature on a spark plug are indicated by clean white, often blistered insulator. This can also be accompanied by excessive wear of the electrode, and the absence of deposits.

CAUSE: Check for the correct spark plug heat range. A plug which is too hot for the engine can result in overheating. A car operated mostly at high speeds can require a colder plug. Also check ignition timing, cooling system level, fuel mixture and leaking intake manifold.

RECOMMENDATION: If all ignition and engine adjustments are known to be correct, and no other malfunction exists, install spark plugs one heat range colder.

Photos Courtesy Champion Spark Plug Co.

Carbon Deposits

APPEARANCE: Carbon fouling is easily identified by the presence of dry, soft, black, sooty deposits.

CAUSE: Changing the heat range can often lead to carbon fouling, as can prolonged slow, stop-and-start driving. If the heat range is correct, carbon fouling can be attributed to a rich fuel mixture, sticking choke, clogged air cleaner, worn breaker points, retarded timing or low compression. If only one or two plugs are carbon fouled, check for corroded or cracked wires on the affected plugs. Also look for cracks in the distributor cap between the towers of affected cylinders.

RECOMMENDATION: After the problem is corrected, these plugs can be cleaned and reinstalled if not worn severely.

MMT Fouled

APPEARANCE: Spark plugs fouled by MMT (Methycyclopentadienyl Maganese Tricarbonyl) have reddish, rusty appearance on the insulator and side electrode.

CAUSE: MMT is an anti-knock additive in gasoline used to replace lead. During the combustion process, the MMT leaves a reddish deposit on the insulator and side electrode.

RECOMMENDATION: No engine malfunction is indicated and the deposits will not affect plug performance any more than lead deposits (see Ash Deposits). MMT fouled plugs can be cleaned, regapped and reinstalled.

High Speed Glazing

APPEARANCE: Glazing appears as shiny coating on the plug, either yellow or tan in color.

CAUSE: During hard, fast acceleration, plug temperatures rise suddenly. Deposits from normal combustion have no chance to fluff-off; instead, they melt on the insulator forming an electrically conductive coating which causes misfiring.

RECOMMENDATION: Glazed plugs are not easily cleaned. They should be replaced with a fresh set of plugs of the correct heat range. If the condition recurs, using plugs with a heat range one step colder may cure the problem.

Ash (Lead) Deposits

APPEARANCE: Ash deposits are characterized by light brown or white colored deposits crusted on the side or center electrodes. In some cases it may give the plug a rusty appearance.

CAUSE: Ash deposits are normally derived from oil or fuel additives burned during normal combustion. Normally they are harmless, though excessive amounts can cause misfiring. If deposits are excessive in short mileage, the valve guides may be worn.

RECOMMENDATION: Ash-fouled plugs can be cleaned, gapped and reinstalled.

Detonation

APPEARANCE: Detonation is usually characterized by a broken plug insulator.

CAUSE: A portion of the fuel charge will begin to burn spontaneously, from the increased heat following ignition. The explosion that results applies extreme pressure to engine components, frequently damaging spark plugs and pistons.

Detonation can result by over-advanced ignition timing, inferior gasoline (low octane) lean air/fuel mixture, poor carburetion, engine lugging or an increase in compression ratio due to combustion chamber deposits or engine modification.

RECOMMENDATION: Replace the plugs after correcting the problem.

Photos Courtesy Fram Corporation

EMISSION CONTROLS

13. Be aware of the general condition of the emission control system. It contributes to reduced pollution and should be serviced regularly to maintain efficient engine operation.

14. Check all vacuum lines for dried, cracked or brittle conditions. Something as simple as a leaking vacuum hose can cause poor performance and loss of economy.

15. Avoid tampering with the emission control system. Attempting to improve fuel econ-

FUEL SYSTEM

Check the air filter with a light behind it. If you can see light through the filter it can be reused.

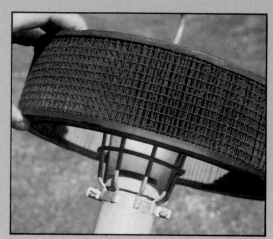

Extremely clogged filters should be discarded and replaced with a new one.

18. Replace the air filter regularly. A dirty air filter richens the air/fuel mixture and can increase fuel consumption as much as 10%. Tests show that 1/3 of all vehicles have air filters in need of replacement.

19. Replace the fuel filter at least as often as recommended.

20. Set the idle speed and carburetor mixture to specifications.

21. Check the automatic choke. A sticking or malfunctioning choke wastes gas.

22. During the summer months, adjust the automatic choke for a leaner mixture which will produce faster engine warm-ups.

COOLING SYSTEM

29. Be sure all accessory drive belts are in good condition. Check for cracks or wear.

30. Adjust all accessory drive belts to proper tension.

31. Check all hoses for swollen areas, worn spots, or loose clamps.

32. Check coolant level in the radiator or expansion tank.

33. Be sure the thermostat is operating properly. A stuck thermostat delays engine warm-up and a cold engine uses nearly twice as much fuel as a warm engine.

34. Drain and replace the engine coolant at least as often as recommended. Rust and scale

TIRES & WHEELS

38. Check the tire pressure often with a pencil type gauge. Tests by a major tire manufacturer show that 90% of all vehicles have at least 1 tire improperly inflated. Better mileage can be achieved by over-inflating tires, but never exceed the maximum inflation pressure on the side of the tire.

39. If possible, install radial tires. Radial tires deliver as much as 1/2 mpg more than bias belted tires.

40. Avoid installing super-wide tires. They only create extra rolling resistance and decrease fuel mileage. Stick to the manufacturer's recommendations.

41. Have the wheels properly balanced.

omy by tampering with emission controls is more likely to worsen fuel economy than improve it. Emission control changes on modern engines are not readily reversible.

16. Clean (or replace) the EGR valve and lines as recommended.

17. Be sure that all vacuum lines and hoses are reconnected properly after working under the hood. An unconnected or misrouted vacuum line can wreak havoc with engine performance.

23. Check for fuel leaks at the carburetor, fuel pump, fuel lines and fuel tank. Be sure all lines and connections are tight.

24. Periodically check the tightness of the carburetor and intake manifold attaching nuts and bolts. These are a common place for vacuum leaks to occur.

25. Clean the carburetor periodically and lubricate the linkage.

26. The condition of the tailpipe can be an excellent indicator of proper engine combustion. After a long drive at highway speeds, the inside of the tailpipe should be a light grey in color. Black or soot on the insides indicates an overly rich mixture.

27. Check the fuel pump pressure. The fuel pump may be supplying more fuel than the engine needs.

28. Use the proper grade of gasoline for your engine. Don't try to compensate for knocking or "pinging" by advancing the ignition timing. This practice will only increase plug temperature and the chances of detonation or pre-ignition with relatively little performance gain.

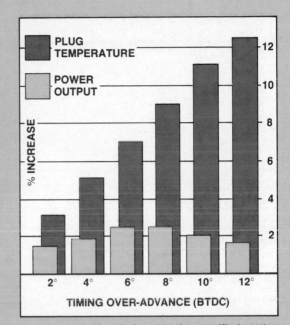

Increasing ignition timing past the specified setting results in a drastic increase in spark plug temperature with increased chance of detonation or preignition. Performance increase is considerably less. (Photo courtesy Champion Spark Plug Co.)

that form in the engine should be flushed out to allow the engine to operate at peak efficiency.

35. Clean the radiator of debris that can decrease cooling efficiency.

36. Install a flex-type or electric cooling fan, if you don't have a clutch type fan. Flex fans use curved plastic blades to push more air at low speeds when more cooling is needed; at high speeds the blades flatten out for less resistance. Electric fans only run when the engine temperature reaches a predetermined level.

37. Check the radiator cap for a worn or cracked gasket. If the cap does not seal properly, the cooling system will not function properly.

42. Be sure the front end is correctly aligned. A misaligned front end actually has wheels going in different directions. The increased drag can reduce fuel economy by .3 mpg.

43. Correctly adjust the wheel bearings. Wheel bearings that are adjusted too tight increase rolling resistance.

Check tire pressures regularly with a reliable pocket type gauge. Be sure to check the pressure on a cold tire.

GENERAL MAINTENANCE

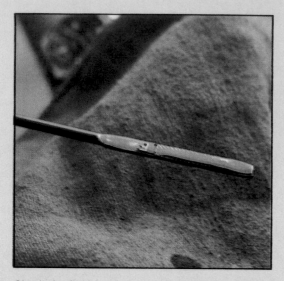

Check the fluid levels (particularly engine oil) on a regular basis. Be sure to check the oil for grit, water or other contamination.

A vacuum gauge is another excellent indicator of internal engine condition and can also be installed in the dash as a mileage indicator.

44. Periodically check the fluid levels in the engine, power steering pump, master cylinder, automatic transmission and drive axle.

45. Change the oil at the recommended interval and change the filter at every oil change. Dirty oil is thick and causes extra friction between moving parts, cutting efficiency and increasing wear. A worn engine requires more frequent tune-ups and gets progressively worse fuel economy. In general, use the lightest viscosity oil for the driving conditions you will encounter.

46. Use the recommended viscosity fluids in the transmission and axle.

47. Be sure the battery is fully charged for fast starts. A slow starting engine wastes fuel.

48. Be sure battery terminals are clean and tight.

49. Check the battery electrolyte level and add distilled water if necessary.

50. Check the exhaust system for crushed pipes, blockages and leaks.

51. Adjust the brakes. Dragging brakes or brakes that are not releasing create increased drag on the engine.

52. Install a vacuum gauge or miles-per-gallon gauge. These gauges visually indicate engine vacuum in the intake manifold. High vacuum = good mileage and low vacuum = poorer mileage. The gauge can also be an excellent indicator of internal engine conditions.

53. Be sure the clutch is properly adjusted. A slipping clutch wastes fuel.

54. Check and periodically lubricate the heat control valve in the exhaust manifold. A sticking or inoperative valve prevents engine warm-up and wastes gas.

55. Keep accurate records to check fuel economy over a period of time. A sudden drop in fuel economy may signal a need for tune-up or other maintenance.

Procedure	Method
Check timing gear backlash and runout:	Mount a dial indicator with its stem resting on a tooth of the camshaft gear (as illustrated). Rotate the gear until all slack is removed, and zero the indicator. Rotate the gear in the opposite direction until slack is removed, and record gear backlash. Mount the indicator with its stem resting on the edge of the camshaft gear, parallel to the axis of the camshaft. Zero the indicator, and turn the camshaft gear one full turn, recording the runout. If either backlash or runout exceed specifications, replace the worn gear(s).

Checking camshaft gear backlash
(© Chevrolet Div. G.M. Corp.)

Checking camshaft gear runout
(© Chevrolet Div. G.M. Corp.)

Completing the Rebuilding Process

Following the above procedures, complete the rebuilding process as follows:

Fill the oil pump with oil, to prevent cavitating (sucking air) on initial engine start up. Install the oil pump and the pickup tube on the engine. Coat the oil pan gasket as necessary, and install the gasket and the oil pan. Mount the flywheel and the crankshaft vibrational damper or pulley on the crankshaft. NOTE: *Always use new bolts when installing the flywheel.* Inspect the clutch shaft pilot bushing in the crankshaft. If the bushing is excessively worn, remove it with an expanding puller and a slide hammer, and tap a new bushing into place.

Position the engine, cylinder head side up. Lubricate the lifters, and install them into their bores. Install the cylinder head, and torque it as specified in the car section. Insert the pushrods (where applicable), and install the rocker shaft(s) (if so equipped) or position the rocker arms on the pushrods. If solid lifters are utilized, adjust the valves to the "cold" specifications.

Mount the intake and exhaust manifolds, the carburetor(s), the distributor and spark plugs. Adjust the point gap and the static ignition timing. Mount all accessories and install the engine in the car. Fill the radiator with coolant, and the crankcase with high quality engine oil.

Break-in Procedure

Start the engine, and allow it to run at low speed for a few minutes, while checking for leaks. Stop the engine, check the oil level, and fill as necessary. Restart the engine, and fill the cooling system to capacity. Check the point dwell angle and adjust the ignition timing and the valves. Run the engine at low to medium speed (800-2500 rpm) for approximately ½ hour, and retorque the cylinder head bolts. Road test the car, and check again for leaks.

Follow the manufacturer's recommended engine break-in procedure and maintenance schedule for new engines.

4 · Emission Controls and Fuel System

Emission Controls

POSITIVE CRANKCASE VENTILATION

All models covered in this guide are equipped with a PCV system (Positive Crankcase Ventilation). A simple valve, operated by intake manifold vacuum, is used to meter the flow of air and vapors through the crankcase. Air is drawn in through the carburetor air cleaner (closed system). When the car is decelerating or the engine is idling, high manifold vacuum closes the valve; this restricts the flow of crankcase vapor into the intake manifold. During acceleration or at a constant speed, the intake manifold vacuum drops, the valve spring forces the valve open, and more vapors flow into the intake manifold from the crankcase. If a backfire occurs the valve closes, preventing the vapor in the crankcase from being ignited. If the vapor is ignited, an explosion will result.

Emission control equipment other than PCV will be covered by model year.

1968–69

The General Motors Corporation had elected to adopt a special system of terminal exhaust treatment. This plan su-persedes (in most cases) the method used to conform to 1966–67 California laws. The new system cancels out (except with stick shift and special purpose engine applications) the use of the A.I.R. method previously used.

The new concept, Combustion Control System (C.C.S.) utilizes engine modification. Essentially the C.C.S. increases combustion efficiency through carburetor and distributor calibrations and by increasing engine operating temperature.

Carburetors are calibrated leaner and initial ignition timing is retarded. Another carburetor feature is the idle fuel mixture limiting orifice. It is located at the base of the idle mixture screw and makes sure that, even if the idle mixture screw is turned too far, the fuel enrichment will not greatly affect exhaust emissions.

The C.C.S. also incorporates a higher engine operating temperature. A 195° thermostat is used. Engines that run hotter provide a more complete vaporation of the fuel and reduce quench area in the combustion chamber. Quench area is the relatively cool area near the cylinder wall and combustion chamber surfaces. Fuel in these areas does not burn properly because of the lower temperatures. This increases emissions.

The C.C.S. uses a thermostatically con-

94

trolled air cleaner called the Auto-Therm air cleaner. It is designed to keep the temperature of the air entering the carburetor at approximately 100°. This allows the lean carburetor to work properly, minimizes carburetor icing, and improves engine warm-up characteristics. A sensor unit located on the clean air side of the air filter senses the temperature of the air passing over it and regulates the vacuum supplied to a vacuum diaphragm in the inlet tube of the air cleaner. The colder the air, the greater the amount of vacuum supplied to the vacuum diaphragm. The vacuum diaphragm, depending on the vacuum supplied to it, opens or closes a damper door in the inlet tube of the air cleaner. If the door is open, it allows air from the engine compartment to go to the carburetor. If the door is closed, air flows from the heat stove located on the exhaust manifold into the carburetor. In this way, heated air is supplied to the carburetor on cold days, and when first starting the engine and warming it up.

Since 1968, all car manufacturers have posted idle speeds and other pertinent data relative to the specific engine-car application in a conspicuous place in the engine compartment.

1970

The more stringent 1970 laws require tighter control of emissions. Crankcase emissions are controlled by the Positive Crankcase Ventilation System, and exhaust emissions by the engine Controlled Combustion System (C.C.S.), in conjunction with the new Transmission Controlled Spark System (T.C.S.).

In addition, cars sold in California are equipped with an Evaporation Control System that limits the amount of gasoline vapor discharged into the atmosphere (usually from the carburetor and fuel tank).

The T.C.S. system consists of a transmission switch, a solenoid valve, and a temperature switch. Under normal conditions, the system permits the vacuum distributor (spark) advance to operate only in high gear (both manual and automatic transmissions) and reverse.

The transmission switch is located on the transmission and senses when the transmission is in one of the lower gears. When it is in a lower gear, the switch activates the vacuum solenoid valve. This valve is located in the vacuum line that runs from the carburetor to the distributor and it shuts off vacuum to the distributor advance when it is activated. There is also an engine-temperature sensing switch which overrides the transmission switch. It will allow vacuum advance in the lower gears when engine temperature is below 85° or above 220°. There is always vacuum advance in high gear and reverse.

1971

In 1971, the Combination Emission Control System (C.E.C.) was introduced. It uses the C.C.S. of 1968–69 and incorporates several, but not all, of the features in the T.C.S. of 1970. Although distributor vacuum advance is eliminated in the lower gears, as in the T.C.S. system, it is eliminated in a different manner. A C.E.C. solenoid valve is used to regulate distributor vacuum advance.

The C.E.C. solenoid valve is mounted on the carburetor. Vacuum from the intake manifold passes through a port at the base of the solenoid before it reaches the distributor. When the solenoid receives an electrical signal, the plunger extends, opening the port, which allows vacuum to the distributor. At the same time, the plunger head contacts the carburetor throttle lever increasing the idle speed. When the solenoid is de-energized, the spring-loaded plunger returns to its unextended position closing the port and allowing the throttle lever to rest against the idle speed adjusting screw.

The switch is energized by two switches and one relay.

The time-delay relay is used to energize the C.E.C. solenoid and provide vacuum advance for the first 15 seconds after the ignition is turned on. This happens regardless of engine temperature. After the 15 seconds, the solenoid is again regulated by the temperature switch and the transmission switch.

One of the controlling switches is an engine temperature switch. It allows vacuum advance in all gears, by energizing the C.E.C. solenoid, when the engine temperature is below 82° or above 220°. In between 82° and 220°, this switch will allow no vacuum advance and the solenoid will be de-energized.

The other switch is the transmission

switch. When the transmission is in the lower gears, this switch keeps the C.E.C. solenoid in the de-energized position eliminating vacuum advance. In high gear, the solenoid is energized by current from the battery and vacuum advance is supplied.

Engine dieseling is controlled by use of lower throttle plate openings (lower carburetor idle speeds).

On air-conditioned (A/C), automatic transmission cars, a solid-state time device engages the A/C compressor for about three seconds after the ignition is turned off. The load from the compressor effectively stalls the engine and prevents dieseling or overrun.

The evaporation control system was added to all cars in 1971. This system limits the amount of gasoline vapor discharged into the air from the gas tank and carburetor. The fuel tank has a non-vented cap. As vapors are generated in the fuel tank, they flow through a liquid vapor separator to a canister where they are stored. From the canister, the vapors are routed to the carburetor where they are burned when the engine is running.

1972

All six-cylinder models with manual transmissions use the C.E.C. system. A description of this system can be found under the above 1971 head. All six-cylinder models with automatic transmissions use the A.I.R. system. A description of this system can be found under the above 1968 head. All V8s equipped with a manual four-speed transmission use the T.C.S. system which is described under the above 1970 head. All V8 models equipped with a three-speed manual transmission or an automatic transmission use the new Speed Control Spark System (S.C.S.).

Every engine/transmission combination uses the Auto-Therm air cleaner, P.C.V. system, and the evaporation control system of 1971.

The Speed Controlled Spark (S.C.S.) system uses a solenoid valve in the vacuum line running between the carburetor and the distributor. This valve is the same as the transmission-controlled spark valve. The difference in this system is that the valve is regulated by vehicle speed using a speed control spark switch. The S.C.S. solenoid valve is energized below 38 mph in any gear, under normal operating temperature, allowing no vacuum advance. Above 38 mph, in any gear, or any time engine temperature is higher or lower than normal operating temperature, the solenoid valve is de-energized allowing full vacuum advance to the distributor.

Normal S.C.S. engine operating temperatures range from 95° to 230°. An engine-temperature sensing switch is located in the head and de-energizes the solenoid until operating temperature is reached regardless of vehicle speed.

1973

The Controlled Combustion System (C.C.S.) is standard on all engines. The Air Injection Reactor (A.I.R.) is used on all 6 cyl and 350 two bbl. and 350 California engines. A combination of the Transmission Controlled Spark and Exhaust Gas Re-Circulation (EGR) is found on all V8 engines.

EGR is a system used to reduce nitrous oxide (NO_x) emissions. It functions by allowing a small amount of exhaust gas into the air fuel mixture in the intake manifold, under certain conditions.

The EGR TCS system consists of a temperature switch which senses when the engine temperature is under 71° or over 230°, a second temperature switch sensing engine temperature between 140° and 230°, an EGR solenoid, a vacuum advance solenoid, a transmission switch, and a time delay relay.

The under 71° and over 230° switch is mounted on the left cylinder head. The 140° to 230° switch is mounted in the right cylinder head. The time delay relay is mounted on the vacuum advance solenoid.

The 71° to 230° switch grounds the circuit for the solenoids below 71° and above 230°. The 140° switch passes current to the transmission switch when engine temperature is between 140° and 230°. The transmission switch then grounds the circuit for the solenoids in First gear only. Between 71° and 140° the temperature switches are both open and the solenoids are in the normal positions.

The vacuum advance solenoid is normally closed, allowing no vacuum advance. The EGR solenoid is normally open, allowing exhaust gas recirculation.

Below 71° there is a complete circuit and both solenoids are energized, allowing vacuum advance and cutting off EGR.

From 71° to 140° there is an open circuit, the solenoids return to their normal positions, and vacuum advance is cut off and EGR is allowed.

From 140 to 230, in First gear, there is an open circuit and the solenoids are in their normal positions. The time delay relay maintains the open circuit for 33 to 55 seconds after the transmission shifts into Second gear. However, after the time delay in Second and Third gear, the solenoids are energized to allow vacuum advance and cut off EGR.

Over 235° the solenoids are energized and vacuum advance occurs and there is no EGR.

COMPONENTS

Removal and Installation

PCV VALVE

1. Pull the valve from its grommet.
2. Remove the valve from the hose.
3. Insert a new valve into the hose and replace the valve into the rubber grommet.

C.C.S. SENSOR

1. Remove the hoses at the sensor.
2. Remove the tabs on the sensor retaining clip.
3. Remove the clip and the sensor from the air cleaner.
4. Install a new sensor, gasket, and replace the hoses.

C.E.C. MOTOR

1. Drill out the two welds with a 1/16 inch drill as required to remove the motor retaining strap.
2. Remove the motor.
3. Drill a 7/64 inch hole in the snorkel tube of the air cleaner (see illustration).
4. Install the motor to the tube.

A.I.R. PUMP FILTER

1. Remove the drive belt and pulley.
2. Remove the disc of the filter fan.
3. Pull the filter out with pliers.

Removing Filter From Air Pump (© Pontiac Div., G.M. Corp.)

A.I.R. PUMP

1. Remove the hoses from the pump.
2. Remove the mounting bolts and remove the pump.
3. To install, reverse these procedures.

Adjustments

E.G.R. AIR PUMP

1. Loosen the pump mounting bolt and adjust the drive belt to ½ inch play.

CARBON CANISTER

Replace the canister base filter every 12 months or 12,000 miles.

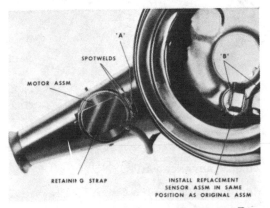

Therm—AC Motor and Sensor (© Pontiac Div., G.M. Corp.)

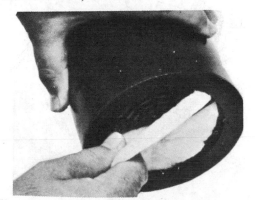

Replacing Canister Filter (© Pontiac Div., G.M Corp.)

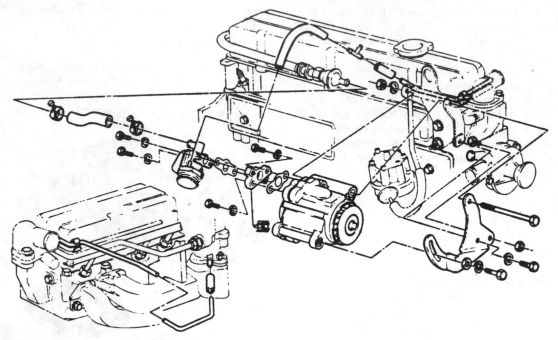

Installing Air Pump—6 Cylinder (© Pontiac Div., G.M. Corp.)

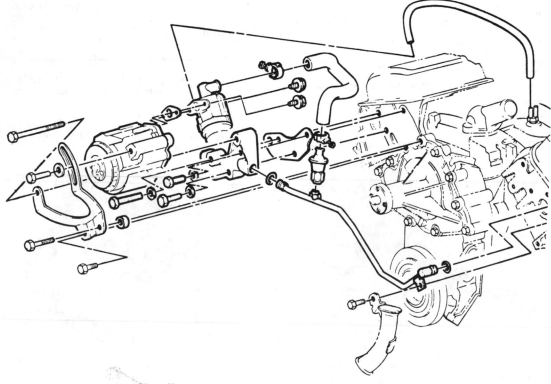

Installing Air Pump—V8 (© Pontiac Div., G.M. Corp.)

Fuel System

FUEL PUMP

Removal and Installation

1. Disconnect the fuel inlet, outlet, and vapor return lines at the pump and plug the pump inlet line.

2. Remove the two pump mounting bolts and lockwashers; remove the pump and gasket.

3. On engines, if the rocker arm pushrod is to be removed, take out the two adapter bolts and lockwashers and remove the adapter and gasket.

4. Install the pump with a new gasket coated with sealer. Coat the mounting bolts threads with sealer and tighten the bolts.

5. Connect the inlet and outlet lines, start the engine, and check for leaks.

FUEL FILTER

1. Disconnect the fuel line connection at the carburetor.

2. Remove the inlet fuel filter nut from the carburetor using a box wrench.

3. Remove the filter element and spring.

4. If the filter element is bronze, blow through the cone end—this should allow air to pass freely.

5. Install the element spring and new element into the carburetor. Bronze elements are installed with the small section of cone facing outward.

6. Install a new gasket on the fitting nut and install the nut.

7. Install the fuel line and tighten it securely. Start the engine and check for leaks.

Fuel Pump Testing

To test the fuel pump, remove the gas inlet line at the carburetor, hold the line over a cup, and crank the engine to see if gas is being pumped. Then attach the line to a pressure gauge, crank the engine, and check for pressure. (See "Tune-Up Chart" for specifications.)

CARBURETORS

Overhaul

ALL TYPES

Efficient carburetion depends greatly on careful cleaning and inspection during overhaul since dirt, gum, water, or varnish in or on the carburetor parts are often responsible for poor performance.

Overhaul your carburetor in a clean, dust-free area. Carefully disassemble the carburetor, referring often to the exploded views. Keep all similar and look-alike parts segregated during disassembly and cleaning to avoid accidental interchange during assembly. Make a note of all jet sizes.

When the carburetor is disassembled, wash all parts (except diaphragms, electric choke units, pump plunger, and any other plastic, leather, fiber, or rubber parts) in clean carburetor solvent. Do not leave parts in the solvent any longer than is necessary to sufficiently loosen the deposits. Excessive cleaning may remove the special finish from the float bowl and choke valve bodies, leaving these parts unfit for service. Rinse all parts in clean solvent and blow them dry with compressed air or allow them to air dry. Wipe clean all cork, plastic, leather, and fiber parts with a clean, lint-free cloth.

Blow out all passages and jets with compressed air and be sure that there are no restrictions or blockages. Never use wire or similar tools to clean jets, fuel passages, or air bleeds. Clean all jets and valves separately to avoid accidental interchange.

Check all parts for wear or damage. If wear or damage is found, replace the defective parts. Especially check the following:

1. Check the float needle and seat for wear. If wear is found, replace the complete assembly.

2. Check the float hinge pin for wear and the float(s) for dents or distortion. Replace the float if fuel has leaked into it.

3. Check the throttle and choke shaft bores for wear or an out-of-round condition. Damage or wear to the throttle arm, shaft, or shaft bore will often require replacement of the throttle body. These parts require a close tolerance of fit; wear may allow air leakage, which could affect starting and idling.

NOTE: *Throttle shafts and bushings are not included in overhaul kits. They can be purchased separately.*

4. Inspect the idle mixture adjusting needles for burrs or grooves. Any such condition requires replacement of the needle, since you will not be able to obtain a satisfactory idle.

5. Test the accelerator pump check valves. They should pass air one way but not the other. Test for proper seating by blowing and sucking on the valve. Replace the valve if necessary. If the valve is satisfactory, wash the valve again to remove breath moisture.

6. Check the bowl cover for warped surfaces with a straightedge.

7. Closely inspect the valves and seats for wear and damage, replacing as necessary.

8. After the carburetor is assembled, check the choke valve for freedom of operation.

Carburetor overhaul kits are recommended for each overhaul. These kits contain all gaskets and new parts to replace those that deteriorate most rapidly. Failure to replace all parts supplied with the kit (especially gaskets) can result in poor performance later.

Some carburetor manufacturers supply overhaul kits of three basic types: minor repair; major repair; and gasket kits. Basically, they contain the following:

Minor Repair Kits:
    All gaskets
    Float needle valve
    All diaphragms
    Spring for the pump diaphragm
Major Repair Kits:
    All jets and gaskets
    All diaphragms
    Float needle valve
    Idle mixture screw
    Pump ball valve
    Main jet carrier
    Float
    Complete intermediate rod
    Intermediate pump lever
    Complete injector tube
    Some cover hold-down screws and washers
Gasket Kits:
    All gaskets

After cleaning and checking all components, reassemble the carburetor, using new parts and referring to the exploded view. When reassembling, make sure that all screws and jets are tight in their seats, but do not overtighten, as the tips will be distorted. Tighten all screws gradually, in rotation. Do not tighten needle valves into their seats; uneven jetting will result. Always use new gaskets. Be sure to adjust the float level when reassembling.

Removal and Installation

1. Remove the air cleaner.
2. Remove all hoses, linkage, and fuel lines.
3. Remove the retaining bolts and remove the carburetor.
4. Reverse the removal order to install.

Float and Fuel Level

NOTE: *See the carburetor chart for float level setting. Use a small ruler as a gauge.*

MV Monojet

1. Remove the float bowl.
2. Adjust the float level as shown in the illustration.
3. After the adjustment, install the metering rod and tension spring.
4. Install the air horn gasket and the float bowl.

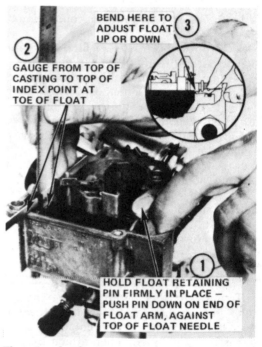

Float Level Adjustment—MV Carburetor (© Pontiac Div., G.M. Corp.)

2 GV

1. Remove the air horn.
2. Adjust the float level as in the illustration.
3. Install the air horn assembly.

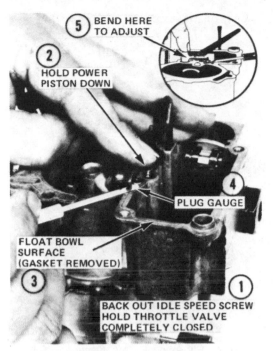

Metering Rod Adjustment—MV Carburetor (© Pontiac Div., G.M. Corp.)

Removing Air Horn—2 GV Carburetor (© Pontiac Div., G.M. Corp.)

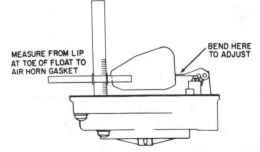

Adjusting Float Level—2 GV Carburetor (© Pontiac Div., G.M. Corp.)

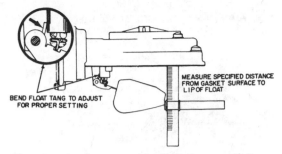

Float Level Adjustment—2 GC Carburetor (© Pontiac Div., G.M. Corp.)

2 GC, 4MV QUADRAJET

1. Remove the air horn.
2. Adjust the float assembly as in the illustration.
3. Install the air horn.

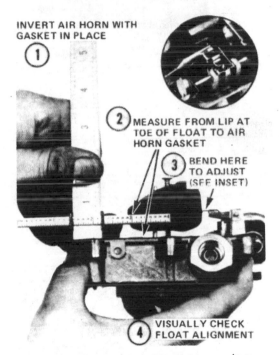

Float Level Adjustment—2 GC Carburetor (© Pontiac Div., G.M. Corp.)

4 MC QUADRAJET

1. Remove the air horn.
2. Adjust the float level as in the illustration.
3. Install the air horn.

FAST IDLE ADJUSTMENTS

Start the engine, turn the fast idle screw until the engine reaches the desired idle. (See the Carburetor Chart.)

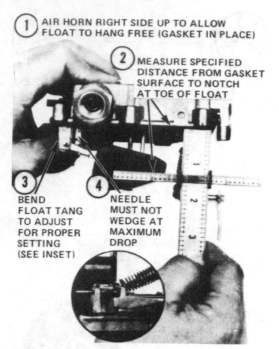

① AIR HORN RIGHT SIDE UP TO ALLOW FLOAT TO HANG FREE (GASKET IN PLACE)

② MEASURE SPECIFIED DISTANCE FROM GASKET SURFACE TO NOTCH AT TOE OF FLOAT

③ BEND FLOAT TANG TO ADJUST FOR PROPER SETTING (SEE INSET)

④ NEEDLE MUST NOT WEDGE AT MAXIMUM DROP

Float Drop Adjustment—2 GC Carburetor (© Pontiac Div., G.M. Corp.)

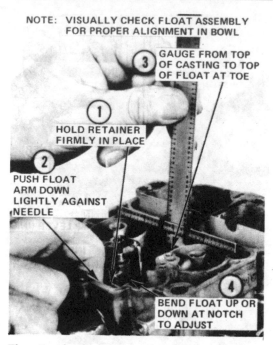

NOTE: VISUALLY CHECK FLOAT ASSEMBLY FOR PROPER ALIGNMENT IN BOWL

③ GAUGE FROM TOP OF CASTING TO TOP OF FLOAT AT TOE

① HOLD RETAINER FIRMLY IN PLACE

② PUSH FLOAT ARM DOWN LIGHTLY AGAINST NEEDLE

④ BEND FLOAT UP OR DOWN AT NOTCH TO ADJUST

Float Level Adjustment—4 MC Quadrajet (© Pontiac Div., G.M. Corp.)

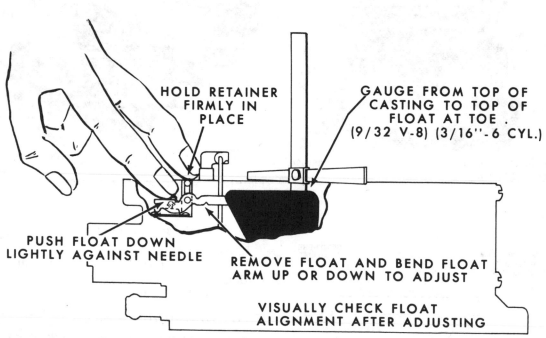

HOLD RETAINER FIRMLY IN PLACE

GAUGE FROM TOP OF CASTING TO TOP OF FLOAT AT TOE . (9/32 V-8) (3/16''-6 CYL.)

PUSH FLOAT DOWN LIGHTLY AGAINST NEEDLE

REMOVE FLOAT AND BEND FLOAT ARM UP OR DOWN TO ADJUST

VISUALLY CHECK FLOAT ALIGNMENT AFTER ADJUSTING

Float Level Adjustment—4 MV Carburetor (© Pontiac Div., G.M. Corp.)

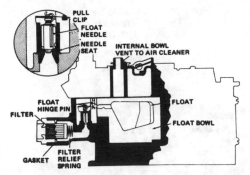

Float System—4 MC Quadrajet (© Pontiac Div., G.M. Corp.)

Automatic Choke Adjustment

1. Make sure the engine is cold.
2. Loosen the screws on the choke spring housing.
3. Turn the housing until the mark on the housing aligns with the desired mark on the housing plate. (See Carburetor Chart.)

Fast Idle Adjustment—MV Carburetor (© Pontiac Div., G.M. Corp.)

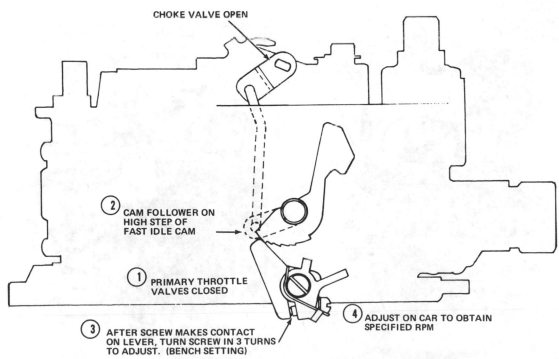

Fast Idle Adjustment—4 MV Carburetor (© Pontiac Div., G.M. Corp.)

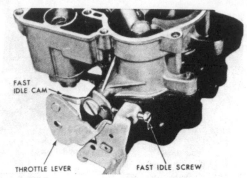

FAST IDLE CAM

THROTTLE LEVER

FAST IDLE SCREW

Fast Idle Adjustment—2GV Carburetor (© Pontiac Div., G.M. Corp.)

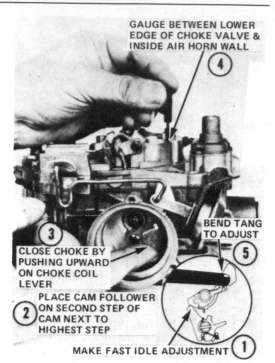

GAUGE BETWEEN LOWER EDGE OF CHOKE VALVE & INSIDE AIR HORN WALL

④

③ CLOSE CHOKE BY PUSHING UPWARD ON CHOKE COIL LEVER

② PLACE CAM FOLLOWER ON SECOND STEP OF CAM NEXT TO HIGHEST STEP

⑤ BEND TANG TO ADJUST

① MAKE FAST IDLE ADJUSTMENT

Fast Idle Adjustment—4MC Quadrajet (© Pontiac Div., G.M. Corp.)

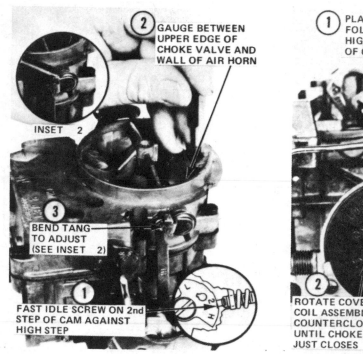

② GAUGE BETWEEN UPPER EDGE OF CHOKE VALVE AND WALL OF AIR HORN

INSET 2

③ BEND TANG TO ADJUST (SEE INSET 2)

① FAST IDLE SCREW ON 2nd STEP OF CAM AGAINST HIGH STEP

Fast Idle Adjustment—2 GC Carburetor (© Pontiac Div., G.M. Corp.)

① PLACE CAM FOLLOWER ON HIGHEST STEP OF CAM

③ SEE INDEX MARK AS SPECIFIED

② ROTATE COVER AND COIL ASSEMBLY COUNTERCLOCKWISE UNTIL CHOKE VALVE JUST CLOSES

Automatic Choke Adjustment—4MC Carburetor (© Pontiac Div., G.M. Corp.)

Choke Linkage and Unloader Adjustment

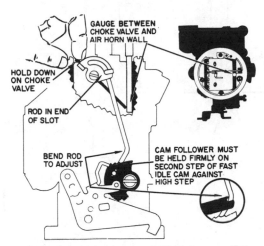

Choke Linkage Adjustment—MV Carburetor (© Pontiac Div., G.M. Corp.)

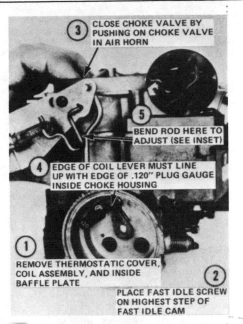

Choke Linkage Adjustment—4MC Quadrajet (© Pontiac Div., G.M. Corp.)

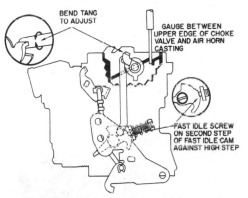

Choke Linkage Adjustment—2GV Carburetor (© Pontiac Div., G.M. Corp.)

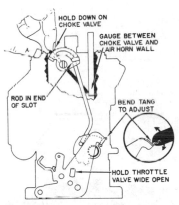

Choke Unloader—MV Carburetor (© Pontiac Div., G.M. Corp.)

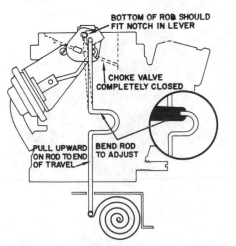

Choke Linkage Adjustment—2GC Carburetor (© Pontiac Div., G.M. Corp.)

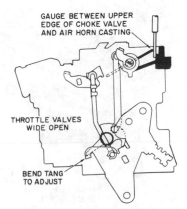

Unloader Adjustment—2 GV Carburetor (© Pontiac Div., G.M. Corp.)

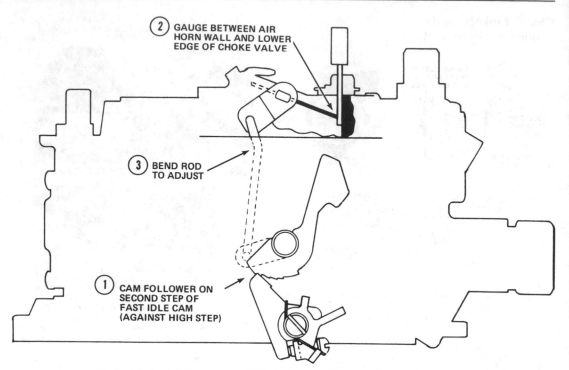

Choke Linkage Adjustment—4MV Carburetor (© Pontiac Div., G.M. Corp.)

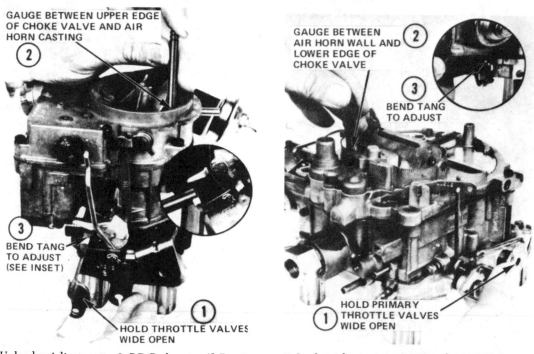

Unloader Adjustment—2 GC Carburetor (© Pontiac Div., G.M. Corp.)

Unloader Adjustment—4 MV and 4 MC Carburetor (© Pontiac Div., G.M. Corp.)

Carburetor Specifications

Year	Model or Type	Float Level (in.) Prim.	Sec.	Float Drop (in.) Prim.	Sec.	Pump Travel Setting (in.)	Choke Setting Unloader (in.)	Housing
'68	MV-7028075-067	$5/16$	—	—	—	—	0.245	—
'68	2BV-All	$9/16$	—	$1\frac{3}{4}$	—	$1^{11}/32$	0.180	—
'68	4MV-6 Cyl.	$5/16$	—	—	—	$9/32$	0.300	—
'68	4MV-All others	$1/4$	—	—	—	$9/32$	0.300	—
'68	BV-7028168	$1^{19}/32$	—	$1\frac{3}{4}$	—	—	0.300	—
'69	MV-7029165-67, Std.	$9/32$	—	—	—	—	0.450	—
'69	MV-7029166-68, Auto.	$9/32$	—	—	—	—	0.450	—
'69	2GV-7029062, Auto.	$9/16$	—	$1\frac{3}{4}$	—	$1^{11}/32$	0.180	—
'69	4MV	$9/32$	—	—	—	$9/32$	0.300	Center Notch
'69	4MV-Ram-Air	$9/32$	—	—	—	$1/4$	0.300	Center Notch
'70	MV-7040014-250, Auto.	$1/4$	—	—	—	—	0.350	—
'70	MV-7040017-250, Std.	$1/4$	—	—	—	—	0.350	—
'70	2GV-7040060-400, Auto.	$11/16$	—	$1\frac{3}{4}$	—	$1^{11}/32$	0.180	—
'70	2GV-7040460-400, Auto. Calif.	$11/16$	—	$1\frac{3}{4}$	—	$1^{11}/32$	0.180	—
'70	2GV-7040461-400, Auto. w/AC Calif.	$11/16$	—	$1\frac{3}{4}$	—	$1^{11}/32$	0.180	—
'70	2GV-7040062-350, Auto.	$9/16$	—	$1\frac{3}{4}$	—	$1^{11}/32$	0.180	—
'70	2GV-7040462-350, Auto. Calif.	$9/16$	—	$1\frac{3}{4}$	—	$1^{11}/32$	0.180	—
'70	2GV-7040063-350, Auto. w/AC Calif.	$9/16$	—	$1\frac{3}{4}$	—	$1^{11}/32$	0.180	—
'70	2GV-7040064-400, Altitude, Auto.	$11/16$	—	$1\frac{3}{4}$	—	$1^{11}/32$	0.180	—
'70	2GV-7040066-400, Std.	$11/16$	—	$1\frac{3}{4}$	—	$1^{11}/32$	0.180	—
'70	2CV-7040466-400, Std. Calif.	$11/16$	—	$1\frac{3}{4}$	—	$1^{11}/32$	0.180	—
'70	2GV-7040071-350, Std.	$9/16$	—	$1\frac{3}{4}$	—	$1^{11}/32$	0.180	—
'70	2GV-7040471-350, Std. Calif.	$9/16$	—	$1\frac{3}{4}$	—	$1^{11}/32$	0.180	—
'70	2GV-7040072-350, Altitude, Std.	$9/16$	—	$1\frac{3}{4}$	—	$1^{11}/32$	0.180	—
'70	4MV-7040263-400, Std. exc. Ram-Air	$9/32$	—	—	—	—	—	Center Notch
'70	4MV-7040263-400, Std. exc. Ram-Air Calif.	$9/32$	—	—	—	—	—	Center Notch
'70	4MV-7040264-400, Auto. exc. Ram-Air	$9/32$	—	—	—	—	—	Center Notch
'70	4MV-7040564-400, Auto. exc. Ram-Air Calif.	$9/32$	—	—	—	—	—	Center Notch
'70	4MV-7040267-455, Std.	$9/32$	—	—	—	—	—	Center Notch
'70	4MV-7040567-455, Std. Calif.	$9/32$	—	—	—	—	—	Center Notch
'70	4MV-7040268-455, Auto.	$9/32$	—	—	—	—	—	Center Notch
'70	4MV-7040568-455, Auto. Calif.	$9/32$	—	—	—	—	—	Center Notch
'70	4MV-7040270-400, Auto. Ram-Air III, IV	$9/32$	—	—	—	—	—	Center Notch
'70	4MV-7040570-400, Auto. Ram-Air III, IV Calif.	$9/32$	—	—	—	—	—	Center Notch
'70	4MV-7040273-400, Std. Ram-Air III, IV	$9/32$	—	—	—	—	—	Center Notch

Carburetor Specifications (cont.)

Year	Model or Type	Float Level (in.)		Float Drop (in.)		Pump Travel Setting (in.)	Choke Setting	
		Prim.	Sec.	Prim.	Sec.		Unloader (in.)	Housing
'70	4MV-7040274-455, Altitude, Auto.	$9/32$	—	—	—	—	—	Center Notch
'71	MV-250	$1/4$	—	—	—	—	0.350	—
'71	2GV-350, All	$9/16$	—	$1 3/4$	—	$1 11/32$	0.180	—
'71	2GV-400, All	$11/16$	—	$1 3/4$	—	$1 11/32$	0.180	—
'71	4MV-All	$9/32$	—	—	—	—	—	Center Notch
'72	2GV-7042060, 7042061	$1/4$	—	$1 9/32$	—	$1 11/32$	0.180	—
'72	2GV-7042062	$9/16$	—	—	—	$1 11/32$	0.180	—
'72	2GV-7042064	$5/8$	—	$1 9/32$	—	$1 11/32$	0.180	—
'72	2GV-702100	$25/32$	—	$1 31/32$	—	$1 5/16$	0.040	—
'72	2GV-7042101	$25/32$	—	$1 31/32$	—	$1 5/16$	0.075	—
'72	4MV-7042262, 7042263, 7042264	$1/4$	—	—	—	$13/32$	0.310	—
'72	4MV-7042270, 7042273	$1/4$	—	—	—	$7/16$	0.310	—
'72	MV-7042014, 7042984	$1/4$	—	—	—	0.160	0.500	—
'72	MV-7042017, 7042987	$1/4$	—	—	—	0.180	0.500	—
'73	MV-7043014	$1/4$	—	—	—	—	0.500	—
'73	MV-7043017	$3/4$	—	—	—	—	0.500	—
'73	2GV-All	$13/32$	—	—	—	$13/32$	0.310	—
'73	4MC-All	$21/32$	—	$1 9/32$	—	$1 5/16$	0.180	—

5 · Chassis Electrical

Heater

BLOWER

Removal and Installation

ALL WITHOUT AC

1. Jack up the front of the car and remove the right front wheel.
2. Cut an access hole along the stamped outline on the right fender skirt, using an air chisel.
3. Disconnect the blower power wire.
4. Remove the blower.
5. To install, replace the blower.
6. Connect the wires.

7. Cover the access hole with a metal plate secured with sealer and sheet metal screws.
8. Install the wheel and lower the car to the ground.

1968–69 WITH AC

1. Remove the fender brace, battery, and tray.
2. Scribe alignment marks and remove the hood.
3. Remove the right front fender and skirt as an assembly.
4. Disconnect the motor wire and cooling tube from the motor.
5. Remove the motor attaching screws and the motor.

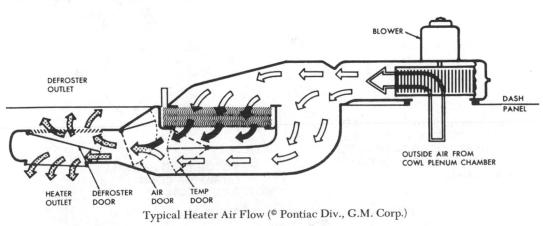

Typical Heater Air Flow (© Pontiac Div., G.M. Corp.)

6. Install the motor and attaching screws.

7. Connect the wire and the cooling tube.

8. Install the right fender and skirt.

9. Install the hood; make sure you align it with the marks.

10. Install the battery, fender brace, and tray.

1970–73 WITH AC

1. Raise the car and remove the right front wheel.

2. Cut an access hole along the outline stamped in the right-hand fender skirt.

3. Disconnect the blower wire, remove the blower attaching bolts, and remove the blower.

4. Install the blower, attaching screws, and wire.

5. Install the wheel and lower the car to the ground.

HEATER CORE

Removal and Installation

1968 WITHOUT AC

1. Drain the radiator and remove the glove compartment.

2. Disconnect the heater hoses at the heater.

3. Disconnect the heater control cables at the heater.

4. Remove the front wheel.

5. Remove the wire connector from the resistor at the top left side of the heater air outlet by prying the connector up with a screwdriver.

6. Cut a 1 in. hole in the skirt.

7. Remove the six nuts from the heater-to-air inlet duct and remove the heater.

8. Install the heater and attaching nuts.

9. Install the wire connector.

10. Install the front wheel.

11. Connect the heater control cables.

12. Connect the heater hoses.

13. Install the glove compartment and fill the radiator to the proper level.

1969–73 WITHOUT AC

1. Drain the radiator.

2. Disconnect the heater hoses at the air inlet assembly.

NOTE: *The water pump hose goes to the top heater core pipe; the other hose (from the rear of the right cylinder head on V8, center of block on 6) goes to the lower heater core pipe.*

3. Remove the nuts from the core studs on the firewall (under hood).

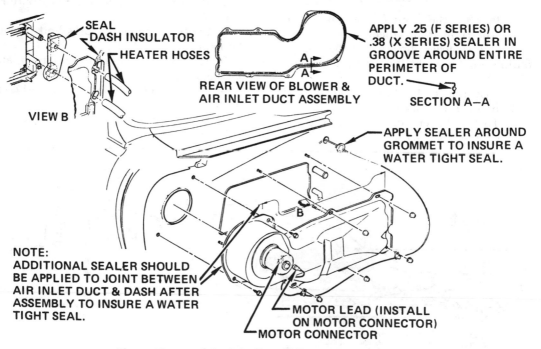

SEAL
DASH INSULATOR
HEATER HOSES
VIEW B

REAR VIEW OF BLOWER & AIR INLET DUCT ASSEMBLY

APPLY .25 (F SERIES) OR .38 (X SERIES) SEALER IN GROOVE AROUND ENTIRE PERIMETER OF DUCT.

SECTION A–A

APPLY SEALER AROUND GROMMET TO INSURE A WATER TIGHT SEAL.

NOTE: ADDITIONAL SEALER SHOULD BE APPLIED TO JOINT BETWEEN AIR INLET DUCT & DASH AFTER ASSEMBLY TO INSURE A WATER TIGHT SEAL.

MOTOR LEAD (INSTALL ON MOTOR CONNECTOR)
MOTOR CONNECTOR

Blower Motor and Air Inlet Duct (© Pontiac Div., G.M. Corp.)

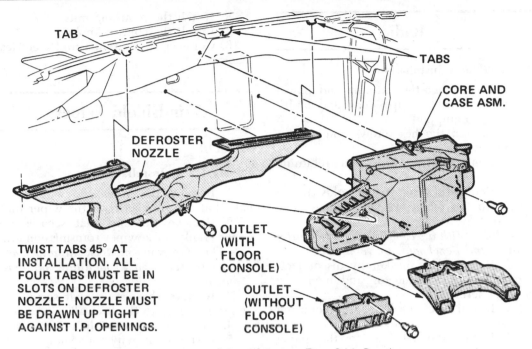

TAB

TABS

CORE AND
CASE ASM.

DEFROSTER
NOZZLE

TWIST TABS 45° AT
INSTALLATION. ALL
FOUR TABS MUST BE IN
SLOTS ON DEFROSTER
NOZZLE. NOZZLE MUST
BE DRAWN UP TIGHT
AGAINST I.P. OPENINGS.

OUTLET
(WITH
FLOOR
CONSOLE)

OUTLET
(WITHOUT
FLOOR
CONSOLE)

Heater Duct and Core (© Pontiac Div., G.M. Corp.)

4. From inside the car, pull the heater assembly from the firewall.

5. Disconnect the control cables and wires, then remove the heater assembly.

6. To remove the core, unhook the retaining springs.

7. Install the heater core.

8. Connect the heater control cables and wires and install the heater assembly.

9. Install the attaching nuts at the firewall.

10. Connect the heater hoses at the air inlet.

11. Fill the cooling system to the proper level.

All with AC

1. Remove the glove box.

2. Remove the lower instrument panel air-conditioning duct and outlet assembly by removing the five attaching screws and the retainer.

3. Lower the duct and outlet assembly after disconnecting the right and left-side nozzle connections.

4. Disconnect the temperature control cable and vacuum hose.

5. Drain the cooling system and remove the two water hoses attached to the heater core.

6. Remove the six heater core to cowl attaching nuts. It is necessary to cut a 1 in. diameter hole in the right-hand fender skirt to remove the lower nut.

7. Remove the two screws from the heater core and case evaporator housing seal and remove the seal and retainer.

8. Remove the core and case assembly.

9. Mark the heater cam and bracket assembly to ensure proper reinstallation and remove the heater cam and bracket.

10. Remove the front case-to-rear case attaching screws and separate the cases.

11. Remove the heater core retaining screws and core.

12. Install the heater core and attaching screws.

13. Connect the two cases.

14. Install the heater cam and bracket.

15. Install the core.

16. Install the heater core-to-cowl attaching nuts.

17. Connect the hoses and fill the cooling system.

18. Connect the temperature control cable.

19. Install the instrument panel.

20. Install the glove compartment.

Radio

Removal and Installation

1. Disconnect the antenna and power leads. Remove the tape deck and multiplex, if so equipped.

2. Loosen the hex screws and remove the knobs.

3. Remove the escutcheon retaining nuts.

4. Remove the screw that holds the receiver to the panel bracket, then remove the ash tray.

NOTE: *With air conditioning, the outlet duct and bezel must be removed.*

5. Remove the speaker by disconnecting the output connector and mounting bracket screws.

6. Install the speaker and mounting bracket.

7. Install the receiver to the panel bracket. Install the ash tray.

8. Install the retaining nuts.

9. Install the control knobs.

10. Connect the antenna and electrical leads.

Windshield Wipers

MOTOR

Removal and Installation

1. Remove the hoses and wire terminals that are connected to the wiper unit.

2. Remove the clip that secures the wiper crank to the wiper transmission arm.

NOTE: *On some models, the wiper arm must be removed to facilitate motor removal.*

3. Remove the screws that secure the wiper assembly to the firewall.

4. Install a gasket on the motor.

5. Position the wiper assembly on the firewall and secure it.

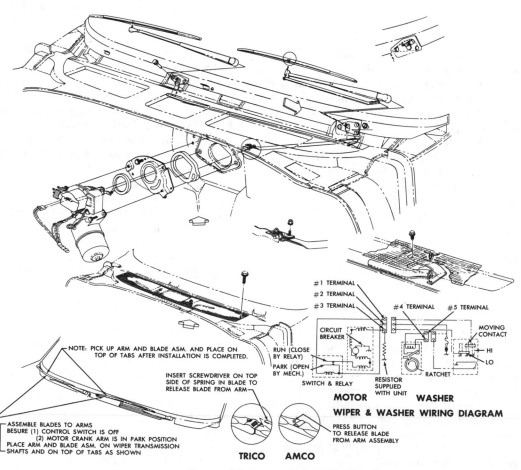

Wiper Motor Removal (© Pontiac Div., G.M. Corp.)

6. Connect the wire terminals and hoses.

7. Connect the wiper crank with the wiper transmission arm.

8. To install, connect the wiper transmission arm and the wiper crank.

9. Connect the electrical terminals.

10. Install the wiper assembly to the firewall.

11. Install the hoses and wire terminals.

Instrument Cluster

Removal and Installation

1968

1. Disconnect the battery.

2. Remove the screws which hold the bezel and cluster assembly to the instrument panel.

3. Remove the speedometer cable.

4. Disconnect the heater control cables.

5. Lower the steering column by removing the trim plate and loosening the nuts on the column bracket.

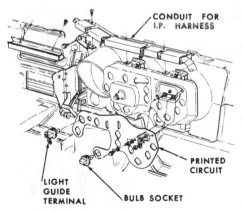

CONDUIT FOR I.P. HARNESS

PRINTED CIRCUIT

LIGHT GUIDE TERMINAL

BULB SOCKET

Tempest Instrument Cluster—1968 (© Pontiac Div., G.M. Corp.)

6. Pull the cluster and bezel away from the instrument panel to gain access to wiring and other connections.

7. Remove the bulbs, wiring, and other connections, as necessary.

8. Remove the screws which hold the cluster to the bezel. Remove the cluster.

9. Install the cluster and the bezel.

10. Install the wiring and bulbs.

11. Place the steering column into position.

12. Connect the heater control cables.

13. Connect the speedometer cables.

14. Connect the battery.

1969–1970

1. Disconnect the battery.

2. Remove the glove compartment and on 1970 models, the lower panel trim.

3. Disconnect the speedometer cable, the wire connectors at the headlight switch, the wipers, the turn signals, the ignition switch, the heater, the air conditioner, and the printed circuit board.

4. Remove the lower column trim and disconnect the heater cable; remove the lower air conditioner duct, if necessary.

5. Lower the steering column.

6. Remove the three instrument panel screws at the gauge clusters.

7. Remove the three upper right instrument panel screws at the gauge clusters.

8. Remove the ground strap retaining screws, if present, then disconnect the harness conduit.

9. Remove the cluster retaining screws, then the cluster.

NOTE: *It may be necessary to shift the instrument panel around to gain access to some wires.*

10. Connect the harness conduit and install the ground strap.

11. Install the panel retaining screws and nuts.

12. Place the steering column into position.

13. Install the column trim and connect the heater cable.

14. Connect the wire connectors.

15. Connect the battery.

1971–73

1. Disconnect the battery cable and remove the lower A/C duct, if so equipped.

2. Remove the lower instrument panel trim and glove box.

3. Lower the steering column.

4. Disconnect the speedometer cable and heater cable (at the case).

5. Remove the three instrument panel screws at the gauges and the three nuts at the upper right.

6. Remove the lower instrument panel bolts at the right and left of the column.

7. Pull the crash pad away from the

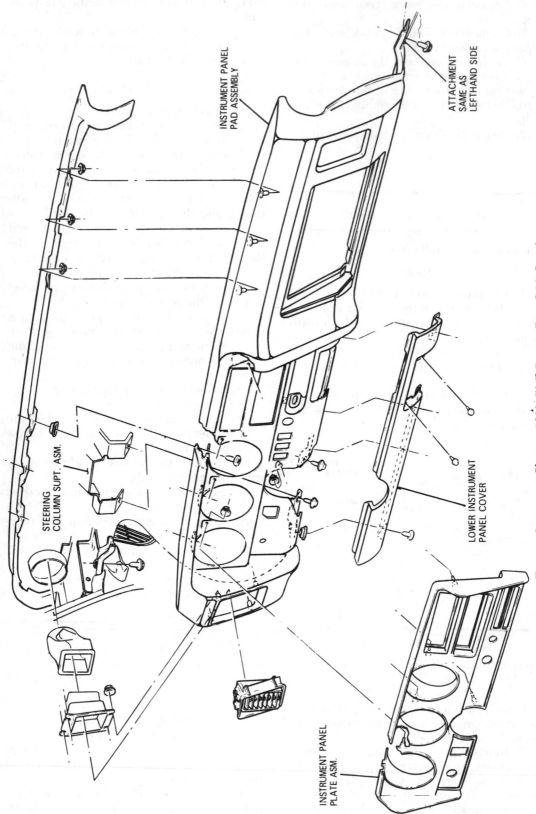

ATTACHMENT
SAME AS
LEFTHAND SIDE

INSTRUMENT PANEL
PAD ASSEMBLY

STEERING
COLUMN SUPT. ASM.

LOWER INSTRUMENT
PANEL COVER

INSTRUMENT PANEL
PLATE ASM.

Tempest Instrument Cluster—1969–70 (© Pontiac Div., G.M. Corp.)

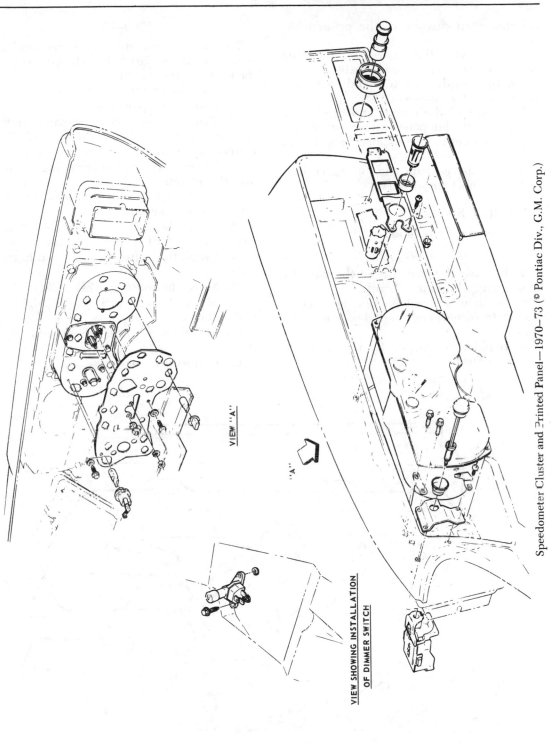

VIEW "A"

"A"

VIEW SHOWING INSTALLATION
OF DIMMER SWITCH

Speedometer Cluster and Printed Panel—1970–73 (© Pontiac Div., G.M. Corp.)

column, then disconnect the printed circuit.

8. Remove the harness retaining screws, cluster screws, and cluster.

9. Install the cluster and retaining screws and the harness.

10. Connect the circuit and crash pad.

11. Install the panel attaching screws.

12. Connect the speedometer and heater cables.

13. Install the trim and the glove box.

14. Connect the battery.

IGNITION SWITCH

Removal and Installation

1968

1. Remove the switch from the dash by unscrewing the switch ferrule.

2. Remove the switch from the back of the instrument panel and disconnect the wires.

3. Replace the switch by reversing the above method.

1969–73

The ignition and steering wheel locking switch is located just below the gear selector lever on the steering column.

1. Disconnect the battery.

2. Loosen the pan screws.

3. Remove the column-to-panel nuts, carefully lower steering column, and disconnect the switch wire connectors.

4. Remove the switch attaching screws and the switch.

5. To install, move key lock to the OFF-LOCK position.

6. Move the actuator rod hole in the switch to the OFF-LOCK position.

7. Install the switch with the rod in the hole.

8. Move the rod to OFF-LOCK.

9. Move the key lock to OFF-LOCK and install.

10. Install the steering column into position.

12. Connect the battery.

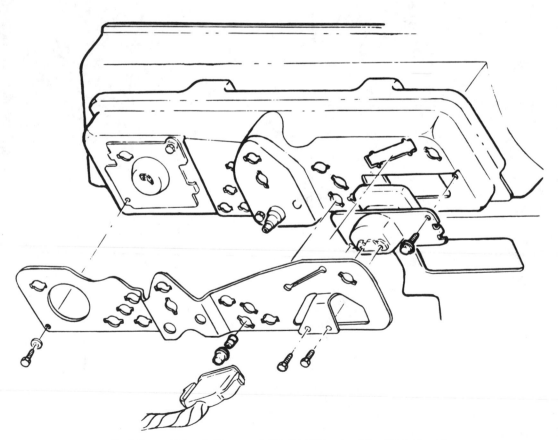

Fuel Gauge Printed Circuit– 1970–73 (© Pontiac Div., G.M. Corp.)

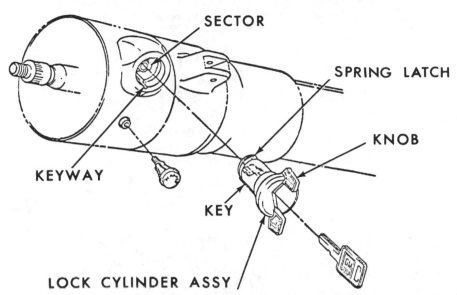

SECTOR

SPRING LATCH

KNOB

KEYWAY

KEY

LOCK CYLINDER ASSY

Installation of Lock Cylinder (© Pontiac Div., G.M. Corp.)

IGNITION SWITCH ADJUSTMENT

1909–73 STANDARD COLUMN

1. Place the switch in the OFF position.
2. Position the switch on the column, then move the slider to the extreme left (toward the wheel.)

Depressing Lock Cylinder Spring Latch—1969–73 (© Pontiac Div., G.M. Corp.)

3. Move the slider back two positions to the right of the ACCESSORY position.
4. Place the key in any run position and shift the transmission into any position but Park for automatics or Reverse for manual.
5. Position the lock toward ACCESSORY with a light finger pressure and secure the switch.

1969–73 TILT COLUMN

1. Place the key in the ACCESSORY position; leave the key in the lock.

2. Loosen the switch mounting screws.
3. Push the switch upward toward the wheel to make certain it is in the ACCESSORY detent.
4. Hold the key in the full counterclockwise ACCESSORY position and tighten the switch mounting screws.
5. The switch is properly adjusted if: it will go into the ACCESSORY position, the key can be removed when in lock, and the switch will go into the START position.

Lighting

HEADLIGHTS

Removal and Installation

1. Remove the screws that hold the chrome bezel around the headlight and remove the bezel.
2. Remove the screws that hold the ring around the headlight and remove the ring and headlight and the wire terminal.
NOTE: *Do not remove or disturb the headlight adjusting screws.*
3. To install, connect the wire to the headlight, install the ring around the headlight and the screws that hold the ring to the bracket.
4. Install the bezel.

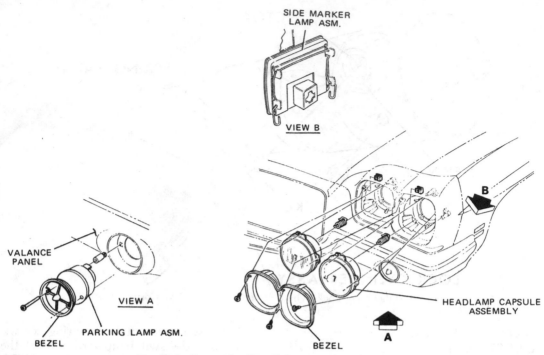

Headlight Removal—GTO (© Pontiac Div., G.M. Corp.)

Light Bulbs

1968	1969	1970	1971–73	
1445(1)	1445	——	——	Ash tray
1156	1156	1156	1156	Back-up
1895	1895	1895	1895	Clock
1895	1895	——	——	Console compartment
89	89	89	89	Courtesy
89(1)	89(1)	89	89	Courtesy (console)
211(1)	211(1)	211-1	211-1	Dome
Type 2(2)	Type 2(2)	Type 2(2)	Type 2	Headlamp (high beam)
Type 1(2)	Type 1(2)	Type 1(2)	Type 1	Headlamp (low beam)
1445	1445	1895	1895	Heater/air conditioner
1891	1891	1895	1895	Instrument cluster
67(1)	67(1)	67	67	License
——	——	1004	1004	Map

Light Bulbs (cont.)

1968	1969	1970	1971–73	
1157A	1157A	1157	1157	Parking
1895	1895	1895	1895	Radio
1445	1893	1893	1893	Shift quadrant (column)
1445	1445	1445	1445	Shift quadrant (console)
1895	194A	194A	194A	Side marker (front)
1893	194A	194	194	Side marker (rear)
1157	1157	1157	1157	Stop
1157	1157	1157	1157	Tail
89	89	89	89	Trunk
1157	1157	1157	1157	Turn signal
1003	1003	1003	1003	Underhood
194	194	194	194	Warning (dash lights)
——	——	1445	1445	Cigarette lighter light
194	194	194	194	Turn signal indicator
194	194	194	194	Ignition lock
194	194	194	194	Tachometer

Fuses and Circuit Breakers

Fuse Type—Amperage	1968	1969	1970	1971–73
A/C controls lamp	AGC-4	AGC-4	SFE-4	SFE-4
A/C power, blower motor	AGC-30	AGC-30	AGC-30	AGC-30
Ash tray lamps	AGC-4	AGC-4	SFE-4	SFE-4
Back-up lamps	SFE-20	SFE-20	SFE-20	SFE-20
Cigarette lighter	SFE-20	SFE-20	SFE-20	SFE-20
Cigarette lighter lamp	AGC-4	AGC-4	SFE-4	SFE-4
Clock lamp	AGC-4	AGC-4	SFE-4	SFE-4

Fuses and Circuit Breakers (cont.)

Fuse Type—Amperage	1968	1969	1970	1971–73
Clock power	SFE-20	SFE-20	SFE-20	SFE-20
Console comp. lamp	SFE-20	SFE-20	——	——
Console courtesy lamp	SFE-20	SFE-20	——	——
Cruise control	SFE-20	SFE-20	AGC-10	AGC-10
Turn signals	SFE-20	SFE-20	SFE-20	SFE-20
Dome light	SFE-20	SFE-20	SFE-20	SFE-20
Downshift switch	AGC-10	AGC-10	——	——
Heater controls lamp	AGC-4	AGC-4	SFE-4	SFE-4
Heater blower motor	AGC-25	AGC-25	AGC-25	AGC-25
Instrument lamps	AGC-4	AGC-4	SFE-4	SFE-4
Instrument panel lamp	SFE-20	SFE-20	SFE-20	SFE-20
Instrument panel courtesy lamp	SFE-20	SFE-20	SFE-20	SFE-20
License lamp	SFE-20	SFE-20	SFE-20	SFE-20
Trunk lamp	SFE-20	SFE-20	SFE-20	SFE-20
Brake warning lamp	SFE-20	SFE-20	AGC-10	AGC-10
Power antenna	SFE-20	SFE-20	——	——
Power seat C.B.	40	40	40	40
Power tail gate window C.B.	40	40	40	40
Power windows C.B.	40	40	40	40
Radio lamp	AGC-4	AGC-4	SFE-4	SFE-4
Radio power	AGC-10	AGC-10	AGC-10	AGC-10
Rear window defogger	SFE-20	SFE-20	AGC-25	AGC-25
Speedometer safeguard	SFE-20	SFE-20	AGC-25	AGC-25
Shift quadrant lamp	AGC-4	AGC-4	SFE-4	SFE-4
Spot lamp	——	——	——	——

Fuses and Circuit Breakers (cont.)

Fuse Type—Amperage	1968	1969	1970	1971–73
Stop lamp	SFE-20	SFE-20	SFE-20	SFE-20
Tachometer	AGC-4	AGC-4	SFE-4	SFE-4
Tail lamps	SFE-20	SFE-20	SFE-20	SFE-20
Underhood lamp	SFE-20	SFE-20	SFE-20	SFE-20
Windshield washer pump, motor	AGC-25	AGC-25	AGC-25	AGC-25

C.B.—Circuit breaker.

Wiring Diagrams

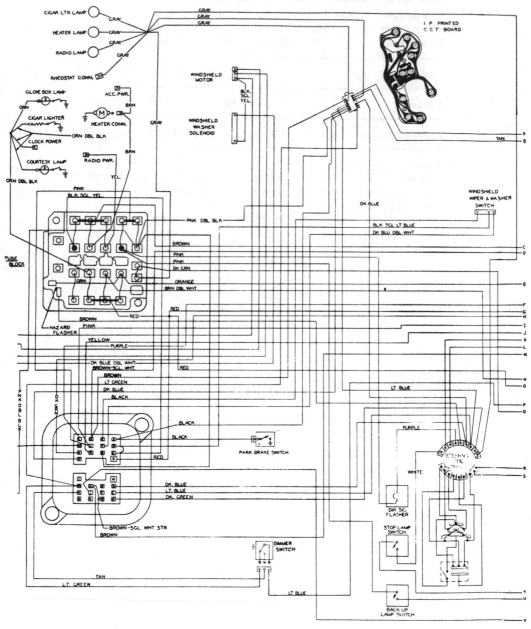

1968 Passenger compartment (left) (© Pontiac Div., G.M. Corp.)

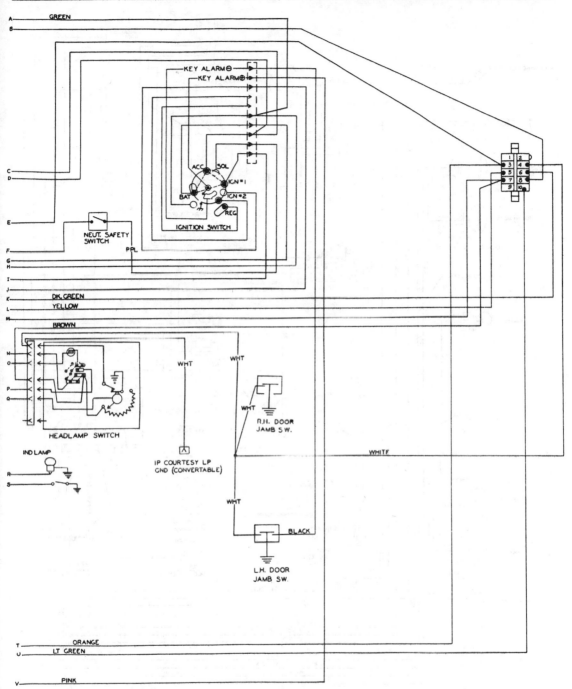

1968 Passenger compartment (right) (© Pontiac Div., G.M. Corp.)

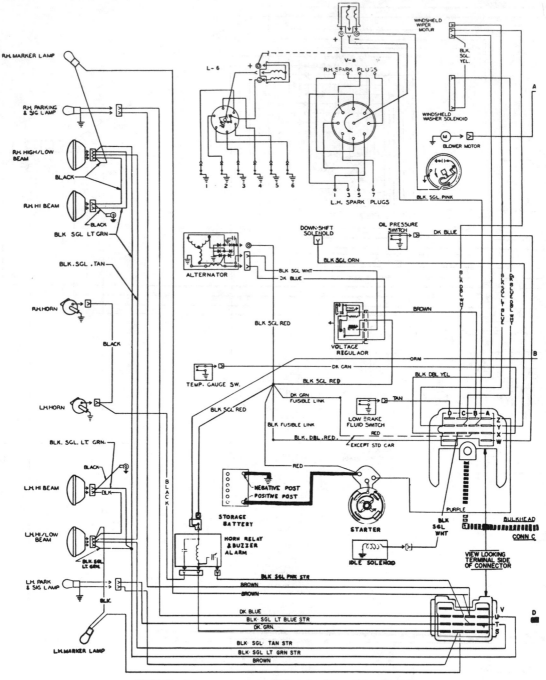

1969 Engine compartment (© Pontiac Div., G.M. Corp.)

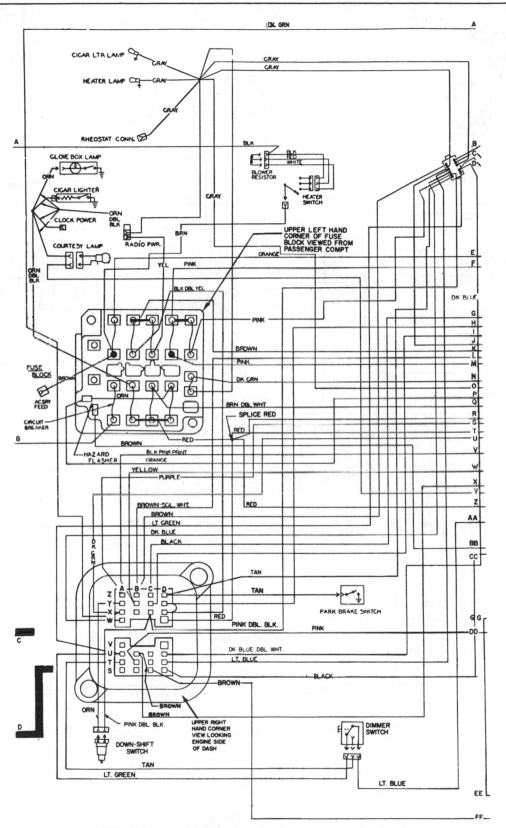

1969 Passenger compartment (left) (© Pontiac Div., G.M. Corp.)

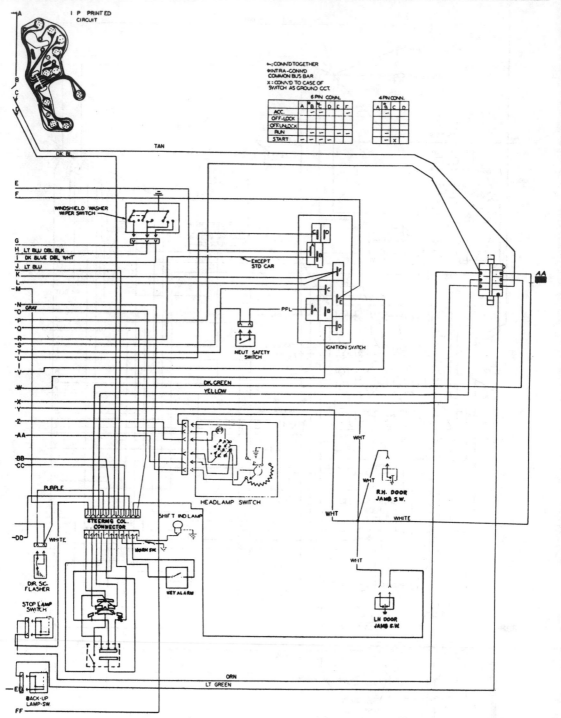

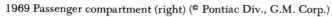

1969 Passenger compartment (right) (© Pontiac Div., G.M. Corp.)

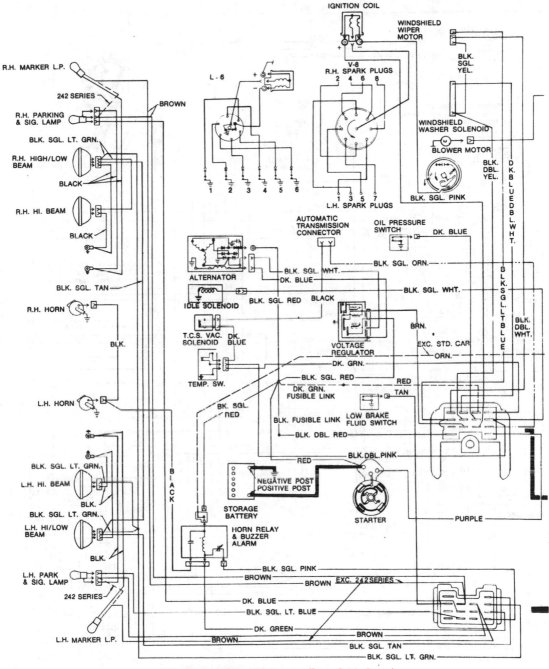

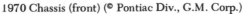

1970 Chassis (front) (© Pontiac Div., G.M. Corp.)

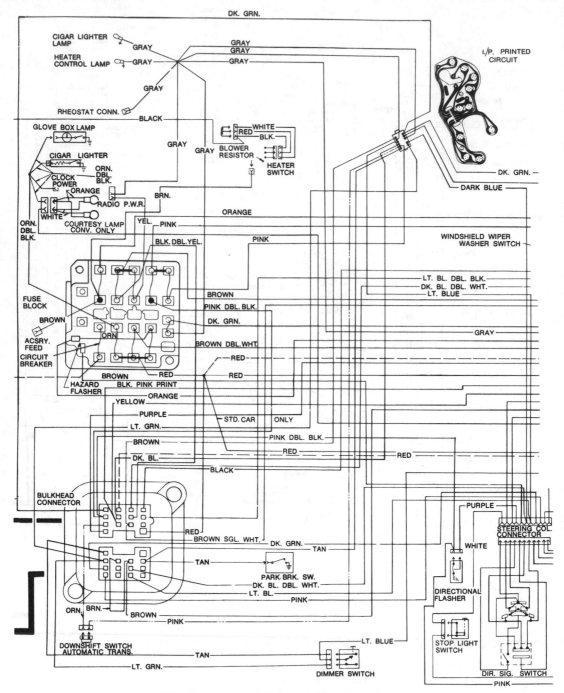

DK. GRN.

CIGAR LIGHTER
LAMP

GRAY
GRAY
GRAY

I/P. PRINTED
CIRCUIT

HEATER
CONTROL LAMP — GRAY

GRAY

GRAY

RHEOSTAT CONN. — BLACK

RED   WHITE
BLK.

DK. GRN. —

DARK BLUE

GLOVE BOX LAMP

GRAY   GRAY

BLOWER
RESISTOR

HEATER
SWITCH

CIGAR LIGHTER
ORN.
DBL.
BLK.

CLOCK
POWER

ORANGE

BRN.

WHITE

RADIO P.W.R.

ORANGE

ORN.
DBL.
BLK.

COURTESY LAMP
CONV. ONLY

YEL.   PINK

WINDSHIELD WIPER
WASHER SWITCH

BLK. DBL. YEL.

PINK

LT. BL. DBL. BLK.
DK. BL. DBL. WHT.
LT. BLUE

FUSE
BLOCK

BROWN

PINK DBL. BLK.

BROWN

DK. GRN.

ORN

BROWN DBL. WHT.

GRAY

ACSRY.
FEED

RED

CIRCUIT
BREAKER

RED

BROWN   RED

HAZARD
FLASHER

BLK. PINK PRINT

YELLOW   ORANGE

PURPLE

STD. CAR   ONLY

LT. GRN.

PINK DBL. BLK.

BROWN

RED

DK. BL.

RED

RED

BLACK

BULKHEAD
CONNECTOR

PURPLE

STEERING COL.
CONNECTOR

RED

BROWN SGL. WHT.   DK. GRN.

TAN

WHITE

TAN

PARK BRK. SW.

DIRECTIONAL
FLASHER

DK. BL. DBL. WHT.

LT. BL.

PINK

ORN. BRN.

BROWN   PINK

STOP LIGHT
SWITCH

LT. BLUE

DOWNSHIFT SWITCH
AUTOMATIC TRANS.

TAN

DIR. SIG. SWITCH

LT. GRN.

DIMMER SWITCH

PINK

1970 Chassis (center) (© Pontiac Div., G.M. Corp.)

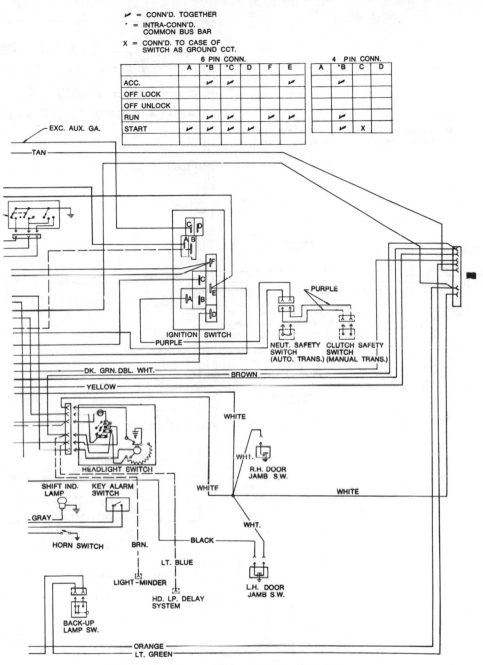

✔ = CONN'D. TOGETHER
* = INTRA-CONN'D. COMMON BUS BAR
X = CONN'D. TO CASE OF SWITCH AS GROUND CCT.

	6 PIN CONN.							4 PIN CONN.			
	A	*B	*C	D	F	E		A	*B	C	D
ACC.		✔	✔			✔			✔		
OFF LOCK											
OFF UNLOCK											
RUN		✔	✔		✔	✔			✔		
START	✔	✔	✔	✔					✔	X	

EXC. AUX. GA.

TAN

PURPLE

IGNITION SWITCH

PURPLE

NEUT. SAFETY SWITCH (AUTO. TRANS.)

CLUTCH SAFETY SWITCH (MANUAL TRANS.)

DK. GRN. DBL. WHT.

BROWN

YELLOW

WHITE

WHT.

R.H. DOOR JAMB S.W.

WHITE

WHITE

HEADLIGHT SWITCH

SHIFT IND. LAMP

KEY ALARM SWITCH

GRAY

WHT.

HORN SWITCH   BRN.   BLACK

LT. BLUE

LIGHT-MINDER

L.H. DOOR JAMB S.W.

HD. LP. DELAY SYSTEM

BACK-UP LAMP SW.

ORANGE

LT. GREEN

1970 Chassis (center) (© Pontiac Div., G.M. Corp.)

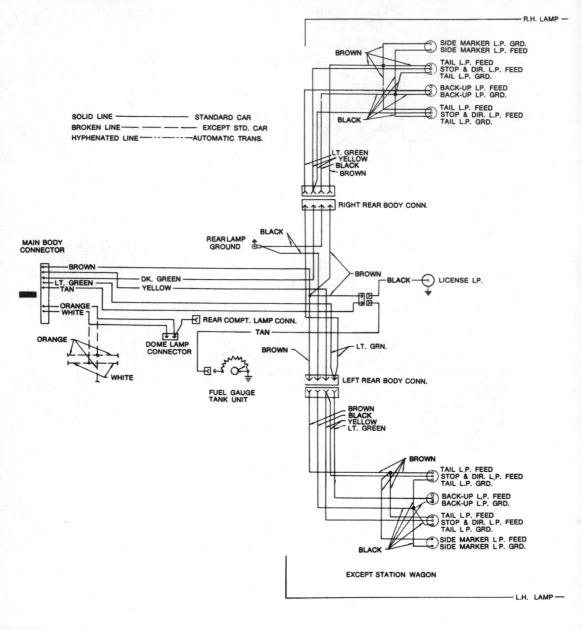

SOLID LINE ————————— STANDARD CAR
BROKEN LINE ——— ——— ——— EXCEPT STD. CAR
HYPHENATED LINE ——·——·——·— AUTOMATIC TRANS.

R.H. LAMP

SIDE MARKER L.P. GRD.
SIDE MARKER L.P. FEED
BROWN

TAIL L.P. FEED
STOP & DIR. L.P. FEED
TAIL L.P. GRD.

BACK-UP LP. FEED
BACK-UP LP. GRD.

TAIL L.P. FEED
STOP & DIR. L.P. FEED
BLACK
TAIL L.P. GRD.

LT. GREEN
YELLOW
BLACK
BROWN

RIGHT REAR BODY CONN.

BLACK

REAR LAMP
GROUND

BROWN — BLACK — LICENSE LP.

MAIN BODY
CONNECTOR

BROWN
DK. GREEN
LT. GREEN
TAN YELLOW

ORANGE
WHITE

REAR COMPT. LAMP CONN.

ORANGE TAN

DOME LAMP
CONNECTOR

BROWN

LT. GRN.

WHITE

LEFT REAR BODY CONN.

FUEL GAUGE
TANK UNIT

BROWN
BLACK
YELLOW
LT. GREEN

BROWN

TAIL L.P. FEED
STOP & DIR. L.P. FEED
TAIL L.P. GRD.

BACK-UP L.P. FEED
BACK-UP L.P. GRD.

TAIL L.P. FEED
STOP & DIR. L.P. FEED
TAIL L.P. GRD.

SIDE MARKER L P. FEED
SIDE MARKER L P. GRD.
BLACK

EXCEPT STATION WAGON

L.H. LAMP

REAR END LAMPS

1970 Chassis (rear except station wagon) (© Pontiac Div., G.M. Corp.)

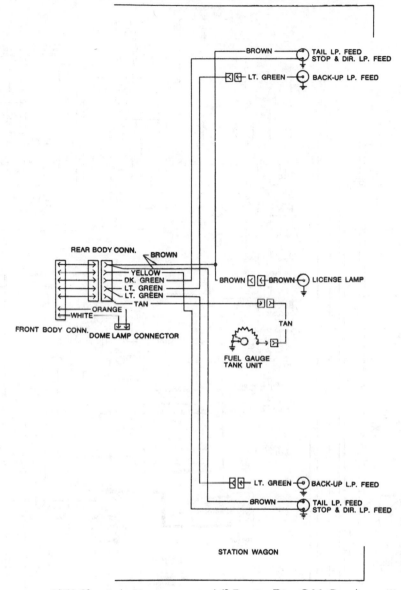

1970 Chassis (station wagon rear) (© Pontiac Div., G.M. Corp.)

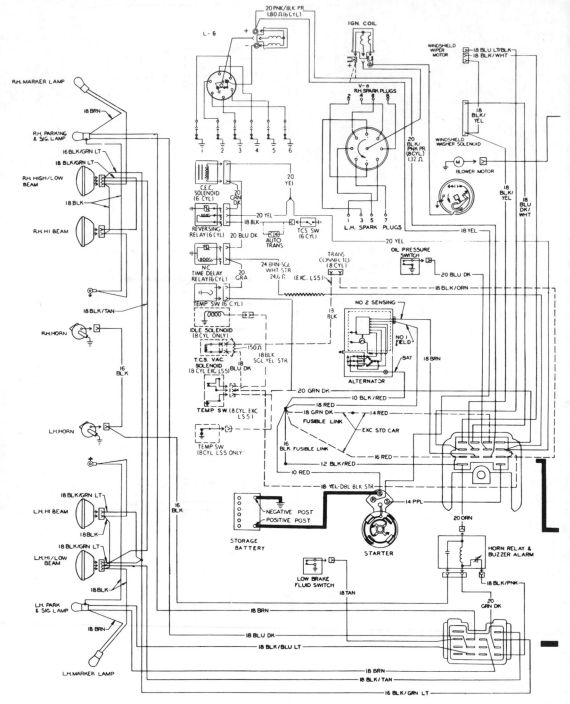

1971 Chassis (front) (© Pontiac Div., G.M. Corp.)

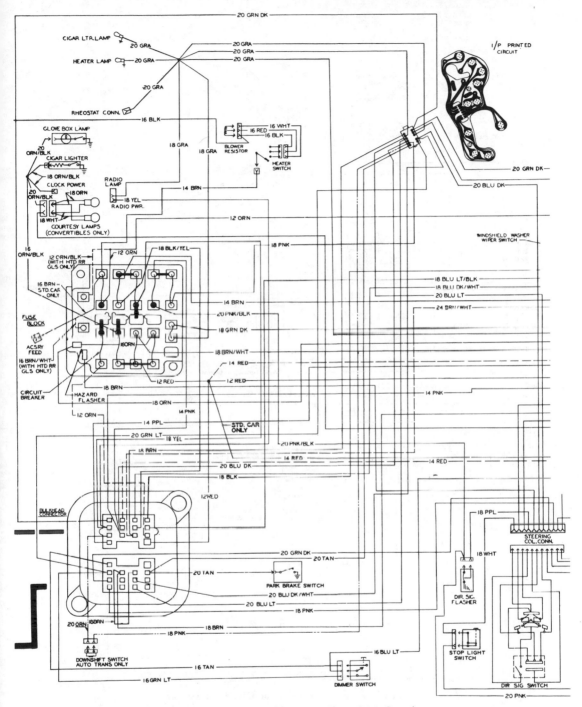

1971 Chassis (center) (© Pontiac Div., G.M. Corp.)

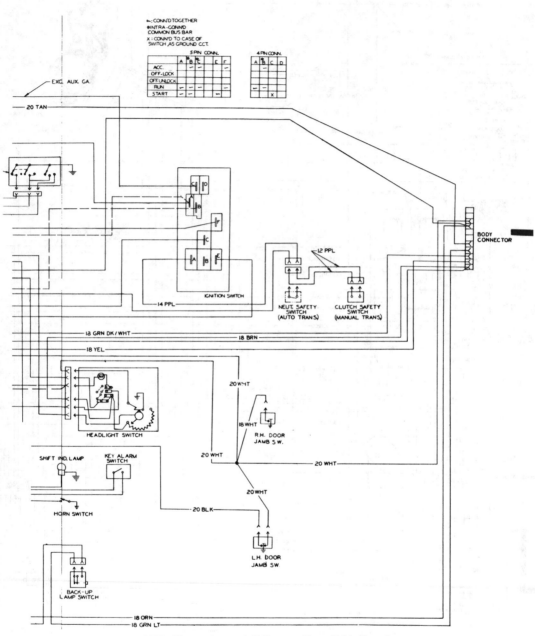

1971 Chassis (center) (© Pontiac Div., G.M. Corp.)

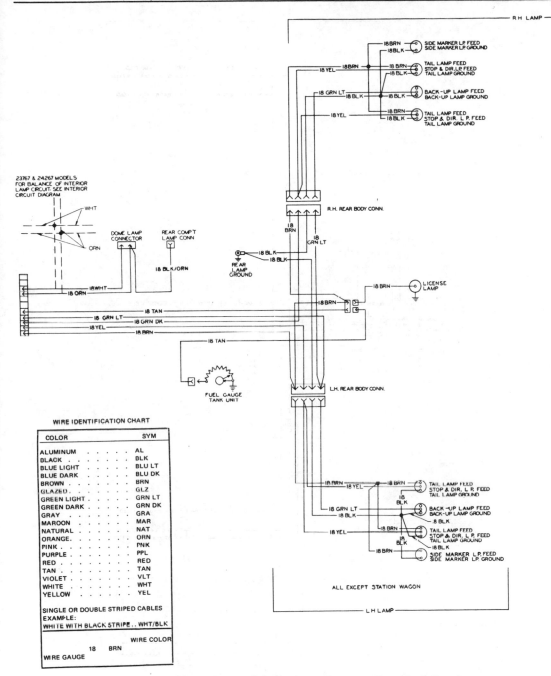

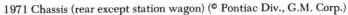

1971 Chassis (rear except station wagon) (© Pontiac Div., G.M. Corp.)

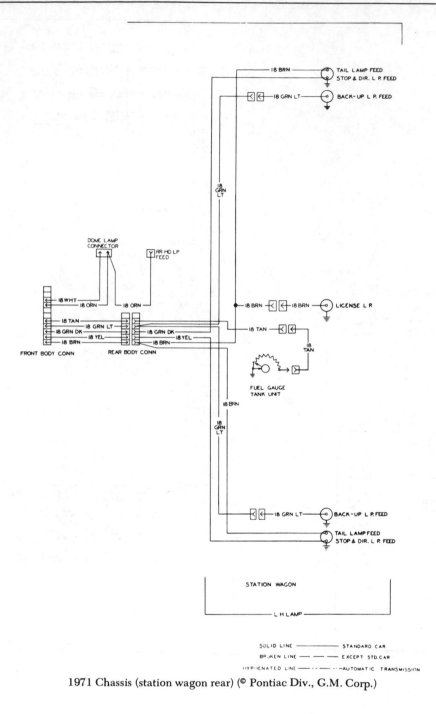

1971 Chassis (station wagon rear) (© Pontiac Div., G.M. Corp.)

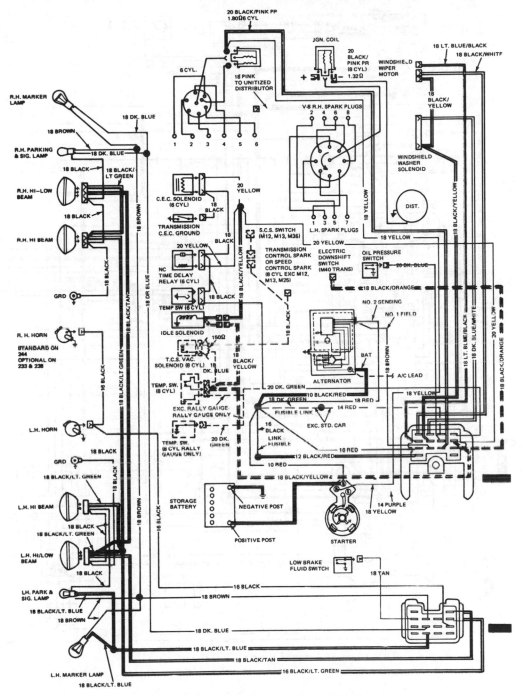

1972 Chassis (front) (© Pontiac Div., G.M. Corp.)

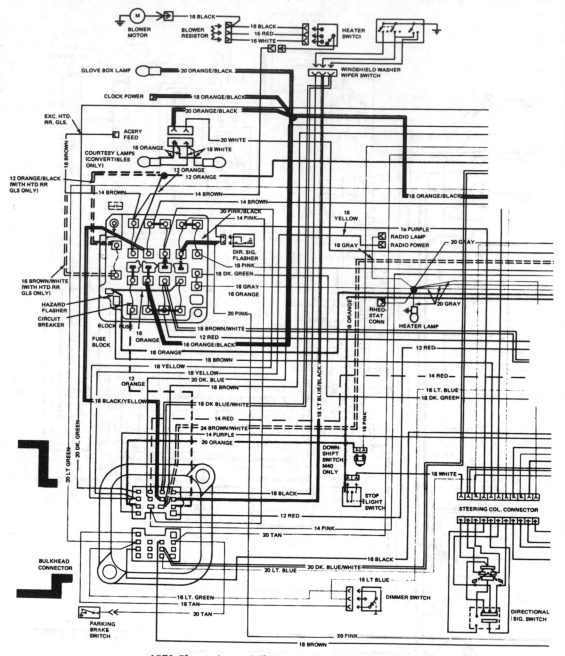

1972 Chassis (center) (© Pontiac Div., G.M. Corp.)

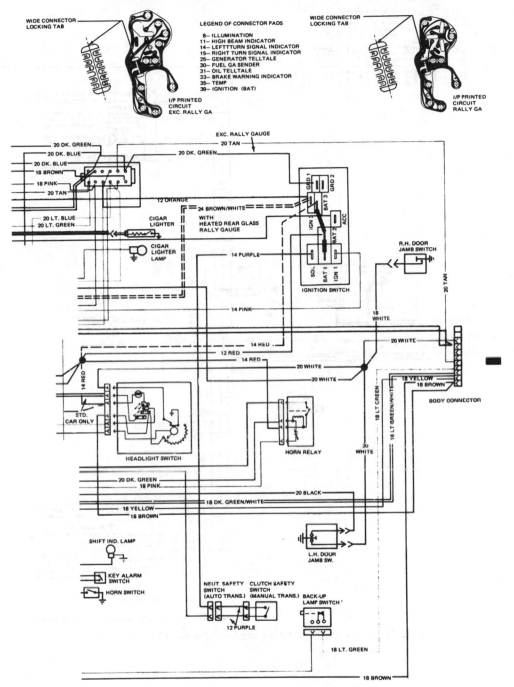

WIDE CONNECTOR
LOCKING TAB

LEGEND OF CONNECTOR PADS

8— ILLUMINATION
11— HIGH BEAM INDICATOR
14— LEFTTTURN SIGNAL INDICATOR
15— RIGHT TURN SIGNAL INDICATOR
25— GENERATOR TELLTALE
30— FUEL GA SENDER
31— OIL TELLTALE
33— BRAKE WARNING INDICATOR
35— TEMP
39— IGNITION (BAT)

WIDE CONNECTOR
LOCKING TAB

I/P PRINTED
CIRCUIT
EXC. RALLY GA

I/P PRINTED
CIRCUIT
RALLY GA

EXC. RALLY GAUGE

20 TAN

20 DK. GREEN
20 DK. BLUE
20 DK. GREEN
20 DK. BLUE
18 BROWN
18 PINK
20 TAN

GRD 1   GRD 2
BAT 3

12 ORANGE
24 BROWN/WHITE
WITH
HEATED REAR GLASS
RALLY GAUGE

IGN 3   BAT 2   ACC

20 LT. BLUE
20 LT. GREEN

CIGAR
LIGHTER

CIGAR
LIGHTER
LAMP

14 PURPLE

SOL.   BAT 1   IGN 1

IGNITION SWITCH

R.H. DOOR
JAMB SWITCH

20 TAN

14 PINK

18
WHITE

14 RED
12 RED
14 RED

20 WHITE

20 WHITE

20 WHITE

14 RED

STD.
CAR ONLY

HEADLIGHT SWITCH

HORN RELAY

20
WHITE

18 LT GREEN
18 LT GREEN/WHITE

18 YELLOW
18 BROWN

BODY CONNECTOR

20 DK. GREEN
18 PINK

20 BLACK

18 DK. GREEN/WHITE

18 YELLOW
18 BROWN

SHIFT IND. LAMP

KEY ALARM
SWITCH

HORN SWITCH

NEUT. SAFETY
SWITCH
(AUTO TRANS.)

CLUTCH SAFETY
SWITCH
(MANUAL TRANS.)

BACK-UP
LAMP SWITCH

L.H. DOOR
JAMB SW.

12 PURPLE

18 LT. GREEN

18 BROWN

1972 Chassis (center) (© Pontiac Div., G.M. Corp.)

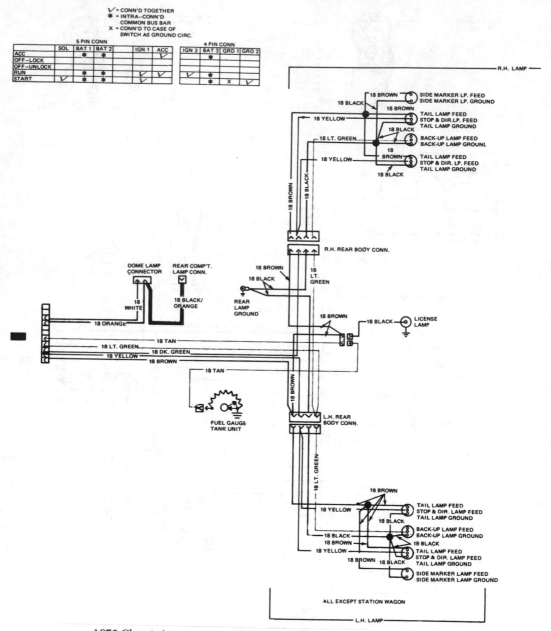

V = CONN'D TOGETHER
* = INTRA–CONN'D COMMON BUS BAR
X = CONN'D TO CASE OF SWITCH AS GROUND CIRC.

	5 PIN CONN					4 PIN CONN			
	SOL	BAT 1	BAT 2	IGN 1	ACC	IGN 3	BAT 3	GRD 1	GRD 2
ACC		*	*		V		*		
OFF–LOCK									
OFF–UNLOCK									
RUN		*	*	V	V	V	*		
START	V	*	*	V			*	X	V

1972 Chassis (rear except station wagon) (© Pontiac Div., G.M. Corp.)

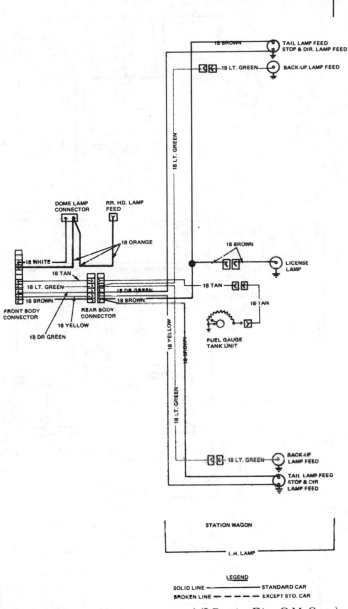

1972 Chassis (station wagon rear) (© Pontiac Div., G.M. Corp.)

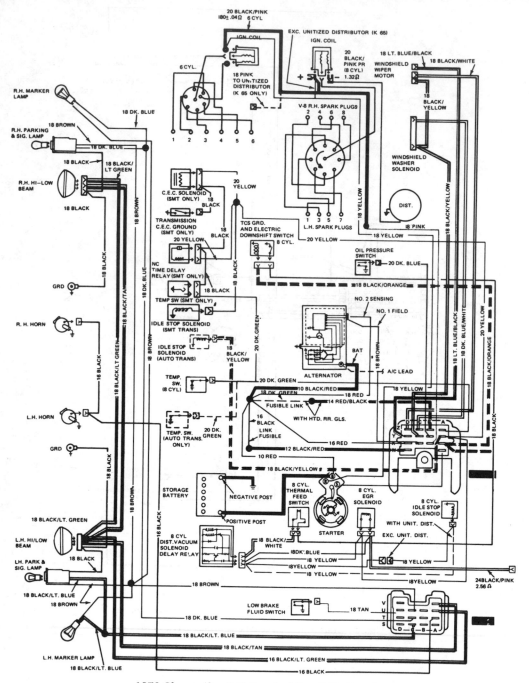

1973 Chassis (front) (© Pontiac Div., G.M. Corp.)

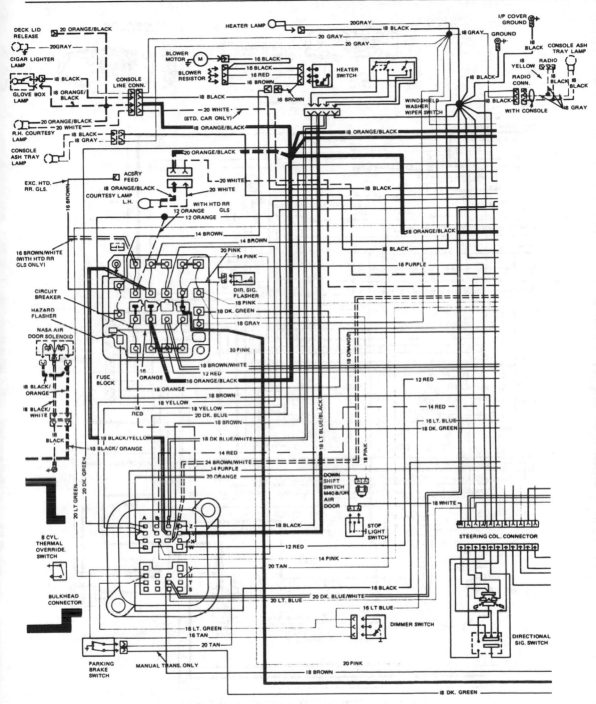

1973 Chassis (center) (© Pontiac Div., G.M. Corp.)

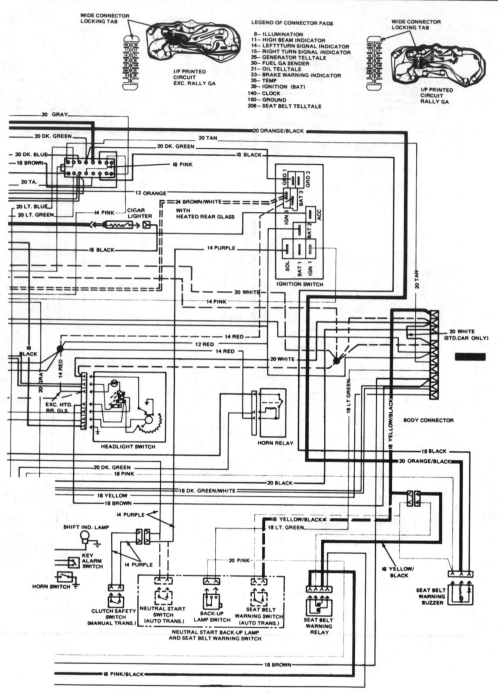

LEGEND OF CONNECTOR PADS

8 — ILLUMINATION
11 — HIGH BEAM INDICATOR
14 — LEFT TURN SIGNAL INDICATOR
15 — RIGHT TURN SIGNAL INDICATOR
25 — GENERATOR TELLTALE
30 — FUEL GAS SENDER
31 — OIL TELLTALE
33 — BRAKE WARNING INDICATOR
35 — TEMP
39 — IGNITION (BAT)
140 — CLOCK
150 — GROUND
206 — SEAT BELT TELLTALE

1973 Chassis (center) (© Pontiac Div., G.M. Corp.)

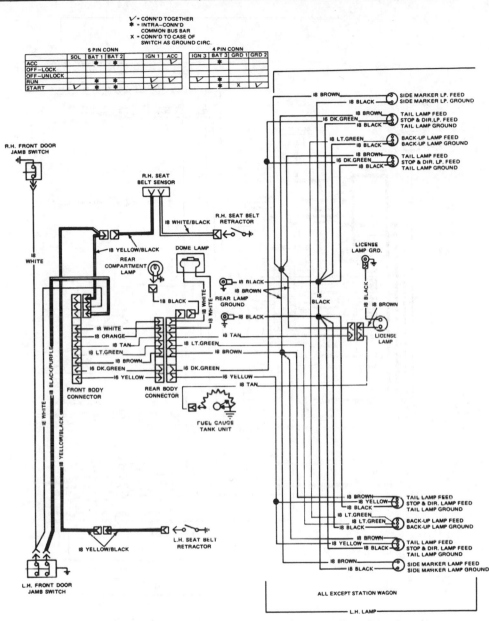

1973 Chassis (rear except station wagon) (© Pontiac Div., G.M. Corp.)

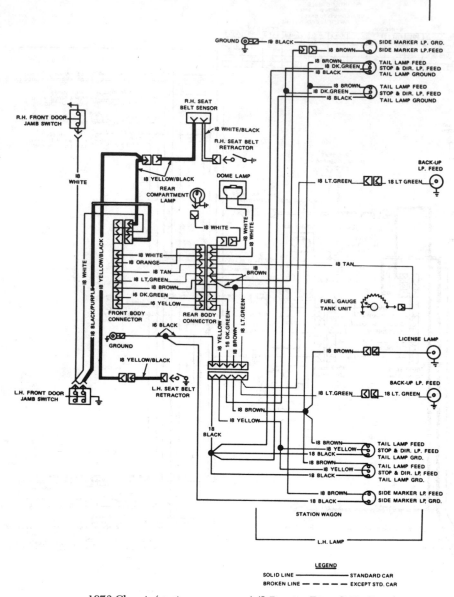

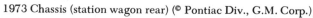

1973 Chassis (station wagon rear) (© Pontiac Div., G.M. Corp.)

6 · Clutch and Transmission

Manual Transmission

Three different three speed and two different four speed transmissions have been used on the models covered in this guide. The heavy duty three speed transmission, used in 1969, was a fully synchronized unit manufactured by Ford (Dearborn). Since 1970, the heavy duty three speed has been a Muncie model.

The Saginaw four speed is an optional floor-shift model used with smaller engines. The four speed Muncie is an optional model used on the 400 and 455 cu in. engines. Both transmissions are fully synchronized in all forward gears.

Removal and Installation

THREE SPEED TRANSMISSIONS

1. Disconnect the battery and release the parking brake before raising the car.
2. Disconnect the speedometer cable.
3. Disconnect the transmission shifter levers from the transmission shifter shafts. On six-cylinder engines, disconnect the electrical lead from the T.C.S. switch. On floorshift models, remove the two shifter assembly-to-shifter support bolts and remove the shifter from the transmission. If it is not necessary to remove the shifter from the car, it may be left hanging from its floor seal. Mark the differential flange

and the driveshaft yoke to assure proper reassembly. Remove the driveshaft.

4. Support the rear of the engine and remove the transmission mount. Do not dent the oil pan or it could hit the crankshaft.
5. Remove the four crossmember bolts and slide the member rearward.
6. Remove the four transmission-to-bellhousing bolts.
7. Slide the transmission rearward until it clears the clutch assembly and bellhousing, then remove the transmission.
8. Position the transmission and then slide it into place.
9. Install the four transmission-to-bellhousing bolts.
10. Install the crossmember and the bolts.
11. Install the driveshaft, aligning it with the marks. Install the shift linkage.
12. Connect the speedometer cable.
13. Connect the battery.

FOUR SPEED TRANSMISSION

1. Disconnect the battery and release the parking brake before raising the car.
2. Disconnect the speedometer cable.
3. Disconnect the transmission shifter levers from the transmission shifter shafts. On six-cylinder engines, disconnect the electrical lead from the T.C.S. switch. On floor-shift models, remove the two shifter assembly-to-shifter support bolts and remove the shifter from the transmission. If

it is not necessary to remove the shifter from the car, it may be left hanging from its floor seal. Mark the differential flange and the driveshaft yoke to assure proper assembly. Remove the driveshaft.

4. Support the rear of the engine and remove the transmission mount. Do not dent the oil pan severely as it will hit the crankshaft.

5. Remove the four crossmember bolts and slide the member rearward.

6. Remove the four transmission-to-bellhousing bolts.

7. Slide the transmission rearward until it clears the clutch assembly and bellhousing, then remove the transmission.

8. Position the transmission and then slide it into place.

9. Install the four transmission-to-bellhousing bolts.

10. Install the crossmember and the bolts.

11. Install the driveshaft, aligning it with the marks. Install the shift linkage.

12. Connect the speedometer cable.

13. Connect the battery.

Linkage Adjustment

1968 Saginaw Three Speed Column Shift

1. Set the transmission shift levers in Neutral.

NOTE: *Align the shift levers in Neutral by inserting a 0.185 in. pin through the holes in the levers.*

2. Loosen the screw on each adjusting swivel clamp.

3. Set both shift levers on the transmission in Neutral.

4. Tighten the screws on each adjusting swivel clamp to 20 ft lbs.

5. Remove the gauge pin and check the shift pattern.

1069–73, Saginaw Three Speed Column Shift

1. Place the gearshift lever in the Reverse position.

2. Loosen the swivel clamp bolt at the rear transmission shift lever (First and Reverse) and the bolt at the equalizer shaft and lever assembly.

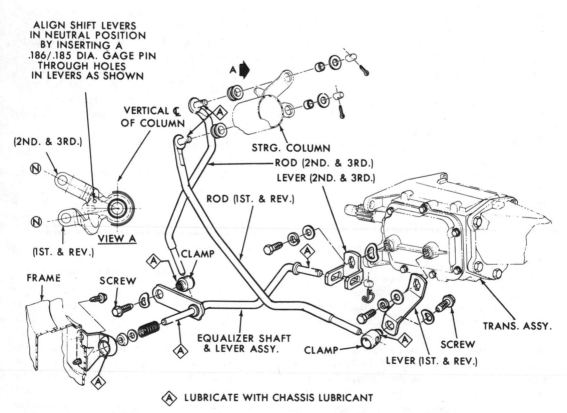

LUBRICATE WITH CHASSIS LUBRICANT

Tempest Shift Column Controls—1968 (© Pontiac Div., G..M. Corp.)

3. Position the front transmission shift lever (Second and Third) in Neutral and the rear transmission shift lever (First and Reverse) in Reverse.

4. Tighten the swivel clamp bolt or nut to 20 ft lbs, then unlock the steering column and shift into Neutral.

5. Align the lower gearshift levers (on the column) in the Neutral position, then insert a 0.185 in. diameter gauge pin through the hole in the lower control levers.

6. Tighten the swivel clamp bolt or nut to 20 ft lbs, then remove the gauge pin and check the shift pattern.

1968–73 THREE SPEED HD DEARBORN AND SAGINAW COLUMN SHIFT

1. Place the gearshift lever in Neutral.
2. Loosen the swivel clamp on the gearshift control rod.
3. Loosen the trunnion locknuts on

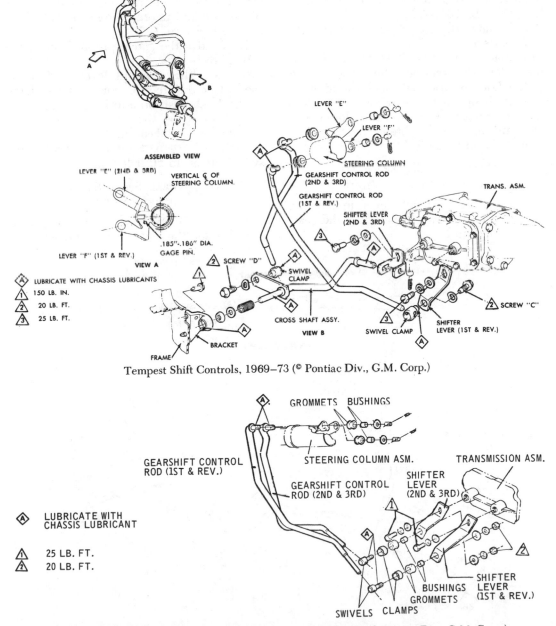

Tempest Shift Controls, 1969–73 (© Pontiac Div., G.M. Corp.)

Tempest Shift Controls, H.D. Dearborn Transmission 1968–73 (© Pontiac Div., G.M. Corp.)

First-Reverse and Second-Third transmission control rods.

4. Insert a ¼ in. drill rod into the shifter assembly.

5. If the gearshift lever is not properly aligned with the floor opening:

    a. Console—loosen the two shifter-to-support bolts and align the shifter. Tighten the bolts.

    b. Without Console—loosen the two shifter-to-support bolts and center the shifter in the boot; tighten the bolts.

6. Position both transmission shift levers in Neutral and tighten the locknuts to 30 ft lbs (25 ft lbs 1971–72).

7. Remove the gauge pin and check the shift pattern.

8. Place the gearshift lever in Reverse, then place the steering column lower lever in the Lock position and lock the ignition.

9. Push up on the gearshift control rod to take up the lash in the column lock mechanism, then tighten the adjusting swivel clamp to 20 ft lbs.

1970–73 Three Speed HD Muncie Column Shift

1. Place the gearshift lever in Neutral.

2. Loosen the swivel clamp on the gearshift control rod.

3. Loosen the trunnion locknuts on the First-Reverse and Second-Third transmission control rods.

4. Insert a ¼ in. drill rod into the shifter assembly.

5. If the gearshift lever is not properly aligned with the floor opening:

    a. Console—loosen the two shifter-to-support bolts and align the shifter; tighten the bolts.

    b. Without Console—loosen the two shifter-to-support bolts and center the shifter in the boot; tighten the bolts.

6. Position both transmission shift levers in Neutral and tighten the locknuts to 30 ft lbs (25 ft lbs 1971–72).

7. Remove the gauge pin and check the shift pattern.

8. Place the gearshift lever in Reverse then place the steering column lower lever in the Lock position and lock the ignition.

9. Push up on the gearshift control rod to take up the lash in the column lock mechanism, then tighten the adjusting swivel clamp to 20 ft lbs.

1968 Three Speed Saginaw Floor Shift

1. Place the gearshift lever in Neutral.
2. Loosen the two swivel nut assemblies.

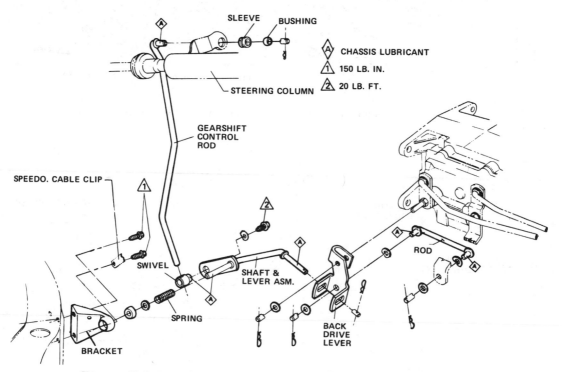

Tempest Shift Controls Column, Muncie, 1970–73 (© Pontiac Div., G.M. Corp.)

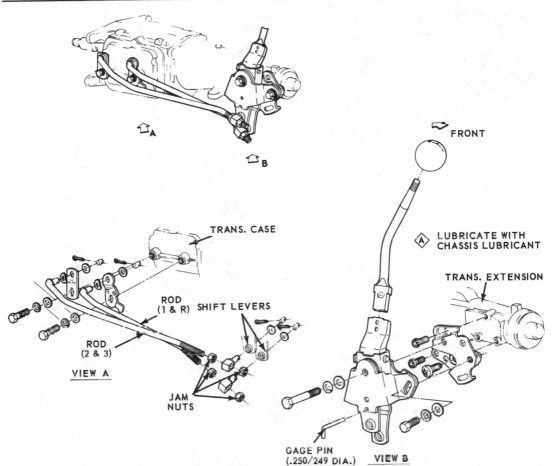

Floor Shift Control, 1968 Three Speed (© Pontiac Div., G.M. Corp.)

3. Insert a ¼ in. drill rod into the bracket and lever assembly and align the shift levers in the Neutral position.

4. Position the transmission shift levers in the Neutral position.

5. Tighten the swivel nut assemblies to 8–12 ft lbs.

6. Remove the gauge pin and check the shift pattern.

1968 Four Speed Floor Shift

1. Place the gearshift lever in Neutral.

2. Loosen the three swivel nut assemblies.

3. Insert a ¼ in. drill rod into the gauge pin hole in the shifter.

4. Position the transmission shift levers in Neutral.

5. Install the swivel assemblies, adjusting the length so that they fit into the transmission shift levers without binding; tighten the swivel nuts to 30 ft lbs.

1969–73 Muncie and 1969 Saginaw Four Speed Floor Shift

1. Place the gearshift lever in Neutral.

2. Loosen the adjusting swivel clamp on the gearshift control rod.

3. For the 1969 Saginaw, loosen the trunnion locknuts on First-Second and Reverse shift rods, then disconnect the trunnion from the lever. Loosen the locknuts for the Muncie-equipped 1969 and up Tempest and GTO.

4. Insert a ¼ in. drill rod into the gauge pin hole in the shifter.

5. If the gearshift lever is not properly aligned with floor opening:

a. Console—loosen the two shifter-to-support bolts and align the shifter; tighten the bolts.

b. Without Console—loosen the two shifter-to-support bolts and center the shifter in the boot; tighten the bolts.

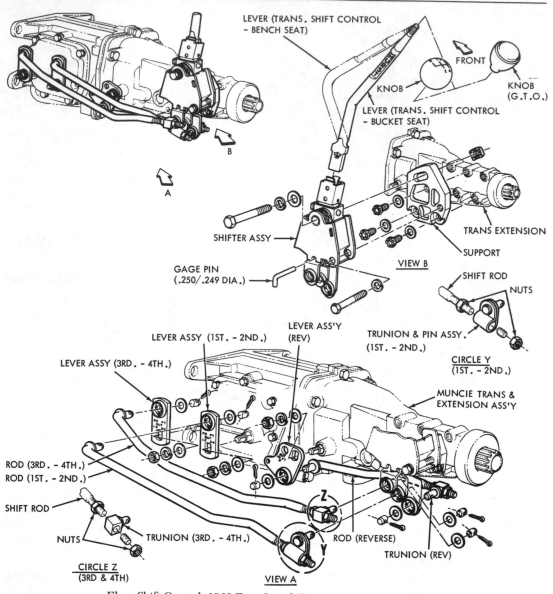

LEVER (TRANS. SHIFT CONTROL – BENCH SEAT)

FRONT

KNOB

KNOB (G.T.O.)

LEVER (TRANS. SHIFT CONTROL – BUCKET SEAT)

SHIFTER ASSY

TRANS EXTENSION

SUPPORT

VIEW B

GAGE PIN (.250/.249 DIA.)

SHIFT ROD

NUTS

LEVER ASS'Y (REV)

TRUNION & PIN ASSY. (1ST. – 2ND.)

LEVER ASSY (1ST. – 2ND.)

CIRCLE Y (1ST. – 2ND.)

LEVER ASSY (3RD. – 4TH.)

MUNCIE TRANS & EXTENSION ASS'Y

ROD (3RD. – 4TH.)

ROD (1ST. – 2ND.)

SHIFT ROD

Z

NUTS

TRUNION (3RD. – 4TH.)

ROD (REVERSE)

Y

TRUNION (REV)

CIRCLE Z (3RD & 4TH)

VIEW A

Floor Shift Control, 1968 Four Speed (© Pontiac Div., G.M. Corp.)

6. Place the transmission shift levers in Neutral and tighten the locknuts to 30 ft lbs for the 1969 Saginaw.

7. Align the trunnion with the hole in the Third-Fourth shifter lever, insert the trunnion and secure it with a washer and cotter pin for the 1969 Saginaw. Tighten the locknuts to 30 ft lbs for the 1969 and up Muncie.

8. Remove the gauge pin and check the shift pattern.

9. Place the gearshift lever in Reverse, set the steering column lower lever in the Lock position and lock the ignition.

10. Push up on the gearshift control rod to take up the lash in the steering column lock mechanism, then tighten the adjusting clamp to 20 ft lbs.

Clutch

A single-plate, dry-disc, diaphragm spring clutch is used on all Tempest, GTO and LeMans models. The clutch assembly consists of the driven plate, the pressure plate, and the release mechanism. Grooves

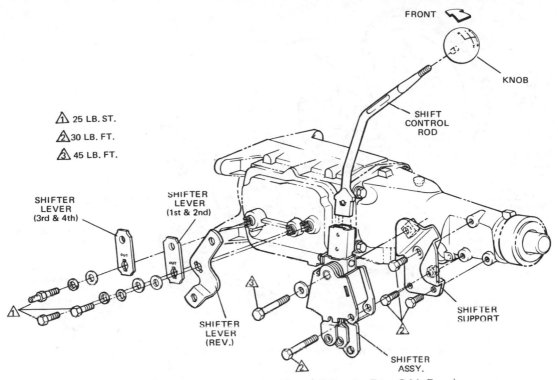

FRONT

KNOB

SHIFT
CONTROL
ROD

⚠1 25 LB. ST.

⚠2 30 LB. FT.

⚠3 45 LB. FT.

SHIFTER
LEVER
(3rd & 4th)

SHIFTER
LEVER
(1st & 2nd)

OUT

OUT

SHIFTER
LEVER
(REV.)

SHIFTER
SUPPORT

SHIFTER
ASSY.

Floor Shift Controls, 1969–73 Four Speed (© Pontiac Div., G.M. Corp.)

on both sides of the driven plate prevent the plate from sticking to the flywheel and the pressure plate due to vacuum.

Two types of diaphragm type pressure plates are used—a bent finger type, for the high performance OHC six-cylinder and all V8s and a flat finger type for the six-cylinder standard engines.

The clutch release mechanism consists of a ball thrust (throwout) bearing and different linkage configurations (for the various models) to control this bearing. The throwout bearing slides on the front transmission extension housing (nose piece), which is concentric with and encloses the transmission main drive gear. When pedal pressure is applied, the clutch fork pivots on its ball socket, through linkage action, and the inner end of the fork forces the throwout bearing against the release levers.

On 1969–72 models, a clutch safety switch prevents the engine from cranking unless the clutch is disengaged. The only periodic clutch service required, other than adjustment for normal wear, is the lubrication of all linkage pivot points every 6,000 miles.

Removal and Installation

1. Raise the car and support it on jackstands. Disconnect the battery.

2. Support the rear of the engine with jackstands.

3. Remove the driveshaft.

4. Remove the rear crossmember bolts from the frame and transmission mounts and remove the crossmember.

NOTE: *See "Transmission Removal" for procedure variations.*

5. Disconnect the transmission shift linkage, the speedometer cable, and the clutch return spring. The clutch fork pushrod will now hang free.

6. Remove the clutch housing cover plate screws and let the plate hang from the starter gear housing.

7. Lower the engine enough to gain access to the clutch housing bolts at the engine block, then remove all but the uppermost bolt.

8. Hold the transmission and clutch housing assembly against the block over the dowel pins while removing the last bolt. Remove the transmission and clutch housing as an assembly.

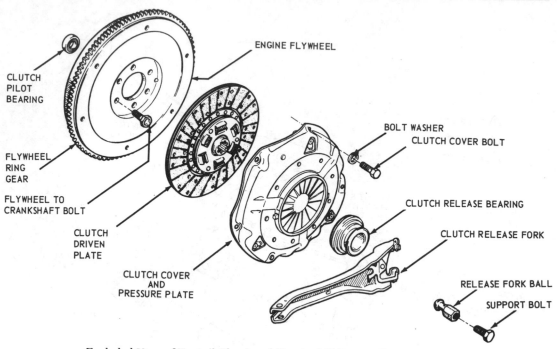

CLUTCH PILOT BEARING

ENGINE FLYWHEEL

FLYWHEEL RING GEAR

FLYWHEEL TO CRANKSHAFT BOLT

CLUTCH DRIVEN PLATE

CLUTCH COVER AND PRESSURE PLATE

BOLT WASHER
CLUTCH COVER BOLT

CLUTCH RELEASE BEARING

CLUTCH RELEASE FORK

RELEASE FORK BALL
SUPPORT BOLT

Exploded View of Typical Clutch and Flywheel (© Pontiac Div., G.M. Corp.)

9. Matchmark the pressure plate and flywheel with paint to make sure the correct balance is maintained.

10. Loosen the six cover plate attaching screws a little at a time, until the clutch diaphragm spring tension is released. Remove the bolts, clutch assembly, and pilot tool.

11. The pilot bearing is an oil impregnated type bearing pressed into the crankshaft. Inspect and renew it if necessary.

12. Install the clutch disc with the long hub forward (toward the flywheel).

13. Install the pressure plate and the cover assembly, then align the clutch disc by inserting a pilot tool, or an old transmission mainshaft, into the splines. Align the mark on the clutch cover with the mark on the flywheel, then align the nearest bolt holes.

14. Install bolts in every other hole in the cover and tighten them alternately. Then install the remaining three bolts and tighten all six to 25 ft lbs.

15. Remove the clutch pilot tool and check to see that it can be reinserted and moved freely.

16. Install the clutch fork and dust boot into the clutch housing. Lubricate the throwout bearing with graphite grease.

17. Complete the reassembly by revers-

ing the removal procedures. Tighten the housing bolts to 40 ft lbs.

18. Adjust the shifter and clutch release linkage.

Clutch Pedal Adjustment

1. Disconnect the return spring.

2. With the pedal against the stop, loosen the locknut to allow the adjusting rod to be turned out of the swivel (V8), or the pushrod (6 cylinder), until the throwout bearing contacts the release fingers in the pressure plate.

3. Turn the adjusting rod into the swivel or pushrod 3½ turns; tighten the locknut to 8–12 ft lbs for 1968, 30 ft lbs for 1969–72.

4. Install the return spring and check the pedal lash; it should be approximately 1 in.

Automatic Transmission

Removal and Installation

1. Raise the car and provide support for the front and rear of the car.

2. Disconnect the front exhaust pipe

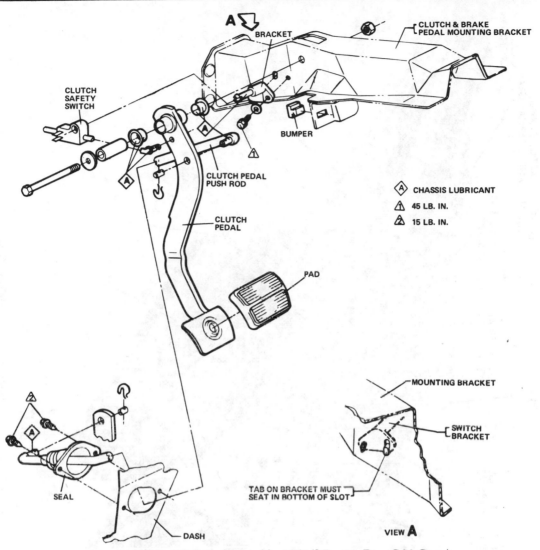

A CHASSIS LUBRICANT

⚠ 45 LB. IN.

⚠ 15 LB. IN.

Clutch Pedal and Push Rod Assembly, 1972 (© Pontiac Div., G.M. Corp.)

bolts at the exhaust manifold and at the connection of the intermediate exhaust pipe location (single exhaust only.) On dual exhaust, the exhaust pipes need not be removed, just loosened.

3. Remove the driveshaft.

4. Place a suitable jack under the transmission and fasten the transmission securely to the jack.

5. Remove the vacuum modulator hose from the vacuum modulator, then remove the T.C.S. wire.

6. Loosen the cooler line bolts and separate the cooler lines from the transmission.

7. Remove the transmission mounting pad-to-crossmember bolts.

8. Remove the transmission crossmem- ber support-to-frame rail bolts. Remove the crossmember.

9. Disconnect the speedometer cable.

10. Loosen the shift linkage and down-shift cable.

11. Disconnect and remove the trans-mission filler pipe.

12. Support the engine at the oil pan.

13. Remove the transmission flywheel cover pan.

14. Mark the flywheel and converter pump for reassembly in the same positions and remove the converter pump-to-fly-wheel bolts.

NOTE: *Starting in 1972 on V8 engines, the flywheel has a locating (NET) hole. This hole is smaller and slightly oval and is specifically located so that when*

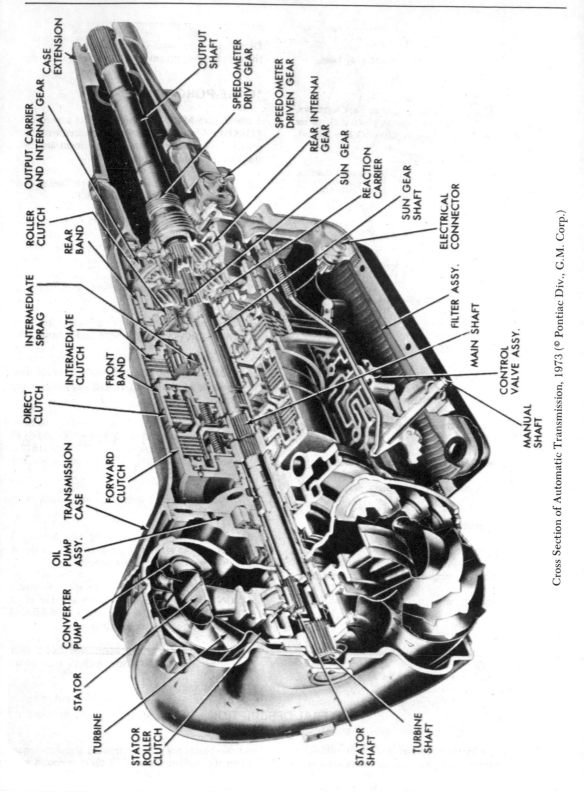

Cross Section of Automatic Transmission, 1973 (© Pontiac Div., G.M. Corp.)

the bolt is started and tightened, the other two holes will line up. When installing and tightening the flywheel bolts, start with the locating hole and torque the bolt to 30 ft lbs. Continue to the second and third bolts, tightening each to 30 ft lbs.

15. Remove the transmission case-to-engine block bolts.

16. Move the transmission rearward to provide clearance between the converter pump and crankshaft. Make sure the converter does not fall off the transmission input shaft during removal.

17. Lower the transmission and move it to a bench.

18. Install the clutch in the reverse order of removal.

Pan Removal and Filter Service

THREE SPEED (M-40, M-38),
TWO SPEED (M-35)

1. Raise the car and drain the oil pan.
2. Remove the oil pan bolts, pan, and gasket.

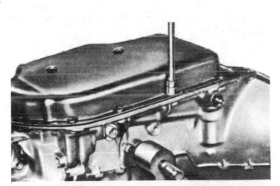

Removing Oil Pan from Transmission, 1973 (© Pontiac Div., G.M. Corp.)

3. Remove the oil strainer-to-valve body screws and the strainer.

4. Clean the oil pan and strainer.

5. Clean the pan gasket surface. Install a new pan gasket and tighten the bolts evenly. Lower the car to the ground and fill with transmission fluid.

Low Band Adjustment

TWO SPEED (M-35) TRANSMISSION

1. Place the shifter lever in Neutral and raise the vehicle.

2. Remove the adjusting screw protecting cap.

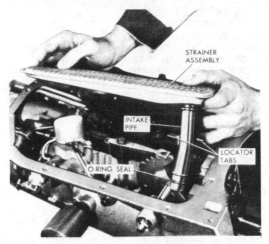

Removing Transmission Filter, M-40 (© Pontiac Div., G.M. Corp.)

3. Loosen the adjusting screw locknut ¼ turn.

Low Band Adjustment, M-35 (© Pontiac Div., G.M. Corp.)

4. Tighten the adjusting screw to 70 ft lbs and then back off *exactly* four complete turns for a band with 6,000 miles or more of use, three turns for a band with less than 6,000 miles of use.

5. Tighten the locknut and install the protective cap.

Band Adjustment

THREE SPEED (M-38 AND M-40)
TRANSMISSIONS

Band adjustments must be made during overhaul and cannot be accomplished without partial disassembly of the transmission. Varying the length of the band apply pin in the servo assemblies determines band adjustment.

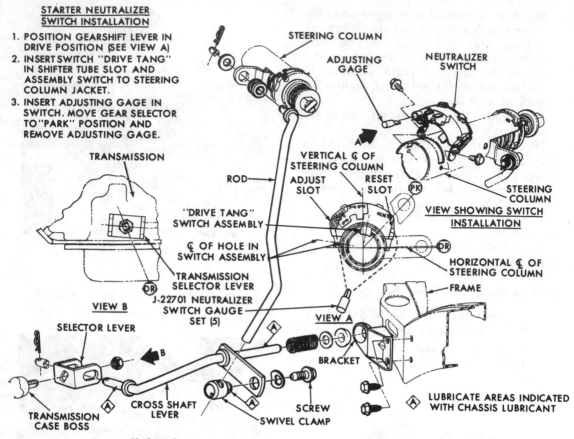

STARTER NEUTRALIZER
SWITCH INSTALLATION

1. POSITION GEARSHIFT LEVER IN DRIVE POSITION (SEE VIEW A)
2. INSERT SWITCH "DRIVE TANG" IN SHIFTER TUBE SLOT AND ASSEMBLY SWITCH TO STEERING COLUMN JACKET.
3. INSERT ADJUSTING GAGE IN SWITCH. MOVE GEAR SELECTOR TO "PARK" POSITION AND REMOVE ADJUSTING GAGE.

STEERING COLUMN

ADJUSTING GAGE

NEUTRALIZER SWITCH

TRANSMISSION

ROD

VERTICAL ₵ OF STEERING COLUMN

ADJUST SLOT

RESET SLOT

PK

STEERING COLUMN

VIEW SHOWING SWITCH INSTALLATION

"DRIVE TANG" SWITCH ASSEMBLY

₵ OF HOLE IN SWITCH ASSEMBLY

DR

HORIZONTAL ₵ OF STEERING COLUMN

TRANSMISSION SELECTOR LEVER

J-22701 NEUTRALIZER SWITCH GAUGE SET (5)

VIEW A

FRAME

VIEW B

SELECTOR LEVER

B

BRACKET

TRANSMISSION CASE BOSS

CROSS SHAFT LEVER

SCREW

SWIVEL CLAMP

LUBRICATE AREAS INDICATED WITH CHASSIS LUBRICANT

Shift Linkage control, column, 1968 (© Pontiac Div., G.M. Corp.).

Shift Linkage Adjustment

1968 COLUMN SHIFT

1. Loosen the nut on the adjusting swivel clamp.
2. Set the transmission selector lever in the Drive detent.
3. Set the shift lever into the Drive position.
4. Tighten the nut on the adjusting swivel clamp.
5. Check the shifting pattern.

1968 CONSOLE SHIFT

1. Disconnect the cable at the transmission.
2. With the gearshift lever in the Park position, adjust the pin as shown in the 1967–68 console gearshift linkage illustrations.
3. Tighten the pin nut and connect the cable.

1969–73 COLUMN SHIFT

1. Loosen the screw on the adjusting swivel clamp.
2. Place the gearshift lever in Park and lock the ignition.
3. Place the transmission shift lever in the Park detent.
4. Push up on the gearshift control rod until the lash is taken up in the steering column lock mechanism, then tighten the screw or nut on the swivel clamp to 20 ft lbs.
5. Readjust the transmission neutral switch if necessary.

1969–73 CONSOLE SHIFT THREE SPEED (M-38, M-40) TRANSMISSIONS

1. Disconnect the shift cable from the transmission shift lever by removing the nut from the pin.
2. Adjust the back drive linkage (as in Step 4, above).
3. Unlock the ignition and rotate the

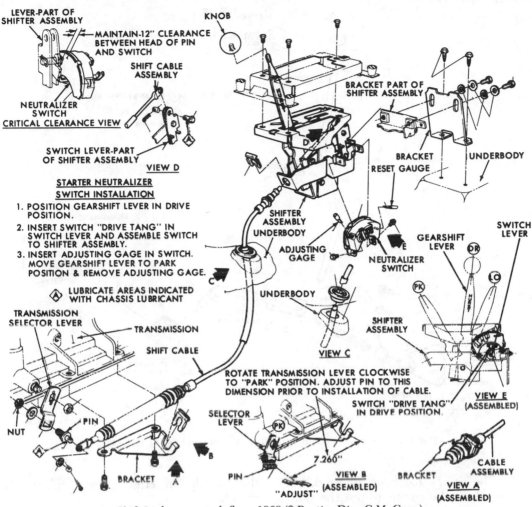

LEVER-PART OF SHIFTER ASSEMBLY

MAINTAIN-12" CLEARANCE BETWEEN HEAD OF PIN AND SWITCH

KNOB

SHIFT CABLE ASSEMBLY

BRACKET PART OF SHIFTER ASSEMBLY

NEUTRALIZER SWITCH
CRITICAL CLEARANCE VIEW

BRACKET RESET GAUGE

UNDERBODY

SWITCH LEVER-PART OF SHIFTER ASSEMBLY
VIEW D

STARTER NEUTRALIZER SWITCH INSTALLATION

1. POSITION GEARSHIFT LEVER IN DRIVE POSITION.
2. INSERT SWITCH "DRIVE TANG" IN SWITCH LEVER AND ASSEMBLE SWITCH TO SHIFTER ASSEMBLY.
3. INSERT ADJUSTING GAGE IN SWITCH. MOVE GEARSHIFT LEVER TO PARK POSITION & REMOVE ADJUSTING GAGE.

SHIFTER ASSEMBLY UNDERBODY

ADJUSTING GAGE

NEUTRALIZER SWITCH

GEARSHIFT LEVER

SWITCH LEVER

Ⓐ LUBRICATE AREAS INDICATED WITH CHASSIS LUBRICANT

UNDERBODY

TRANSMISSION SELECTOR LEVER

TRANSMISSION

SHIFT CABLE

SHIFTER ASSEMBLY

VIEW C

VIEW E
(ASSEMBLED)

ROTATE TRANSMISSION LEVER CLOCKWISE TO "PARK" POSITION. ADJUST PIN TO THIS DIMENSION PRIOR TO INSTALLATION OF CABLE.

SWITCH "DRIVE TANG" IN DRIVE POSITION.

NUT

PIN

SELECTOR LEVER

BRACKET

PIN

7.260"

"ADJUST"

VIEW B
(ASSEMBLED)

BRACKET

CABLE ASSEMBLY

VIEW A
(ASSEMBLED)

Shift Linkage control, floor, 1969 (© Pontiac Div., G.M. Corp.)

transmission shift lever counterclockwise two detents.

4. Place the console lever in Neutral and move it against the forward Neutral stop.

5. Assemble the shift cable and pin to the transmission shift lever so that no binding exists, then tighten the nut to 30 ft lbs (20 ft lbs—1970–72).

6. Readjust the transmission neutral switch if necessary.

1969–73 CONSOLE SHIFT
TWO SPEED (M-35) TRANSMISSION

1. Place the console lever in Park and lock the ignition.

2. Disconnect the shift cable from the transmission shift lever pin. Loosen the screw on the adjusting swivel at the shaft lever.

3. Rotate the transmission shift lever clockwise to the Park position and push up on the control rod to take up the slack.

4. Tighten the swivel to 30 ft lbs (20 ft lbs—1970 up).

5. Unlock the ignition and rotate the range lever on the transmission counterclockwise two positions.

6. Place the shift lever in Neutral and move it forward against the Neutral stop.

7. Assemble the shift cable and pin to the transmission lever (free fit) and tighten the pin nut to 30 ft lbs up to 1969, 20 ft lbs thereafter.

8. Readjust the transmission neutralizer switch if necessary.

Neutral Safety Switch

NOTE: *The neutral safety switch on 1968 console shifters is located on the shifter, not on the steering column.*

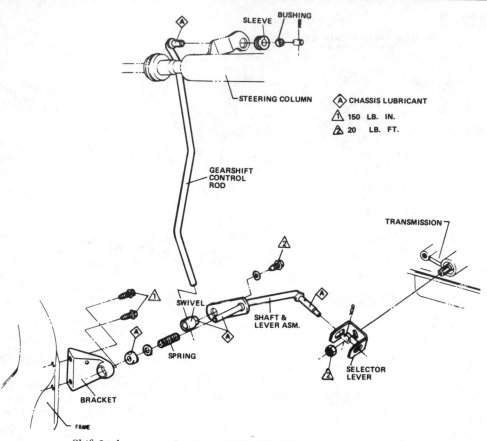

SLEEVE BUSHING

STEERING COLUMN

△A CHASSIS LUBRICANT

⚠1 150 LB. IN.

⚠2 20 LB. FT.

GEARSHIFT
CONTROL
ROD

TRANSMISSION

SWIVEL

SHAFT &
LEVER ASM.

SPRING

SELECTOR
LEVER

BRACKET

FRAME

Shift Linkage control, column, 1969–73 (© Pontiac Div., G.M. Corp.)

After the switch has been adjusted, but before starting the engine to test the shifting pattern, make sure that the brakes are securely locked. This is necessary because a misadjusted neutralizer switch will allow the engine to start in any of the forward or reverse gears.

1. Place the shifter lever in Park.

2. Loosen the switch retaining screws. Make sure that the switch drive tang is engaged in the shifter tube slot and that it stays engaged during adjustment.

3. Rotate the switch in its slot until it is in the Park position and then tighten the screws.

4. After observing the above caution, check the shifter pattern by placing the shifter lever in Neutral. If the transmission does not shift into Neutral, place the lever back in Park and rotate the switch slightly until the shift pattern is correct.

5. If it is possible to move the shift lever a large distance without having the transmission respond, check for a worn switch drive tang or bad electrical contacts inside

the switch. In either case, replace the switch.

Downshift Cable Adjustment

1. With the engine off and the throttle butterflies closed (off fast idle), position the retainer against the insert on the cable (from inside the car).

2. To adjust, grasp the accelerator pedal lever adjacent to the downshift cable and pull the carburetor cable to the wide open throttle position. Check for full cable travel.

Throttle Linkage Adjustment

SIX CYLINDER

1. Remove the air cleaner.

2. Disconnect the TV control rod swivel and clip from the carburetor lever, then disconnect the TV return spring from the bellhousing.

3. Push the TV control rod rearward until the transmission TV lever is against the internal transmission stop.

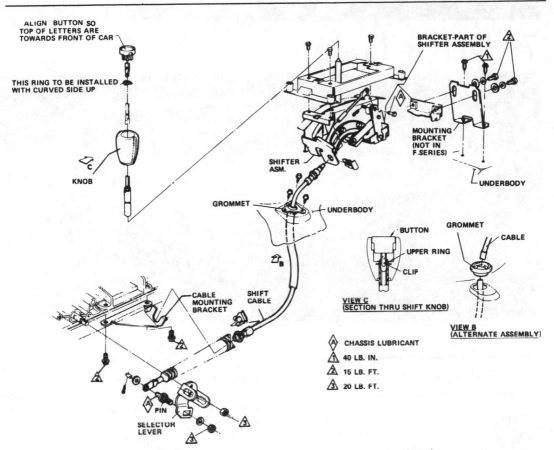

ALIGN BUTTON SO
TOP OF LETTERS ARE
TOWARDS FRONT OF CAR

THIS RING TO BE INSTALLED
WITH CURVED SIDE UP

KNOB

BRACKET-PART OF
SHIFTER ASSEMBLY

MOUNTING
BRACKET
(NOT IN
F SERIES)

UNDERBODY

SHIFTER
ASM.

GROMMET

UNDERBODY

BUTTON

GROMMET

CABLE

UPPER RING

CLIP

VIEW C
(SECTION THRU SHIFT KNOB)

VIEW B
(ALTERNATE ASSEMBLY)

CABLE
MOUNTING
BRACKET

SHIFT
CABLE

CHASSIS LUBRICANT

40 LB. IN.

15 LB. FT.

20 LB. FT.

PIN

SELECTOR
LEVER

Shift Linkage control, floor, 1969–73 (© Pontiac Div., C.M. Corp.)

4. Holding the TV control rod in this position, hold carburetor lever in the wide open throttle position and adjust the TV control rod swivel so that the pin freely enters the hole in the carburetor lever without binding.

5. Secure the swivel, connect the return spring, and check the linkage action for binding.

6. Install the air cleaner.

V8

1. Remove the air cleaner.

2. Disconnect the accelerator linkage at the carburetor.

3. Disconnect the throttle and TV rod return springs.

4. Pull the TV rod forward until the transmission is through its detent; hold it in this position and open the carburetor butterflies to the wide open position.

5. The butterflies must reach the wide open position at the same time that the ball stud contacts the end of the slot in the upper TV rod ($\pm$ $1/32$ in.).

6. If necessary, adjust the swivel end of the upper TV rod.

7. Connect the linkage and springs, then check the linkage for binding.

8. Install the air cleaner.

7 · Drive Train

Differential Operation

The differential is an arrangement of gears that permits the rear wheels to turn at different speeds when cornering and divides the torque between the axle shafts. The differential gears are mounted on a pinion shaft and the gears are free to rotate on this shaft. The pinion shaft is fitted in a bore in the differential case and is at right angles to the axle shafts.

Power flow through the differential is as follows. The drive pinion, which is turned by the driveshaft, turns the ring gear. The ring gear, which is bolted to the differential case, rotates the case. The differential pinion forces the pinion gears against the side gears. In cases where both wheels have equal traction, the pinion gears do not rotate on the pinion shaft because the input force of the pinion gear is divided equally between the two side gears. Consequently the pinion gears revolve with the pinion shaft, although they do not revolve on the pinion shaft itself. The side gears, which are splined to the axle shafts, and meshed with the pinion gears, rotate the axle shafts.

When it becomes necessary to turn a corner, the differential becomes effective and allows the axle shafts to rotate at different speeds. As the inner wheel slows down, the side gear splined to the inner wheel axle shaft also slows down. The pinion gears act as balancing levers by maintaining equal tooth loads to both gears while allowing unequal speeds of rotation at the axle shafts. If the vehicle speed remains constant, and the inner wheel slows down to 90 percent of vehicle speed, the outer wheel will speed up to 110 percent.

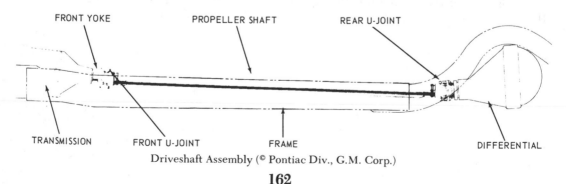

FRONT YOKE   PROPELLER SHAFT   REAR U-JOINT

TRANSMISSION   FRONT U-JOINT   FRAME   DIFFERENTIAL

Driveshaft Assembly (© Pontiac Div., G.M. Corp.)

LIMITED-SLIP DIFFERENTIAL

Limited-slip differentials provide driving force to the wheel with the best traction before the other wheel begins to spin. This is accomplished through clutch plates or cones. The clutch plates or cones are located between the side gears and inner wall of the differential case. When they are squeezed together through spring tension and outward force from the side gears, three reactions occur. Resistance on the side gears causes more torque to be exerted on the clutch packs or clutch cones. Rapid one-wheel spin cannot occur because the side gear is forced to turn at the same speed as the case. Most important, with the side gear and the differential case turning at the same speed, the other wheel is forced to rotate in the same direction and at the same speed as the differential case. Thus driving force is applied to the wheel with the better traction.

Driveline

DRIVESHAFT AND U-JOINTS

Removal and Installation

1. Mark the driveshaft rear yoke and the differential flange to assure correct alignment upon reassembly.
2. Remove the U-bolts and nuts from the differential flange.

3. Remove the driveshaft assembly by first sliding the driveshaft sufficiently forward to disengage the differential flange, then slide the shaft downward and rearward to disengage the front splined yoke from the transmission output shaft.
4. Install the driveshaft and align the marks while doing so.
5. Install the U-bolts and nuts to the differential flange.

U-Joint Overhaul

1. Remove the driveshaft.
NOTE: *The universal may have snaprings or injection molded plastic that are used to retain the bearing cups in the yokes. These snap-rings may be located at the outside of each yoke or in a groove at the base or open end of each bearing cap. In both cases, there are four snap-rings for each universal joint and they must be removed before proceeding further. Repair Kits for the plastic ring type U-joints supply replacement snap-rings.*
2. Support the splined yoke (front universal) or the journal (rear universal) in a manner that will allow the fixed yoke on the driveshaft to be moved. Support the opposite end so that the driveshaft will be in a horizontal position.
3. Using a piece of pipe, or a similar tool with a large enough diameter, apply force to the fixed yoke until the bearing is almost completely pushed out of the yoke

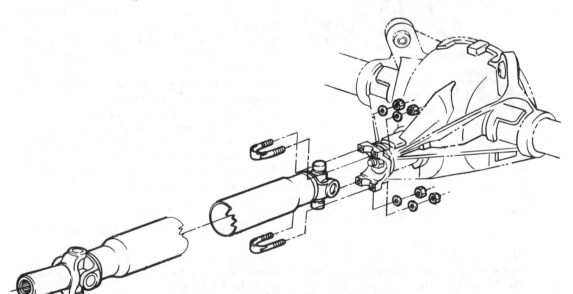

U-joint removal (© Pontiac Div., G.M. Corp.)

and into the pipe. Remove the bearing completely by tapping around the circumference of the exposed portion of the bearing with a punch and small hammer.

4. Remove the rest of the bearings following the same procedure.

5. Install a bearing one-quarter of the way into one side of the splined yoke (front universal) or fixed yoke (rear universal).

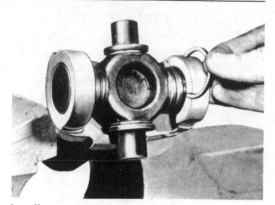

Installing snap ring retainer (© Pontiac Div., G.M. Corp.)

9. Install the rest of the bearings in the same manner.

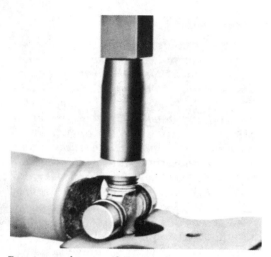

Pressing out bearing (© Pontiac Div., G.M. Corp.)

Installing journal to yoke (© Pontiac Div., G.M. Corp.)

6. Insert the journal into the yoke so that an arm of the journal seats into the bearing.

7. Press in the bearing the remaining distance.

8. Install the opposite bearing. Do not allow the bearing rollers to jam. Continually check for free movement of the journal in the bearings as they are pressed into the yoke.

Rear Axle

Removal and Installation

Two types of axles are used on these models, the C and the non-C type. Axle shafts in the C type are retained by C-shaped locks, which fit grooves at the inner end of the shaft. Axle shafts in the non-C type are retained by the brake backing plate, which is bolted to the axle housing. Bearings in the C type axle consist of an outer race, bearing rollers, and a roller cage retained by snap-rings. The non-C type axle uses a unit roller bearing (inner race, rollers, and outer race), which is pressed onto the shaft up to a shoulder. When servicing C or non-C type axles, it is imperative to determine the axle type before attempting any service. Before attempting any service to the drive axle or axle shafts, remove the axle carrier cover and visually determine if the axle shafts are retained by C-shaped locks at the inner end, or by the brake backing plate at the outer end. If the shafts are *not* retained by C locks, proceed as follows.

Non-C Type

1. Remove the wheel, tire, and brake drum.

2. Remove the nuts which hold the retainer plate to the backing plate. Disconnect the brake line.

3. Remove the retainer and install the

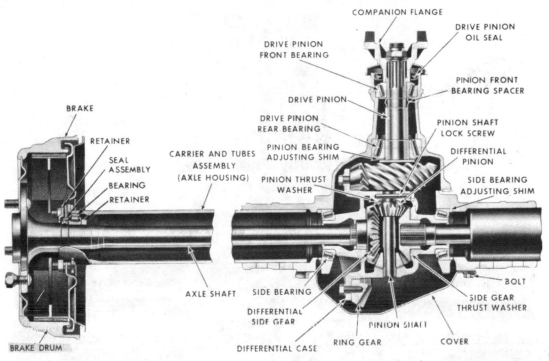

Cross section of non-C rear axle (© Pontiac Div., G.M. Corp.)

nuts fingertight to prevent the brake backing plate from being dislodged.

4. Pull out the axle shaft and bearing assembly, using a slide hammer.

5. Install the axle shaft into the housing. Turn it until the grooves mesh.

6. Install the retainer nuts.

7. Connect the brake line.

8. Install the brake drum, wheel, and tire.

9. Bleed the brakes.

Before attempting any service to the drive axle or axle shafts, remove the carrier cover and visually determine if the axle shaft(s) are retained by C-shaped locks at the inner ends or by a brake backing plate at the outer end. If they are retained by C-shaped locks, proceed as follows.

C Type

1. Raise the vehicle and remove the wheels.

2. The differential cover has already been removed (see NOTE above). Remove the differential pinion shaft lockscrew and the differential pinion shaft.

3. Push the flanged end of the axle shaft toward the center of the vehicle and remove the C lock from the end of the shaft.

4. Remove the axle shaft from the housing, being careful not to damage the oil seal.

5. Install the axle into the housing.

6. Install the C lock to the shaft.

7. Install the differential pinion lockscrew.

8. Install the differential cover.

9. Install the wheels and lower the car to the ground.

GEAR RATIOS

The drive axle of a vehicle is said to have a certain axle ratio. This number (usually a whole number and a decimal fraction) is actually a comparison of the number of gear teeth on the ring gear and the pinion gear. For example, a 4.11 rear means that theoretically, there are 4.11 teeth on the ring gear and one tooth on the pinion. Actually, on a 4.11 rear, there are 37 teeth on the ring gear and nine teeth on the pinion gear. By dividing the number of teeth on the pinion gear into the number of teeth on the ring gear, the numerical axle ratio (4.11) is obtained.

Axle Ratio Determining

Make a horizontal chalk mark on your driveshaft and a vertical mark on the outside of the tire. Jack up the rear of the car

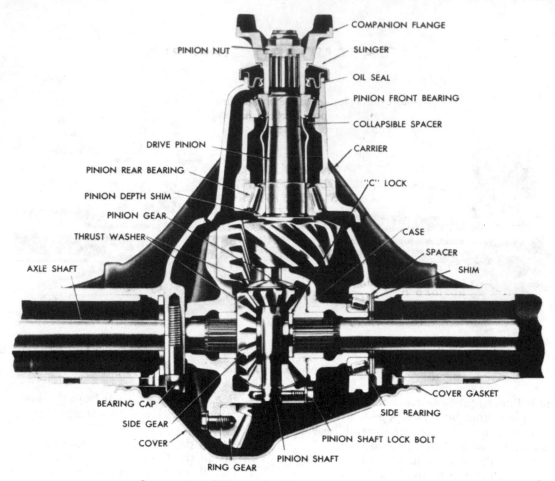

Cross section of C rear axle (© Pontiac Div., G.M. Corp.)

(block the front wheels), making sure both wheels clear the ground. Put the transmission in Neutral and slowly turn the driveshaft. While an assistant watches the tire, count the number of revolutions the driveshaft makes and stop when the tire has made exactly one complete revolution. Check the chart for the available axle ratios. If the driveshaft turns about 3⅓ times, the ratio is probably a 3.36. If it turns 3½ turns, it is probably a 3.55 or a 4.10 if it turns a little over 4 times.

8 · Suspension and Steering

Rear Suspension

The rear wheels are fastened to axle shafts within a Salisbury-type, solid axle housing. The axle housing is connected to the frame by a four-link suspension system, consisting of two upper and two lower control arms pivoted in rubber at each end. These control arms locate the axle laterally and axially with relation to the frame and oppose torque reaction under acceleration and braking.

Two coil springs are mounted between seats in the frame and axle housing to carry the load of the vehicle. A stabilizer bar is mounted on some GTO models to improve side roll stability. This bar attaches to the lower control arms and is positioned under the axle housing.

Shock absorbers are direct double-action hydraulic units and are mounted between the lower control arms and the frame.

SHOCK ABSORBERS

Removal and Installation

1. Raise the car at the axle housing.
2. Remove the nut, retainer, and grommet or nut, and lockwasher, as equipped, which attach the lower end of the shock absorber to its mounting.

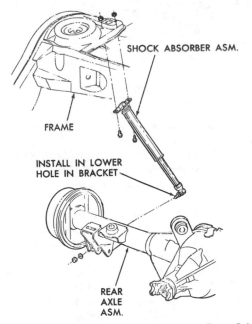

Installation of shock absorber (© Pontiac Div., G.M. Corp.)

3. Remove the two shock absorber upper attaching screws and the shock absorber.
4. Install the shock absorbers and the upper attaching screws.
5. Install the nut lockwasher and grommet to the lower end of the shock.
6. Lower the car to the ground.

SPRINGS

Removal and Installation

LEAF SPRING

1. Jack up the car at the rear axle. Then support the major portion of the weight of the car on the frame rails, leaving the jack in place under the axle. At this point the jack should be supporting the axle only; there should be no tension on the spring.

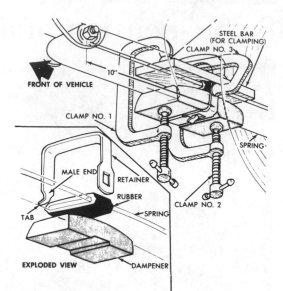

Installation of spring damper (© Pontiac Div., G.M. Corp.)

Installation of rear leaf springs (© Pontiac Div., G.M. Corp.)

2. Disconnect the shock at the axle and move it out of the way.

3. Remove the spring and shock absorber anchor plate nuts and remove the anchor plate and lower spring cushion pad.

4. Raise the axle with the jack and remove the upper spring cushion pad.

5. Loosen the upper and lower spring shackle pin nuts.

6. Loosen the front spring eye bolt.

7. Remove the screws which secure the spring front mounting bracket to the floor pan and carefully let the spring swing down.

8. Remove the lower shackle pin from the rear of the spring and remove the spring from the car.

CAUTION: *Torque values must be used as specified during reassembly. To ensure proper retention, always replace any worn parts.*

9. Install the front spring mounting bracket on the front spring eye and loosely insert the bolt and nut. Do not tighten the spring eyebolt until the weight of the car is on the springs.

10. Place the spring into the shackles at the rear of the car and loosely install the lower shackle pin and nut. Do not tighten them.

11. Raise the front end of the spring and install the spring mounting bracket to the floor pan and torque the bolts to 25 ft lbs. Make sure the tab on the spring mounting bracket is indexed in the slot in the floor pan and that the parking brake cables are on the top side of the spring.

12. Place the upper spring cushion pan on the spring and lower the axle onto the spring.

13. Install the lower spring cushion and shock absorber anchor plate and torque the anchor plate nuts to 40 ft lbs.

14. Install the shock absorber.

15. Put the weight of the car on the springs and torque the shackle pin nuts and front eyebolt to 50 ft lbs.

COIL SPRINGS

1. Raise the rear of the car and support it solidly on the frame rails.

2. Remove the clip that attaches the brake hose to its bracket on the frame crossmember.

3. Support the rear axle with a jack.

4. Remove the nut and lockwasher from the shock absorber and disconnect the

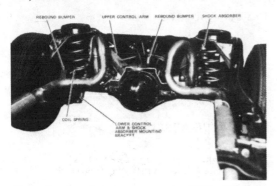

Typical coil spring rear suspension (© Pontiac Div., G.M. Corp.)

shock from the axle. It may be necessary to adjust the height of the jack to disconnect the shock.

5. Carefully lower the jack until the

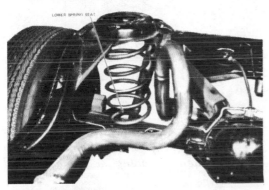

Typical coil spring lower seat (© Pontiac Div., G.M. Corp.)

spring is free and remove the spring. Note the position of the spring and replace it with the lower coil pointing in the same direction.

6. Position the spring and raise the jack until the spring positions correctly.

7. Install the shock, nut, and lockwasher.

8. Install the brake hose clip.

9. Lower the car to the ground.

Front Suspension

Ball joints, located at the outer ends of the upper control arms, act as pivots for both the vertical movement of the wheel and rotation of the steering knuckle. The spherical joints have a fixed boot grease seal to protect against dirt and water. Steering knuckles and spindles are one-piece forgings.

Rubber bushings at the upper inner control arm ends pivot on shafts attached to the frame. By varying shim thickness at this point, caster and camber adjustment is accomplished. The inner ends of the lower control arms are also rubber mounted and are attached to the front crossmember through brackets.

The upper ends of the coil springs are seated in the frame, while the lower ends

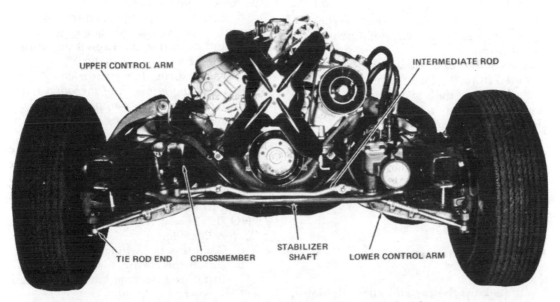

Independent front suspension (© Pontiac Div., G.M. Corp.)

rest on the lower control arms. Double-action shock absorbers are located inside the coil springs; the rubber insulated upper end of each unit is fastened to the frame, the similarly insulated lower end is fastened to the lower control arm.

Front Suspension components (© Pontiac Div., G.M. Corp.)

For increased roll stability, a stabilizer bar is rubber mounted to the frame and is connected to the lower control arms via links at each end.

SHOCK ABSORBERS

Removal and Installation

1. Remove the nut, retainer, and grommet which are attached to the upper end of the shock absorber and seat against the frame bracket.

NOTE: *It may be necessary to hold the shock absorber shaft to remove the nut. This may be done with a wrench on the end of the shaft.*

2. Raise the car to allow the shock to be dropped from the lower control arm.

3. Remove the two shock absorber lower attaching screws and lower the shock from the control arm.

4. Install the new shock, the attaching screws, and the lower control arm.

5. Lower the car to the ground.

6. Install the shock against the frame bracket; install the grommet, nut, and retainer.

SPRINGS

Removal and Installation

1968

1. Jack up the car and allow the lower control arm to hang free. Support the car

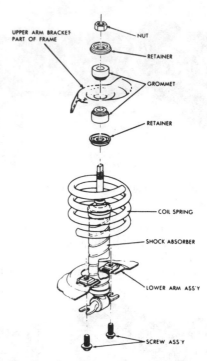

Shock Absorber Installation (© Pontiac Div., G.M. Corp.)

on jackstands under the frame side rails.

CAUTION: *Extreme caution should be used when removing or installing coil springs.*

2. Remove the wheel and brake drum.

3. Remove the shock absorber.

4. Disconnect the stabilizer bar from the lower control arm.

5. Insert a spring compressing tool through the shock absorber mounting holes and compress the coil spring until it lifts from its seat.

NOTE: *A spring compressor can be fabricated using a length of threaded rod, a support plate, and a support hook.*

6. Remove the backing plate and swing it out of the way.

7. Disconnect the lower ball joint stud and swing the steering knuckle out of the way.

8. Pull the lower control arm down far enough to remove the spring.

NOTE: *The spring must be compressed before installation.*

9. Compress the spring.

10. Install the spring.

11. Install the steering knuckle and connect the lower ball joint.

12. Install the backing plate.

13. Connect the stabilizer bar to the lower control arm.

14. Install the shock absorber.

15. Remove the spring compressor.

16. Install the brake drum and wheel.

17. Lower the car to the ground.

1969–73

1. Jack up the front of the car and support it with jackstands at the side frame rails.

2. Remove the shock absorber.

3. Disconnect the stabilizer bar at the lower control arm.

4. Support the lower control arm with a hydraulic floor jack, then remove the two inner control arm-to-front crossmember bolts.

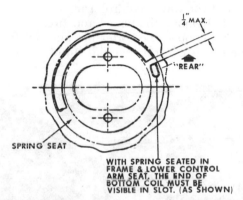

Coil spring position in lower control arm (© Pontiac Div., G.M. Corp.)

5. Carefully lower the control arm, allowing the spring to relax.

6. Reach in and remove the spring. NOTE: *Compress the spring before installation.*

7. Install the spring.

8. Install the control arm.

9. Install the control arm and crossmember nuts.

10. Connect the stabilizer at the lower control arm.

11. Remove the hydraulic jack.

12. Install the shock absorber.

13. Lower the car to the ground.

BALL JOINTS

Inspection

NOTE: *Before performing this inspection, make sure the wheel bearings are adjusted correctly and that the A-arm bushings are in good condition.*

1. Jack up the car under the front lower control arm at the spring seat.

2. Raise the car until there is 1–2 in. of clearance under the wheel.

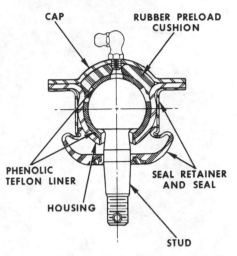

Typical upper ball joint (© Pontiac Div., G.M. Corp.)

3. Insert a bar under the wheel and pry upward. If the wheel raises more than $\frac{1}{8}$ in., the ball joints are worn. Determine whether the upper or lower ball joint is worn by visual inspection while prying on the wheel.

NOTE: *Due to the distribution of forces in the suspension, the lower ball joint is usually the defective joint.*

Removal and Installation

UPPER BALL JOINT

1. Punch the center of each of the four rivets.

2. Drill through the heads of the rivets.

3. Chisel off the rivet heads and tap the rivets out with a punch.

4. Install the new ball joint against the top side of upper control arm. Secure the joint to the control arm with the four special alloy bolts and nuts furnished with the replacement part.

5. Torque these bolts and nuts to 10–12 ft lbs.

NOTE: *Only use the special bolts which are supplied with the ball joint kit.*

LOWER BALL JOINT

NOTE: *It is necessary to remove the lower control arm first to remove the ball joint.*

1. Jack up the front of the car and place jackstands under the side rails.

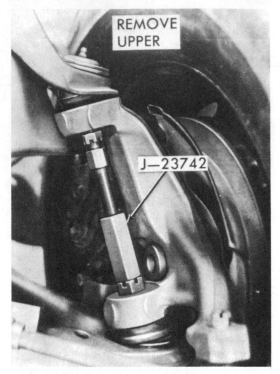

Upper ball joint, removal (© Pontiac Div., G.M. Corp.)

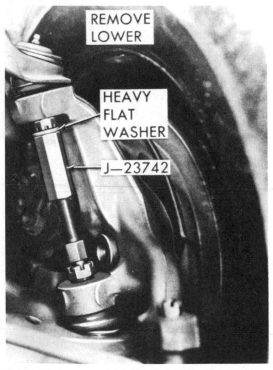

Lower ball joint, removal (© Pontiac Div., G.M. Corp.)

2. Remove the wheel.

3. Place a jack under the lower control arm and remove the nut from the ball joint.

4. Remove the lower ball joint by prying, while hammering on the steering knuckle.

5. Remove the ball joint by pressing it out. (Remove the lower control arm.)

6. Press in a new ball joint.

7. Install the nut and cotter pin and torque to 85–90 ft lbs.

8. Install the wheel and lower the car to the ground.

UPPER CONTROL ARM

Removal and Installation

1. Support the car's weight at the outer end of the lower control arm.

2. Remove the wheel and tire.

3. Remove the cotter pin and nut from the upper control arm ball stud.

Removing upper control arm nuts (© Pontiac Div., G.M. Corp.)

4. Remove the stud from the knuckle with a pry bar, while tapping with a hammer.

5. Remove the two nuts that hold the upper control arm cross-shaft to the front crossmember. Count the number of shims at each bolt.

6. Install bolts through the holes and install the upper control arm to the crossmember.

7. Secure the two nuts and washers to

the bolts which hold the upper control arm shaft to the front crossmember. Install the same number of shims as removed at each bolt. Torque the bolts to 50 ft lbs.

8. Lubricate the ball joint with chassis lube.

9. Install the ball joint stud through the knuckle. Install the nut and torque it to 50 ft lbs.

10. Install the wheel and tire assembly.

11. Lower the car to the floor.

12. Bounce the car to neutralize the front end suspension and torque the pivot shaft nuts to 50 ft lbs on Tempests.

13. Be sure to recheck caster and camber.

LOWER CONTROL ARM

Removal and Installation

1. Remove the coil spring and lower control arm inner bolts.

2. Separate the ball joint.

3. Remove the control arm.

4. Install the control arm and ball joint.

5. Install the lower control arm inner bolts and coil spring.

FRONT END ALIGNMENT

Front wheel alignment is the position of the front wheels relative to each other and to the vehicle. It is determined and must be maintained to provide safe, accurate steering with minimum tire wear. Many factors are involved in wheel alignment and adjustments are provided to return those that might change due to normal wear to their original value. The factors which determine wheel alignment are de-

pendent on one another. Therefore, when one of the factors is adjusted, the others must be adjusted to compensate.

Camber angle is the number of degrees that the centerline of the wheel is inclined from the vertical. Camber reduces loading of the outer wheel bearing and improves the tire contact patch while cornering.

Caster angle is the number of degrees that a line drawn through the steering knuckle pivots is inclined from the vertical, toward the front or rear of the car. Caster improves directional stability and decreases susceptibility to cross-winds or road surface deviations.

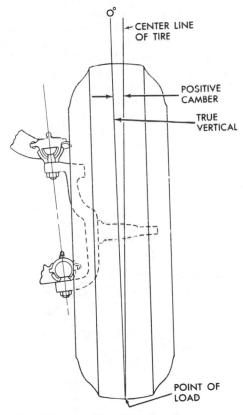

Camber (© Pontiac Div., G.M. Corp.)

Toe-in is the difference of the distance between the centers of the front and rear of the front wheels. It is most commonly measured in inches, but is occasionally referred to as an angle between the wheels. Toe-in is necessary to compensate for the tendency of the wheels to deflect rearward while in motion. Due to this tendency, the wheels of a vehicle with properly adjusted toe-in are traveling straight forward when the vehicle itself is traveling straight for-

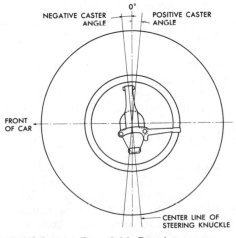

Caster (© Pontiac Div., G.M. Corp.)

ward, resulting in directional stability and minimum tire wear.

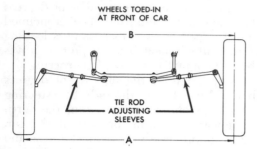

WHEELS TOED-IN
AT FRONT OF CAR

TIE ROD
ADJUSTING
SLEEVES

Toe-in (© Pontiac Div., G.M. Corp.)

Steering wheel spoke misalignment is often an indication of incorrect front end alignment. Care should be exercised when aligning the front end to maintain steering wheel spoke position. When adjusting the tie-rod ends, adjust each an equal amount (in the opposite direction) to increase or decrease toe-in. If, following toe-in adjustment, further adjustments are necessary to center the steering wheel spokes, adjust the tie rod ends an equal amount in the same direction.

Adjustment

Caster and camber are controlled by shims between the frame bracket and the upper suspension arm pivot shaft.

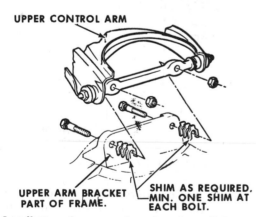

UPPER CONTROL ARM

UPPER ARM BRACKET
PART OF FRAME.
SHIM AS REQUIRED,
MIN. ONE SHIM AT
EACH BOLT.

Installation of caster and camber shims (© Pontiac Div., G.M. Corp.)

To adjust caster, remove shims from the front bolt and replace them at the rear bolt, or vice versa. To adjust camber, add or remove the same number of shims from each bolt. Keep in mind when loosening the bolts that the upper suspension arm is

supporting the weight of the vehicle. Loosen the bolts only a sufficient amount to remove the shims.

Adjust toe-in by loosening the clamps on the sleeves at the outer ends of the tie rod and turning the sleeves an equal amount in the opposite direction to maintain steering wheel spoke alignment while adjusting toe-in.

Steering

The steering system consists of a steering wheel, steering column, universal joint, intermediate steering shaft flexible coupling, manual or power steering gear, and steering linkage.

The manual steering gear is the recirculating-ball nut type. The steering shaft, worm shaft, and worm nut are all in line. The steering shaft and worm shaft are separated by a flexible coupling. This coupling permits the gear to be removed independently of the steering shaft and steering column.

Hydraulic pressure for power steering is provided by a constant displacement vane-type pump. It is located on the left front of the engine and is belt-driven by the engine crankshaft pulley.

STEERING WHEEL

Removal and Installation

1. On deluxe models, remove the screws which hold the trim cover to the wheel, or if equipped with a horn button, lift the button off.

2. Remove the steering wheel nut from the steering shaft.

3. Position the wheels in the straight-ahead position and make match marks on the steering shaft and steering wheel.

4. Using a puller, remove the steering wheel.

5. Disconnect the horn wire insulator by rotating the insulator counterclockwise to the unlock position and then pull up.

6. Reverse the removal procedures for installation. Make sure the match marks are lined up when installing the wheel.

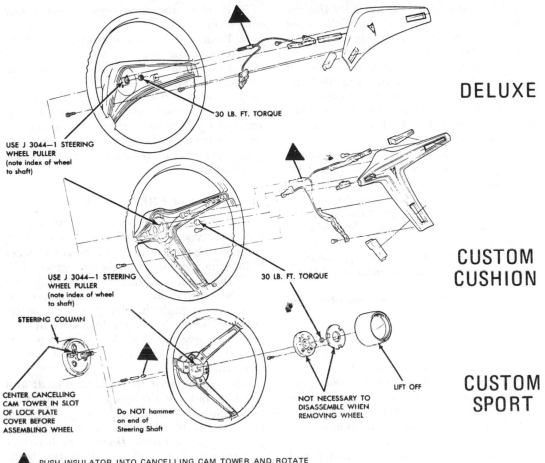

30 LB. FT. TORQUE

DELUXE

USE J 3044—1 STEERING
WHEEL PULLER
(note index of wheel
to shaft)

**CUSTOM
CUSHION**

USE J 3044—1 STEERING
WHEEL PULLER
(note index of wheel
to shaft)

STEERING COLUMN

30 LB. FT. TORQUE

LIFT OFF

**CUSTOM
SPORT**

CENTER CANCELLING
CAM TOWER IN SLOT
OF LOCK PLATE
COVER BEFORE
ASSEMBLING WHEEL

Do NOT hammer
on end of
Steering Shaft

NOT NECESSARY TO
DISASSEMBLE WHEN
REMOVING WHEEL

PUSH INSULATOR INTO CANCELLING CAM TOWER AND ROTATE
COUNTER—CLOCKWISE TO RELEASE OR CLOCKWISE TO LOCK
IN POSITION.

Steering Wheel Removal—all models (© Pontiac Div., G.M. Corp.)

TURN SIGNAL SWITCH

Removal and Installation

1968

CAUTION: *Make sure the steering column is supported at all times as the column is extremely easy to bend.*

1. Remove the bolts which hold the
column bracket.

2. Remove the wire protector, wire
clip, and cover.

3. Remove the steering wheel.

4. Slide the preload springs and turn
signal cancelling cam off of the steering
shaft.

5. Remove the turn signal lever screw
and lever.

6. Push the hazard warning knob in
and remove the knob.

7. Remove the snap-ring from the
steering shaft.

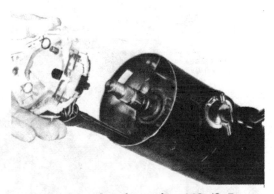

Removing Turn Signal switch—1968 (© Pontiac
Div., G.M. Corp.)

8. Loosen the three switch mounting
screws until the cover assembly can be rotated counterclockwise. Remove the cover
assembly.

9. Remove the three switch attaching
screws entirely and remove the old switch.

NOTE: *These three screws hold the entire assembly together. Carefully note the position and orientation of these parts to aid reassembly.*

10. Place the new switch assembly on top of the housing assembly and feed the switch wires through the switch cover.

11. Align the switch housing and cover holes and install the three mounting screws through the holes.

12. Slide three springs onto the screws and start the screws into the lockplate.

13. Run the wires through the bowl and place the switch assembly on top of the bowl. Make sure the tangs of the lockplate are aligned with the slots on the inside of the bowl.

14. Push down on the housing assembly and turn clockwise. Tighten the three screws.

15. Reverse Steps 1–7 to complete the installation.

1969–73

1. Remove the steering wheel.

2. Remove the three cover screws and lift the cover from the shaft. Do not remove the screws completely.

3. Depress the lockplate and remove the snap-ring.

4. Slide the upper bearing spring and turn signal cam off of the shaft.

5. Remove the turn signal lever screw and lever.

6. Push the hazard warning switch in and remove the knob.

7. Lower the steering column and disconnect the switch wiring.

8. Remove the turn signal switch mounting screws and pull the switch straight up with the wire protector and remove it from the housing.

9. Reverse the removal procedures for installation.

MANUAL STEERING GEAR

The steering gear is of the recirculating ball nut type. The ball nut, mounted on the worm gear, is driven by means of steel balls which circulate in helical grooves in both the worm and nut. Ball return guides attached to the nut serve to recirculate the two sets of balls in the grooves. As the steering wheel is turned to the right, the ball nut moves upward. When the wheel is turned to the left, the ball nut moves downward.

The sector teeth on the pinion shaft and the ball nut are designed so that they fit the tightest when the steering wheel is straight ahead. This mesh action is adjusted by an adjusting screw which moves the pinion shaft endwise until the teeth mesh properly. The worm bearing adjuster

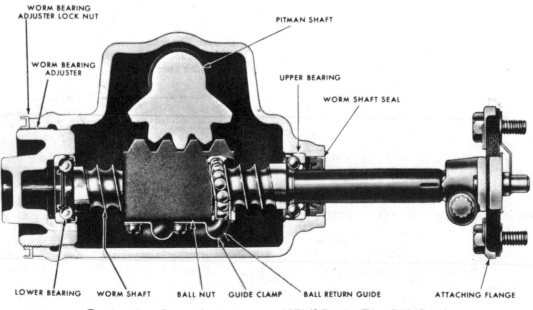

Cross section of manual steering gear—1972 (© Pontiac Div., G.M. Corp.)

provides proper preloading of the upper and lower bearings.

Adjustments

WORM BEARING PRELOAD

CAUTION: *Do not turn the steering wheel against the stops or you could damage the nut and ball assembly.*

1. Disconnect the ball stud from the pitman arm and retighten the pitman arm nut.

2. Loosen the pitman shaft adjusting screw locknut and back off the adjusting screw a few turns.

3. Attach a spring scale to the steering wheel and measure the pull needed to move the steering wheel when off of the high point. The pull should be between 1/8 and 3/8 lbs.

4. To adjust the worm bearing, loosen the worm bearing adjuster locknut with a brass drift and turn the adjuster screw until the proper pull is obtained. When adjustment is correct, tighten the adjuster locknut and recheck with the spring scale.

SECTOR AND BALL NUT BACKLASH

1. After the worm bearing preload has been adjusted correctly, loosen the pitman shaft adjusting screw locknut and turn the pitman shaft adjusting screw clockwise until a pull of 3/4–1 1/8 lbs is shown on the spring scale. When the adjustment is correct, tighten the pitman shaft adjusting screw locknut and recheck the adjustment.

NOTE: *A torque wrench calibrated in in. lbs may be substituted for the spring scale when adjusting the steering gear.*

2. Turn the steering wheel to the center of its turning limits (pitman arm disconnected). If the steering wheel is removed, the mark on the steering shaft should be at top center.

3. Connect the ball stud to the pitman arm, tightening the attaching nut to 115 ft lbs.

POWER STEERING GEAR

The rotary type power steering gear is designed with all components in one housing.

The power cylinder is an integral part of the gear housing. A double-acting piston allows oil pressure to be applied to either side of the piston. The one-piece piston and power rack is meshed to the sector shaft.

The hydraulic control valve is composed of a sleeve and valve spool. The spool is

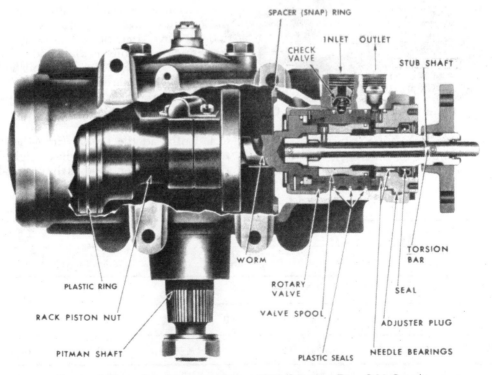

Sectional View of power steering gear—1972 (© Pontiac Div., G.M. Corp.)

held in the neutral position by the torsion bar and spool actuator. Twisting of the torsion bar moves the valve spool, allowing oil pressure to be directed to either side of the power piston, depending on the directional rotation of the steering wheel, to give power assist.

ADJUSTMENTS

Worm Bearing Preload and Sector

MESH ADJUSTMENTS

Disconnect the pitman arm from the sector shaft, then back off on the sector shaft adjusting screw on the sector shaft cover.

Center the steering on the high point, then attach a pull scale to the spoke of the steering wheel at the outer edge. The pull required to keep the wheel moving for one complete turn should be $\frac{1}{2}$–$\frac{2}{3}$ lbs.

If the pull is not within these limits, loosen the thrust bearing locknut and tighten or back off on the valve sleeve adjuster locknut to bring the preload within limits. Tighten the thrust bearing locknut and recheck the preload.

Adjusting Thrust bearing preload (© Pontiac Div., G.M. Corp.)

Slowly rotate the steering wheel several times, then center the steering on the high point. Now, turn the sector shaft adjusting screw until a steering wheel pull of 1–1$\frac{1}{2}$ lbs is required to move the worm through the center point. Tighten the sector shaft adjusting screw locknut and recheck the sector mesh adjustment.

Install the pitman arm and draw the arm into position with the nut.

POWER STEERING PUMP

Removal and Installation

1. Remove the adjusting bolts and remove the drive belt.
2. Remove the fluid hoses.
3. Remove the attaching bolts and remove the pump.
4. To install, position the pump and install the attaching bolts.
5. Install the fluid lines.
6. Install the adjusting bolts and drive belt.
7. Adjust the belt to $\frac{1}{2}$ in. free-play.
8. Check the fluid.

STEERING LINKAGE

Removal and Installation

TIE ROD END

1. Loosen the tie-rod adjuster sleeve clamp nuts.
2. Remove the tie-rod stud nut cotter pin and nut.
3. Remove the tie-rod stud from the steering arm or intermediate rod. This is a taper fit. Removal is accomplished by using a ball joint removal tool or by hitting the tie rod sharply with a hammer. If the ball joint is to be reused, the removal tool must be used.
4. Unthread the tie-rod from the adjuster sleeve. Outer tie-rods have right-hand threads and inner tie-rods have left-hand

Wheel Alignment Chart

Year	Caster Range (deg)	Caster Pref Setting (deg)	Camber Range (deg)	Camber Pref Setting (deg)	Toe-In (in.)	Steering Axis Inclination	Wheel Pivot Ratio (deg) Inner Wheel	Wheel Pivot Ratio (deg) Outer Wheel
68–69	1N–2N	1$\frac{1}{2}$N	$\frac{1}{4}$N–$\frac{3}{4}$P	$\frac{1}{4}$P	0–$\frac{1}{8}$	9	20	22
70–71	1N–2N	1$\frac{1}{2}$N	$\frac{1}{4}$N–$\frac{3}{4}$P	1$\frac{1}{4}$P	0–$\frac{1}{8}$	9	20	22
71–73	2N–1N	1$\frac{1}{2}$N	$\frac{1}{2}$N–$\frac{1}{2}$P	0	$\frac{1}{16}$–$\frac{3}{16}$	9	20	22

N—Negative
P—Positive

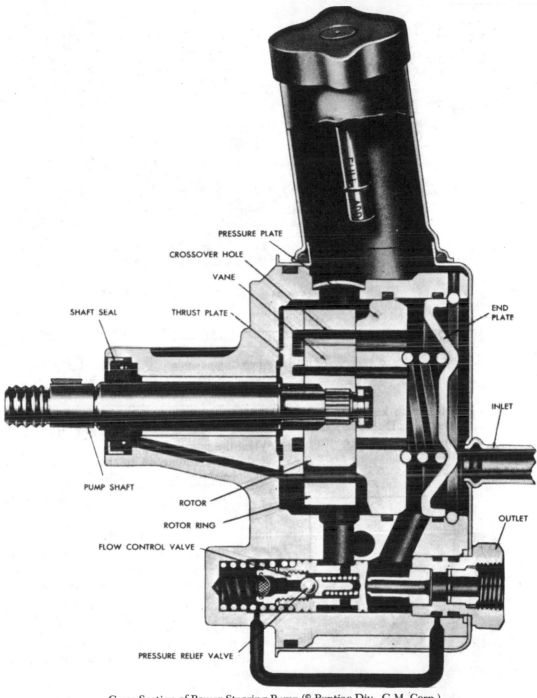

PRESSURE PLATE

CROSSOVER HOLE

VANE

SHAFT SEAL   THRUST PLATE

END PLATE

INLET

PUMP SHAFT

ROTOR

ROTOR RING

OUTLET

FLOW CONTROL VALVE

PRESSURE RELIEF VALVE

Cross Section of Power Steering Pump (© Pontiac Div., G.M. Corp.)

threads. Count the number of turns the tie rod must be rotated to remove it from the adjusting sleeve. This will allow a reasonably accurate realignment upon reassembly.

5. Reverse the removal procedures for installation. Clean all rust and dirt from the threads. Check the alignment and adjust if necessary.

INTERMEDIATE ROD

1. Remove the left and right-side inner tie-rod ends from the intermediate rod. These are taper fits; remove them as described in the "Tie-Rod" section.

2. Remove the intermediate rod studs from the idler and pitman arms. These are taper fits.

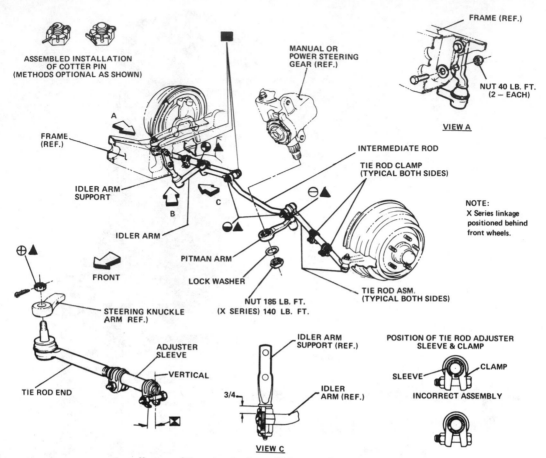

Installation of Steering Linkage (© Pontiac Div., G.M. Corp.)

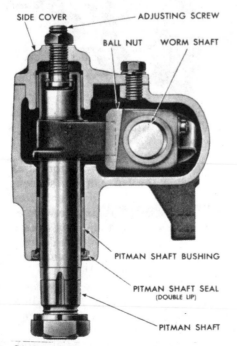

Cross Section of Pitman Arm Shaft (© Pontiac Div., G.M. Corp.)

3. Remove the intermediate rod.

4. Reverse the above steps for installation.

Pitman Arm

1. Remove the intermediate rod stud from the pitman arm.

2. Remove the pitman arm nut and lockwasher from the pitman shaft.

3. Remove the pitman arm from the pitman shaft using a puller. Do not hammer on the end of the puller or serious internal damage will be done to the steering gear box.

4. Reverse the above steps to install.

Idler Arm

1. Remove the intermediate arm stud. This is a taper fit; see the "Tie-Rod" section for the removal procedures.

2. Remove the two bolts which attach the idler arm to the frame.

3. Remove the idler arm.

4. Reverse the above steps for installation.

9 · Brakes

Standard brakes are of the duo servo, self-adjusting type. The self-adjusters only operate when the brakes are applied with car moving in reverse.

Metallic brake linings, used on some early high-performance models, should never be installed on cars equipped with standard brake drums unless the drums are radius ground and honed to a special finish.

The parking brake uses a foot-operated control lever, enclosed cables, rear wheel brake shoe levers, and struts to the rear wheel shoes.

Single-piston, sliding-caliper disc brakes have been available as optional equipment on most models since 1969. The optional disc brakes in 1968 were the four-piston type.

Disc brakes need no adjustment because, during operation, the application and release of hydraulic pressure causes the piston and caliper to move only slightly. In the released position, the pads do not move very far from the rotor; as pads wear down, the piston simply moves farther out of the caliper bore and the caliper repositions itself on its mounting bolts to maintain proper pad-to-rotor clearance.

A metering valve in the front brake circuit prevents the discs from operating until about 75 psi exists in the system. This enables the rear drum brakes to operate in synchronization with the front discs and reduces the possibility of unequal brake application and premature front brake lock-up. A proportioning valve in the rear brake circuit of some models limits the amount of hydraulic pressure that can be applied to the rear brakes, preventing the rear brakes from locking up. Starting in 1971, a two or three-function combination valve replaces the separate units used previously. The pressure required to operate front brakes is now 110–150 psi. Disc brake pads should be examined for wear every 12,000 miles.

Brake System

ADJUSTMENTS

1. Remove the access slot plug from the backing plate or front of the drum. On some late-model cars, there is no access slot in the backing plate. It has been filled in and must be punched out to gain access to the adjuster. Complete the adjustment and cover the hole with the plug to prevent the entrance of dirt and water.

2. Using a brake adjusting spoon or screwdriver, pry downward on the end of the tool (star wheel teeth moving up) to

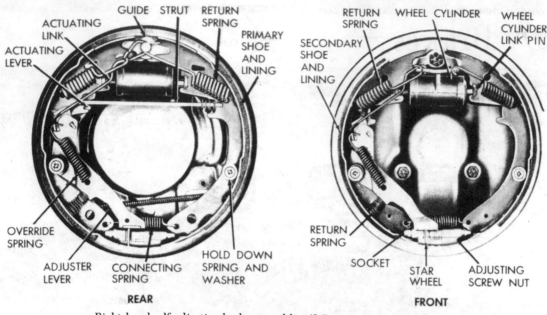

ACTUATING LINK

ACTUATING LEVER

GUIDE   STRUT   RETURN SPRING

PRIMARY SHOE AND LINING

OVERRIDE SPRING

ADJUSTER LEVER   CONNECTING SPRING   HOLD DOWN SPRING AND WASHER

REAR

RETURN SPRING   WHEEL CYLINDER   WHEEL CYLINDER LINK PIN

SECONDARY SHOE AND LINING

RETURN SPRING

SOCKET   STAR WHEEL   ADJUSTING SCREW NUT

FRONT

Right-hand self-adjusting brake assemblies (© Pontiac Div., G.M. Corp.)

tighten the brakes, or upward on the end of the tool (star wheel teeth moving down) to loosen the brakes.

NOTE: *It will be necessary to use a small screwdriver to hold the adjusting lever away from the star wheel. Be careful not to bend the adjusting lever.*

3. When the brakes are tight almost to the point of being locked, back off on the star wheel until the wheel is able to rotate freely. The star wheel on each set of brakes (front or rear) must be backed off the same number of turns to prevent brake pull from side to side.

4. When all four brakes are adjusted, check brake pedal travel and then make several stops, while backing the car up, to equalize all the wheels.

Hydraulic System

MASTER CYLINDER

Dual master cylinders are actually two single master cylinders operating in the same bore. They are designed so that the front and rear brakes have separate hydraulic systems. Malfunction in either system has no effect on the other system but is immediately evident to the driver be-

cause of the additional pedal travel required to actuate the remaining half of the brake system. Service procedure for single master cylinders is identical, except that there is only one piston assembly and no stop-screw. Some master cylinders have bleed screws on the outlet flanges and may be bled without disturbing the wheel cylinders.

Removal and Installation

1. Disconnect the hydraulic line(s) at the master cylinder; disconnect the clevis at the pedal.

2. Remove the two retaining nuts and lockwashers that hold the cylinder to the firewall.

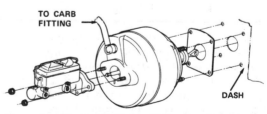

TO CARB FITTING

DASH

Removing Master Cylinder (© Pontiac Div., G.M. Corp.)

3. Remove the master cylinder, gasket, and rubber boot.

4. Position the master cylinder on the firewall; reconnect the pushrod clevis to the brake pedal.

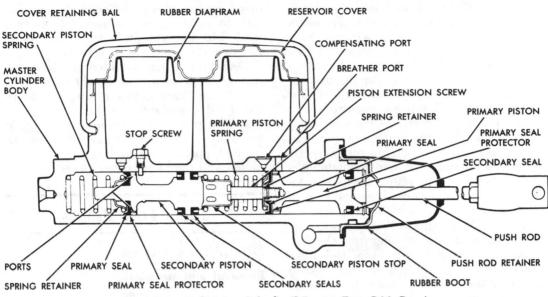

COVER RETAINING BAIL — RUBBER DIAPHRAM — RESERVOIR COVER
SECONDARY PISTON SPRING
MASTER CYLINDER BODY
COMPENSATING PORT
BREATHER PORT
PISTON EXTENSION SCREW
SPRING RETAINER — PRIMARY PISTON
STOP SCREW — PRIMARY PISTON SPRING — PRIMARY SEAL — PRIMARY SEAL PROTECTOR
SECONDARY SEAL
PUSH ROD
PORTS — PRIMARY SEAL — SECONDARY PISTON — SECONDARY PISTON STOP — PUSH ROD RETAINER
SPRING RETAINER — PRIMARY SEAL PROTECTOR — SECONDARY SEALS — RUBBER BOOT

Cross Section of Master Cylinder (© Pontiac Div., G.M. Corp.)

5. Install the nuts and lockwashers.

6. Install the hydraulic line(s) and then check the brake pedal free-play.

7. Bleed the brakes.

NOTE: *Cars having disc brakes do not have a check valve in the front outlet port of the master cylinder. If one is installed, front discs will immediately wear out due to residual hydraulic pressure holding the pads against the rotor.*

Overhaul

1. Remove the master cylinder from the car and drain the brake fluid.

2. Mount the cylinder in a vise so that the outlets are up and remove the seal from the hub.

3. Remove the stop-screw from the bottom of the front reservoir.

4. Remove the snap-ring from the front of the bore and remove the primary piston assembly.

5. Remove the secondary piston assembly using compressed air or a piece of wire. Cover the bore opening with a cloth to prevent damage to the piston.

6. Clean metal parts in brake fluid and discard rubber parts.

7. Inspect the bore for damage or wear and check pistons for damage and proper clearance in the bore.

8. If the bore is only slightly scored or pitted it may be honed. Always use hones that are in good condition and completely clean the cylinder with brake fluid when

honing is completed. If any evidence of contamination exists in the master cylinder, the entire hydraulic system should be flushed and refilled with clean brake fluid. Blow out passages with compressed air.

9. Install new secondary seals in the two grooves in the flat end of the front piston. The lips of the seals will be facing away from each other.

10. Install a new primary seal and the seal protector on the opposite end of the front piston with the lips of the seal facing outward.

11. Coat the seals with brake fluid. Install the spring on the front piston with the spring retainer in the primary seal.

12. Insert the piston assembly, spring end first, into the bore and use a wooden rod to seat it.

13. Coat the rear piston seals with brake fluid and install them into the piston grooves with the lips facing the spring end.

14. Assemble the spring onto the piston and install the assembly into the bore spring first. Install the snap-ring.

15. Hold the piston train at the bottom of the bore and install the stop screw. Install a new seal on the hub. Bench-bleed the cylinder on the car.

PRESSURE DIFFERENTIAL WARNING VALVE

Since the introduction of dual master cylinders to the hydraulic brake system, a pressure differential warning signal has been added. This signal consists of a warning light on the dashboard activated by a differential pressure switch located below the master cylinder. The signal indicates a loss of fluid pressure in either the front or rear brakes and should warn the driver that a hydraulic failure has occurred.

The pressure differential warning valve is a housing with the brake warning light switch mounted centrally on top. Directly below the switch is a bore containing a piston assembly. The piston assembly is located in the center of the bore and kept in that position by equal fluid pressure on either side. Fluid pressure is provided by two brake lines, one coming from the rear brake system and one from the front brakes. If a leak develops in either system (front or rear), fluid pressure to that side of the piston will decrease or stop causing the piston to move in that direction. The plunger on the end of the switch engages with the piston. When the piston moves off center, the plunger moves and triggers the switch to activate the warning light on the dash.

After repairing and bleeding any part of the hydraulic system, the warning light may remain on due to the pressure differential valve remaining in the off-center position. After repairs or bleeding have been performed, center the valve by applying moderate pressure on the brake pedal. This will turn out the light.

NOTE: *Front wheel balancing of cars equipped with disc brakes may also cause a pressure differential in the front branch of the system.*

BLEEDING

1. Clean the bleed screw at each wheel.
2. Attach a small rubber hose to one of the bleed screws and place the end in a container of brake fluid.
3. Top up the master cylinder with brake fluid. (Check often during bleeding.) Pump up the brake pedal and hold it.
4. Open the bleed screw about one-quarter turn, press the brake pedal to the floor, close the bleed screw, and slowly release the pedal. Continue until no more air bubbles are forced from the cylinder on application of the brake pedal.
5. Repeat this procedure on the remaining wheel cylinders.

Master cylinders equipped with bleed screws may be bled independently. When bleeding dual master cylinders, it is necessary to solidly cap one reservoir section while bleeding the other to prevent pressure loss through the cap vent hole.

Disc brakes may be bled in the same manner as drum brakes, except that:

1. It usually requires a longer time to bleed a disc brake thoroughly.
2. The disc should be rotated to make sure that the piston has returned to the unapplied position when bleeding is completed and the bleed screw closed.

Front Disc Brakes

DISC BRAKE PADS

Removal and Installation

1968

1. Siphon off about two-thirds of the brake fluid from a full master cylinder.

CAUTION: *The insertion of the thicker replacement pads will push the caliper pistons back into their bores and will cause a full master cylinder to overflow causing paint damage. In addition to siphoning fluid, it would be wise to keep the cylinder cover on during pad replacement.*

2. Raise the car and support it with jackstands. Remove the wheels.

NOTE: *Replacing the pads on just one wheel will result in uneven braking. Always replace the pads on both wheels.*

3. Extract and discard the pad retaining pin cotter key.
4. Remove the retaining pin and, while removing one pad, insert its replacement before the piston has time to move outward. If you were too slow and the pistons were too fast, it will be necessary to use a wide-bladed putty knife to hold in the pistons while inserting the new pads. If this gives you difficulty, open the bleeder screw on that caliper and release some of the fluid, but do not allow the fluid to drain from the master cylinder. This may reduce the pressure and make it easier to push in on the pistons. After removing the outboard pad, inspect it and compare it with the inboard pad. They may be slightly different; if so, make sure that the replacement pads are installed correctly.
5. After installing the new pads, install the retaining pin and insert a new cotter pin.

6. Refill the master cylinder and bleed the system if necessary.

1969–73

1. Siphon off about two-thirds of the brake fluid from a full master cylinder. CAUTION: *The insertion of the thicker replacement pads will push the piston back into its bore and will cause a full master cylinder to overflow causing paint damage. In addition to siphoning off fluid it would be wise to keep the cylinder cover on during pad replacement.*

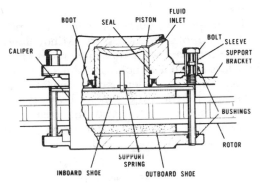

Front Single-Piston Disc Brake Assembly (© Pontiac Div., G.M. Corp.)

2. Raise the car and support it with jackstands. Remove the wheels.
NOTE: *Replacing the pads on just one wheel will result in uneven braking. Always replace the pads on both wheels.*
3. Install a C-clamp on the caliper so that the solid side of the clamp rests against the back of the caliper and so the screw end rests against the metal part of the outboard pad.
4. Tighten the clamp until the caliper moves enough to bottom the piston in its bore. Remove the clamp.
5. Remove the two allen-head caliper mounting bolts enough to allow the caliper to be pulled off the disc.
6. Remove the inboard pad and loosen the outboard pad. Place the caliper where it won't strain the brake hose. It would be best to wire it out of the way.
7. Remove the pad support spring clip from the piston.
8. Remove the two bolt ear sleeves and the four rubber bushings from the ears.
9. Brake pads should be replaced when they are worn to within 1/32 in. of the rivet heads.
10. Check the inside of the caliper for leakage and the condition of the piston dust boot.
11. Lubricate the two new sleeves and four bushings with a silicone spray.
12. Install the bushings in each caliper ear. Install the two sleeves in the two inboard ears.
13. Install the pad support spring clip and the old pad into the center of the piston. Push the pad down until it is flat against the caliper.
14. Place the outboard pad in the caliper with its top ears over the caliper ears and the bottom tab engaged in the caliper cutout.
15. After both pads are installed, lift the caliper and place the bottom edge of the outboard pad on the outer edge of the disc to make sure that there is no clearance between the tab on the bottom of the shoes and the caliper abutment.
16. Clamp a 1/4 x 1 x 2½ in. metal plate across the bottom of the pad. Make sure that the clamp and plate are clean to avoid contaminating the pads. Tighten the clamp moderately.
17. Bend the upper ears of the outboard shoe over the caliper with arc joint pliers. Bend the ears until the clearance between the pad ear and the caliper is 0.005 in. or less.
18. Remove the C-clamp and install the new inboard pad in place of the old pad used for installation purposes.
19. Place the caliper over the disc and line up the mounting holes.
20. Insert the mounting bolts through the inboard caliper ear sleeves and mounting bracket. Make sure that the bolts go under the inboard pad retaining ears.
21. Push the bolts through the outboard pads and caliper ears. Hand-tighten the bolts into the mounting bracket and then tighten them to 35 ft lbs.
22. Install the wheels, lower the car, and refill the master cylinder with new fluid. Pump the brake pedal to make sure that there are no air bubbles in the system.

DISC BRAKE CALIPERS

Removal, Installation, and Overhaul

1968

1. Raise the car and support it on jackstands.
2. Remove the tire and wheel assembly

from the side on which the caliper is being removed.

3. Disconnect the brake hose at the support bracket. Tape the end of the line to prevent contamination.

4. Remove the cotter pin from the brake pad retaining pin and remove the pin.

5. Remove the brake pads and identify them as inboard or outboard if they are being reused.

6. Remove the U-shaped retainer from the hose fitting and pull the hose from the bracket.

7. Remove the two caliper retaining bolts and also the caliper from its mounting bracket.

8. Separate the caliper halves. Remove the two O-rings from the fluid transfer holes in the caliper.

9. Push the piston all the way down into the caliper. Using the piston as a fulcrum, place a screwdriver under the steel ring in the boot and pry the boot from the caliper half.

10. Remove the pistons and springs, being careful not to damage the seal.

11. Remove the boot and seal from the piston.

12. Clean all metal components with clean brake fluid or denatured alcohol. CAUTION: *Do not use gasoline, kerosine, or any other mineral-based solvent for cleaning. These solvents form an oily film on the parts which leads to fluid contamination and the deterioration of rubber parts.*

13. Blow out all fluid passages with an air hose.

14. Discard and replace all rubber parts.

15. Inspect all bores for scoring and pitting and replace if necessary. Minor flaws can be removed with very fine crocus cloth but do so with a circular motion.

16. Using a feeler gauge, check the clearance of the piston in its bore. If the bore is not damaged and the clearance exceeds the maximum limit below, then the piston must be replaced.

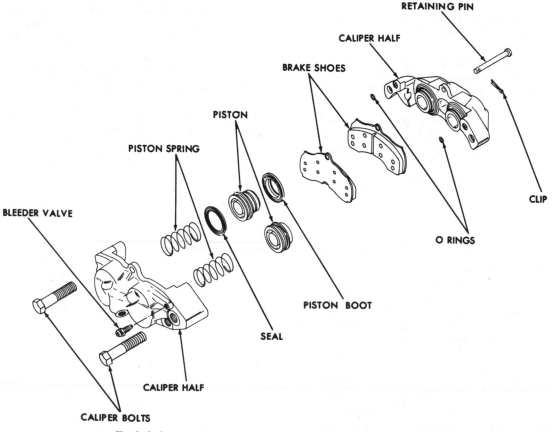

Exploded view of four-piston caliper (© Pontiac Div., G.M. Corp.)

Bore Diameter	Clearance
2¹⁄₁₆ in.	0.0045–0.010 in.
1⅞ in.	0.0045–0.010 in.
1⅜ in.	0.0035–0.009 in.

17. Insert the seal in the piston groove nearest the flat end of the piston. The seal lip must face the large end of the piston. The lips must be in the groove and may not extend beyond.

18. Place the spring in the piston bore.

19. Coat the seal with clean brake fluid.

20. Install the piston assembly into the bore, being careful not to damage the seal lip on the edge of the bore.

21. Install the boot into the piston groove closest to the concave end of the piston.

22. The fold in the boot must face the seal end of the piston.

23. Push the pistons to the bottom of the bore and check for smooth piston movement. The end of the piston must be flush with the end of the bore. If it is not, check the installation of the seal.

24. Seat the piston boot so that its metal ring is even in the counterbore. The ring must be flush or below the machined face of the caliper. If the ring is seated unevenly dirt and moisture could get into the bore.

25. Insert the O-rings around the fluid transfer holes at both ends of the caliper halves.

26. Lubricate the bolts with brake fluid, connect the caliper halves, and torque the bolts to 130 ft lbs.

27. While holding in the brake pistons with a putty knife, mount the caliper over the disc. Be careful not to damage the piston boots on the edge of the disc.

28. Install the two mounting bolts and torque them to 130 ft lbs.

29. Install the brake pads. If the same pads are being reused, return them to their original places (outboard or inboard) as marked during removal. New pads will usually have an arrow on the back indicating the direction of disc rotation. See "Brake Pad Replacement" for details.

30. Install the brake hose into the caliper, passing the female end through the support bracket.

31. Make sure that the tube line is clean and connect the brake line nut to the caliper.

32. Install the hose fitting into the support bracket and install the U-shaped retainer. Turn the steering wheel from side to side to make sure that the hose doesn't interfere with the tire. If it does, turn the hose end one or two points in the bracket until the interference is eliminated.

33. After performing the above check, install the steel tube connector and tighten it.

34. Bleed the brakes as instructed earlier in this chapter.

35. Install the wheels and lower the car.

1969–73

1. Raise the vehicle on a hoist and remove the front wheels.

2. Working on one side at a time only, disconnect the hydraulic inlet line from the caliper and plug the end. Remove the caliper mounting bolts and shims (if used) and slide the caliper off of the disc.

3. Remove the disc pads from the caliper. If the old ones are to be reused, mark them so that they can be reinstalled in their original positions.

4. Open the caliper bleed screw and drain the fluid. Clean the outside of the caliper and mount it in a vise with padded jaws.

CAUTION: *When cleaning any brake components, use only brake fluid or denatured alcohol. Never use a mineral-based solvent, such as gasoline or paint thinner, since it will swell and quickly deteriorate rubber parts.*

5. Remove the bridge bolts, separate the caliper halves, and remove the two O-ring seals from the transfer holes.

6. Pry the lip on each piston dust boot from its groove and remove the piston assemblies and springs from the bores. If necessary, air pressure may be used to force the pistons out of the bores, using care to prevent them from popping out.

7. Remove the boots and seals from the pistons and clean the pistons in brake fluid. Blow out the caliper passages with an air hose.

8. Inspect the cylinder bores for scoring, pitting, or corrosion. Corrosion is a pitted or rough condition not to be confused with staining. Light rough spots may be removed by rotating crocus cloth, using finger pressure, in the bores. Do not polish with an in and out motion or use any other abrasive.

9. If the pistons are pitted, scored, or

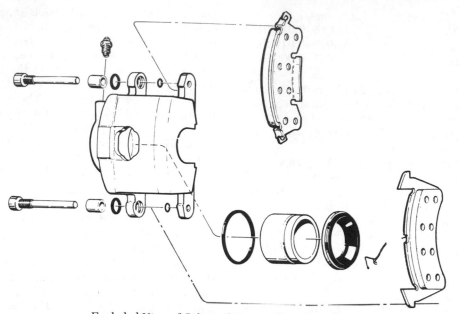

Exploded View of Caliper (© Pontiac Div., G.M. Corp.)

worn, they must be replaced. A corroded or deeply scored caliper should also be replaced.

10. Check the clearance of the pistons in the bores using a feeler gauge. Clearance should be 0.045–0.010 in. If there is excessive clearance, the caliper must be replaced.

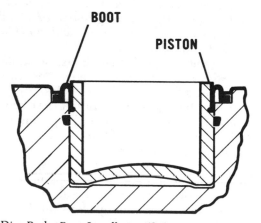

Disc Brake Boot Installation (© Pontiac Div., G.M. Corp.)

11. Replace all rubber parts and lubricate with brake fluid. Install the seals and boots in the grooves in each piston. The seal should be installed in the groove closest to the closed end of the piston with the seal lips facing the closed end. The lip on the boot should be facing the seal.

12. Lubricate the piston and bore with brake fluid. Position the piston return spring, large coil first, in the piston bore.

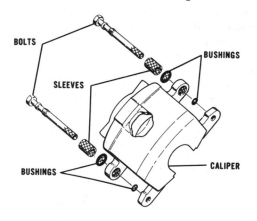

Shoe Supporting Spring (© Pontiac Div., G.M. Corp.)

13. Install the piston in the bore, taking great care to avoid damaging the seal lip as it passes the edge of the cylinder bore.

14. Compress the lip on the dust boot into the groove in the caliper. Be sure the boot is fully seated in the groove, as poor sealing will allow contaminants to ruin the bore.

15. Position the O-rings in the cavities around the caliper transfer holes, and fit the caliper halves together. Install the bridge bolts (lubricated with brake fluid) and be sure to torque to specification.

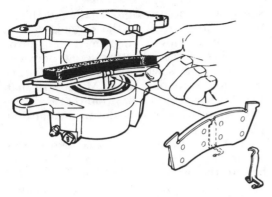

Shoe Installation (© Pontiac Div., G.M. Corp.)

16. Slide the caliper over the disc. A putty knife can be used to hold back the pistons so that the caliper can be completely lowered into position. The caliper should be positioned carefully to avoid tearing the rubber boot on the edge of the disc. Secure the caliper to the mounting bracket and torque to specifications. Install the pads as instructed earlier. When the brake hose is connected, it should not be twisted or touch other parts at any time during suspension or steering travel.

17. Bleed the brakes.

WHEEL BEARINGS

Removal and Installation

1. Raise the front of the car.
2. Remove the hubcap and wheel.
3. Remove the dust cap, cotter pin and nut, and washer.
4. Remove the wheel bearing.
5. Reverse the removal procedure to install.

Front Drum Brakes

BRAKE DRUM

Removal and Installation

1. Raise the front of the car.
2. Remove the hubcap and dust cap and wheel bearing.
3. Remove the wheel.
4. Lay the wheel on the ground and remove the lug nuts. This will release the brake drum.
5. To install, install the drum on the spindle.

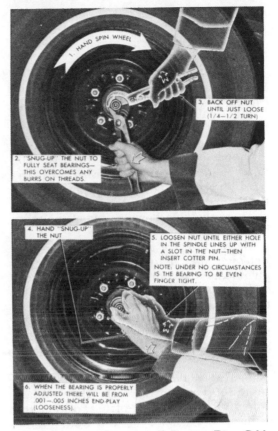

Wheel Bearing Adjustment (© Pontiac Div., G.M. Corp.)

6. Install the wheel bearing and dust cap.
7. Install the wheel and lug nuts and hubcap.
8. Lower the car to the ground.

BRAKE SHOES

Removal and Installation

NOTE: *If you are not thoroughly familiar with the procedures involved in brake replacement, disassemble and assemble one side at a time, leaving the other wheel intact for reference.*

1. Remove the brake drum.
2. Place the hollow end of a brake spring service tool on the brake shoe anchor pin and twist it to disengage one of the brake retaining springs. Repeat this operation to remove the other spring. Grasp the secondary shoe return spring with a pair of pliers and lift upward on the spring to disengage it from the automatic adjuster link.

CAUTION: *Be careful that the springs do not slip off the tool during removal, as the springs could break loose and cause personal injury.*

3. Reach behind the brake backing plate and place a finger on the end of one of the brake hold-down mounting pins. Using a pair of pliers, grasp the washer on the top of the hold-down spring that corresponds to the pin that you are holding. Push down on the pliers and turn them 90° to align the slot in the washer with the head on the spring mounting pin. Remove the spring and washer and repeat this operation on the hold-down spring of the other brake shoe.

4. Remove the automatic adjuster link. Remove the automatic adjuster lever, pivot, and override spring from the secondary spring as an assembly. Move the top of each brake shoe outward to clear the wheel cylinder pins and parking brake link (rear brakes). Lift the brakes from the backing plate and remove the adjusting screw.

5. Apply a light coating of high-temperature grease to the brake shoe contact points on the backing plate. Position the primary brake shoe on the front of the backing plate and install the hold-down spring and washer over the mounting pin. Install the secondary shoe on the rear of the backing plate.

6. Assemble the automatic adjuster lever, pivot, and override spring and install to the secondary spring as an assembly.

7. Install the return spring in the primary brake shoe and, using the tapered end of a brake spring service tool, slide the top of the spring onto the anchor pin. CAUTION: *Make sure that the spring does not slip off of the tool during installation, as the spring could break loose and cause personal injury.*

8. Install the automatic adjuster cable guide in the secondary brake shoe, making sure that the flared hole in the cable guide is inside the hole in the brake shoe. Fit the cable into the groove in the top of the cable guide.

9. Install the secondary shoe return spring through the hole in the cable guide and the brake shoe. Using the brake spring tool, slide the top of the spring onto the anchor pin.

10. Clean the threads on the adjusting screw and apply a *light* coating of high-temperature grease to the threads. Screw the adjuster closed, then open it ½ turn.

11. Install the adjusting screw between the brake shoes with the star wheel nearest to the secondary shoe. Make sure that the star wheel is in a position that is accessible from the adjusting slot in the backing plate.

12. Install the short, hooked end of the automatic adjuster spring in the proper hole in the primary brake shoe.

13. Connect the hooked end of the automatic adjuster cable and the free end of the automatic adjuster spring in the slot in the top of the automatic adjuster lever.

14. Pull the automatic adjuster lever (the lever will pull the cable and spring with it) downward and to the left and engage the pivot hook of the lever in the hole in the secondary brake shoe.

15. Check the entire brake assembly to make sure everything is installed properly. Make sure that the shoes engage the wheel cylinder properly and are flush on the anchor pin. Make sure that the automatic adjuster cable is flush on the anchor pin and in the slot on the back of the cable guide. Make sure that the adjusting lever rests on the adjusting screw star wheel. Pull upward on the adjusting cable until the adjusting lever is free of the star wheel, then release the cable. The adjusting lever should snap back into place on the adjusting screw star wheel and turn the wheel one tooth.

16. Expand the brake adjusting screw until the brake drum will just fit over the brake shoes.

17. Install the wheel and drum and adjust the brakes. (See "Brake Adjustment")

WHEEL CYLINDERS

Removal, Installation, and Overhaul

1. Raise the vehicle on a hoist and remove the wheel and drum from the brake to be serviced.

2. Remove the brake shoes and clean the backing plate and wheel cylinder.

3. Disconnect the brake line from the brake hose. Remove the brake hose retainer clip at the frame bracket and remove the hose from the wheel cylinder. (On rear brakes it will only be necessary to remove the line from the cylinder.)

4. Remove the cylinder mounting bolts and remove the cylinder.

5. Remove the boots from the cylinder ends and discard. Remove the pistons, remove and discard the seal cups, and remove the expanders and spring.

6. Inspect the bore and pistons for damage or wear. Damaged pistons should be discarded, as they cannot be reconditioned. Slight bore roughness can be removed using a brake cylinder hone or crocus cloth. (Cloth should be rotated in the bore under finger pressure. Do not slide lengthwise.) Use only lint-free cloth for cleaning.

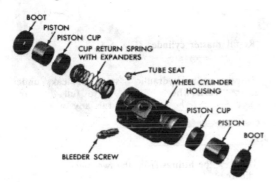

Wheel Cylinder—Exploded View (© Pontiac Div., G.M. Corp.)

7. Clean the cylinder and internal parts using *only brake fluid or denatured alcohol.*

8. Insert the spring expander assembly. Lubricate all rubber parts using only fresh brake fluid.

9. Install new cups with the seal lips facing inward.

10. Install the pistons and rubber boots. Install the cylinder on the car in the reverse order of removal. Bleed the cylinder. (see "Brake Bleeding")

WHEEL BEARINGS

Adjustment

1. Lift the wheel off of the ground by jacking under the lower control arm.

2. Remove the dust cap from the hub.

3. Remove the cotter pin and discard it.

4. Snug up the spindle nut to seat the bearings. Then back off the nut 1/4–1/2 turn.

5. Retighten the nut by hand until it is finger-tight.

6. Loosen the nut until the nearest hole in the spindle lines up with a slot in the

spindle nut and then insert a new cotter pin.

NOTE: *Under no circumstances is the final bearing nut adjustment to be even finger-tight.*

7. Replace the dust cover and lower the car.

Inspection

1. Raise the car and support it under the front lower control arm.

2. Spin the wheel to check for any unusual noise. Bad wheel bearings sometimes squeal or sound as though there is sand in the bearing.

3. If bearings are noisy or loose, they should be cleaned, inspected, and repacked before adjustment.

4. To check for loose bearings, grip the tire at top and bottom and move the wheel in and out. Movement greater than 0.005 in. indicates improper adjustment or excessive wear.

Rear Drum Brakes

BRAKE DRUMS

Removal and Installation

1. Raise the rear of the car.

2. Remove the hubcap and remove the wheel.

3. Pull off the brake drum.

4. Reverse the procedures to install.

BRAKE SHOES

Removal and Installation

1. Remove the brake drum.

2. Place the hollow end of a brake spring service tool on the brake shoe anchor pin and twist it to disengage one of the brake retaining springs. Repeat this operation to remove the other spring. Grasp the secondary shoe return spring with a pair of pliers and lift upward on the spring to disengage it from the automatic adjuster link.

CAUTION: *Be careful that the springs do not slip off of the tool during removal, as the springs could break loose and cause personal injury.*

3. Reach behind the brake backing plate and place a finger on the end of one

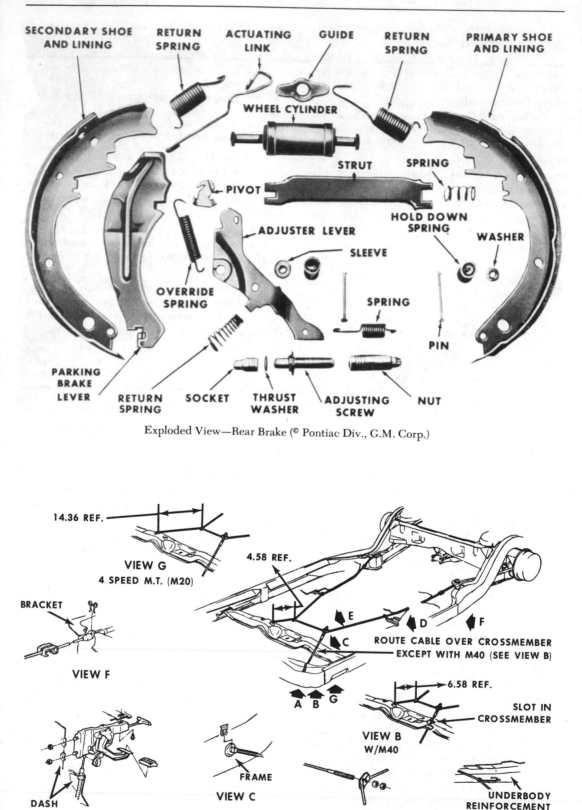

SECONDARY SHOE AND LINING

RETURN SPRING

ACTUATING LINK

GUIDE

RETURN SPRING

PRIMARY SHOE AND LINING

WHEEL CYLINDER

STRUT

SPRING

PIVOT

ADJUSTER LEVER

SLEEVE

HOLD DOWN SPRING

WASHER

OVERRIDE SPRING

SPRING

PARKING BRAKE LEVER

RETURN SPRING

SOCKET

THRUST WASHER

ADJUSTING SCREW

NUT

PIN

Exploded View—Rear Brake (© Pontiac Div., G.M. Corp.)

14.36 REF.

VIEW G
4 SPEED M.T. (M20)

4.58 REF.

BRACKET

E

D

F

C

ROUTE CABLE OVER CROSSMEMBER
EXCEPT WITH M40 (SEE VIEW B)

VIEW F

A B G

6.58 REF.

SLOT IN CROSSMEMBER

VIEW B
W/M40

FRAME

DASH

VIEW A

VIEW C

VIEW E

UNDERBODY REINFORCEMENT

VIEW D

Parking Brake System (© Pontiac Div., G.M. Corp.)

of the brake hold-down mounting pins. Using a pair of pliers, grasp the washer on the top of the hold-down spring that corresponds to the pin that you are holding. Push down on the pliers and turn them 90° to align the slot in the washer with the head on the spring mounting pin. Remove the spring and washer and repeat this operation on the hold-down spring of the other brake shoe.

4. Remove the automatic adjuster link. Remove the automatic adjuster lever, pivot, and override spring from the secondary spring as an assembly. Move the top of each brake shoe outward to clear the wheel cylinder pins and parking brake link (rear brakes). Lift the brakes from the backing plate and remove the adjusting screw.

5. Grasp the end of the brake cable spring with a pair of pliers and, using the brake lever as a fulcrum, pull the end of the spring away from the lever. Disengage the cable from the brake lever.

6. The brake cable must be connected to the secondary brake shoe before the shoe is installed on the backing plate. To do this, transfer the parking brake lever from the old secondary shoe to the new one. This is accomplished by spreading the bottom of the horseshoe clip and disengaging the lever. Position the lever on the new secondary shoe and install the spring washer and the horseshoe clip. Close the bottom of the clip after installing it. Grasp the metal tip of the parking brake cable with a pair of pliers. Position a pair of side cutters on the end of the cable coil spring and, using the pliers as a fulcrum, pull the coil spring back with the side cutters. Position the cable in the parking brake lever.

7. Apply a light coating of high-temperature grease to the brake shoe contact points on the backing plate. Position the primary brake shoe on the front of the backing plate and install the hold-down spring and washer over the mounting pin. Install the secondary shoe on the rear of the backing plate.

8. Assemble the automatic adjuster lever, pivot, and override spring and install to the secondary spring as an assembly.

9. Install the return spring in the primary brake shoe and, using the tapered end of a brake spring service tool, slide the top of the spring onto the anchor pin.

CAUTION: *Make sure that the spring does not slip off of the tool during installation, as the spring could break loose and cause personal injury.*

10. Install the automatic adjuster cable guide in the secondary brake shoe, making sure that the flared hole in the cable guide is inside the hole in the brake shoe. Fit the cable into the groove in the top of the cable guide.

11. Install the secondary shoe return spring through the hole in the cable guide and the brake shoe. Using the brake spring tool, slide the top of the spring onto the anchor pin.

12. Clean the threads on the adjusting screw and apply a *light* coating of high-temperature grease to the threads. Screw the adjuster closed, then open it ½ turn.

13. Install the adjusting screw between the brake shoes with the star wheel nearest to the secondary shoe. Make sure that the star wheel is in a position that is accessible from the adjusting slot in the backing plate.

14. Install the short, hooked end of the automatic adjuster spring in the proper hole in the primary brake shoe.

15. Connect the hooked end of the automatic adjuster cable and the free end of the automatic adjuster spring in the slot in the top of the automatic adjuster lever.

16. Pull the automatic adjuster lever (the lever will pull the cable and spring with it) downward and to the left, and engage the pivot hook of the lever in the hole in the secondary brake shoe.

17. Check the entire brake assembly to make sure everything is installed properly. Make sure that the shoes engage the wheel cylinder properly and are flush on the anchor pin. Make sure that the automatic adjuster cable is flush on the anchor pin and in the slot on the back of the cable guide. Make sure that the adjusting lever rests on the adjusting screw star wheel. Pull upward on the adjusting cable until the adjusting lever is free of the star wheel, then release the cable. The adjusting lever should snap back into place on the adjusting screw star wheel and turn the wheel one tooth.

18. Expand the brake adjusting screw until the brake drum will just fit over the brake shoes.

Handbrake

ADJUSTMENT

The automatic self-adjusting feature incorporated in the rear brake mechanism normally maintains proper parking brake adjustment. For this reason, the rear brake adjustment must be checked before any adjustment of the parking brake cables is done. Check the parking brake mechanism and cables for free movement and lubricate all working surfaces before proceeding.

CAUTION: *It is very important that the* parking brake cables not be too tight. If the cables are too tight, they create a drag and position the secondary shoes so that the self-adjusters continue to operate in compensation for drag wear. The result is rapidly worn rear brake linings.

1. Jack up both rear wheels.
2. Push the parking brake pedal 5–7 notches from the full release position.
3. Loosen the rear equalizer locknut and adjust the forward nut until a light rear brake drag is felt as the wheels are rotated by hand.
4. Tighten the locknut and release the parking brake pedal; no drag should be felt.

Brake Specification Chart
(All measurements are given in in.)

Year	Model	Master Cylinder Bore		Wheel Cylinder Bore			Brake Disc or Drum Diameter		
				Front			Front		
		Disc	Drum	Disc	Drum	Rear	Disc	Drum	Rear
1968	Tempest, LeMans, GTO	1.125	1.0	2.062	1.125	0.875	11.0	9.5	9.5
1969–73	Tempest, LeMans, GTO	1.125	1.0	2.938	1.125	0.875	11.0	9.5	9.5

10 · Body

Doors

Removal and Installation

1. Scribe lines on the door hinges.
2. Remove the hinge attaching bolts.
3. Remove the door.
4. Install the door making sure to align the scribe marks on the hinge.
5. Install the attaching bolts.

DOOR PANELS

Removal and Installation

1. Remove the door handle attaching screw.
2. Remove the window handle attaching screw.
3. Remove the two armrest attaching bolts and the armrest.
4. Insert a screw driver between the door trim panel and the door and lift outward on the trim panel to free the attaching clips from the holes in the door.
5. Remove the door panel from the door.
6. Position the trim panel on the door, making sure the clips align with the holes in the door.
7. Press the trim panel to seat the clips in the holes.

8. Install the armrest.
9. Install the door and window handles.

WINDOWS

Adjustments

1. Remove the trim panel from the door.
2. Remove the weathersheet from the door.
3. Loosen the screw on the rear window run.
4. Loosen the nut on the front window run.
5. Raise or lower the window until the top edge of the glass is about 4 in. above the window opening in the door.
6. Tighten the rear run adjusting screw, then raise the window to the full up position.
7. Adjust the front nut run against the window, then tighten the front screw. Do the same with the rear.
8. Install the weathersheet and panel.

LOCKS

NOTE: *The key code for the ignition and door locks is stamped on the front door lock cylinder.*

1. Remove the trim panel from the door.
2. Remove the weather sheet from the door.

3. Disconnect the lock button-to-lock cylinder rod at the lock cylinder.

4. Remove the lock cylinder retainer clip and remove the cylinder from the door.

5. Transfer the lock cylinder arm to the new lock cylinder.

6. Position the cylinder in the door and install the lock cylinder retaining clip.

7. Connect the lock button rod to the lock cylinder.

8. Install the weathersheet and the trim panel.

HOOD

Alignment

REAR

1. Loosen the hood hinge mounting bracket bolts.

2. Force the hood open.

3. Tighten the hinge mounting bolts.

FRONT

1. Close the hood.

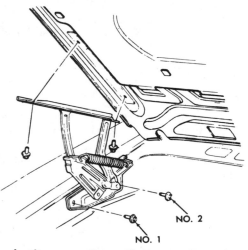

Hood Alignment—Front (© Pontiac Div., G.M. Corp.)

2. See how much adjustment you need.

3. Open the hood.

4. Loosen the jam nut on the hood, bumper and adjust the bumper as needed.

5. Tighten the nut.

HOOD LATCH

Adjustment

HORIZONTAL

Loosen the hood latch bracket-to-hood attaching screws and lower the hood. Move the hood latch bracket as required

to align the hood latch hook with the hood latch striker bar. Tighten the screws.

VERTICAL

Loosen the hood latch-to-hood latch bracket attaching screws. Move the hood as required to align the top of the hood with the tops of the fenders. Tighten the screws. Raise or lower the rubber hood bumpers on the radiator support to remove.

FUEL TANK

Removal and Installation

1. Drain the fuel from the tank if the tank is equipped with a drain plug.

2. Remove all fuel lines, pollution equipment lines, and wires from the fuel tank.

3. Support the tank.

4. Remove the mounting bolts from the mounting straps.

5. Remove the tank.

6. Position the tank and install the mounting straps and bolts.

7. Connect all wiring and lines.

Bumpers

To remove and install the bumpers, remove or install the attaching bolts. Make sure to remove any wire connectors to lights in the bumper if so equipped.

Fenders

Removal and Installation

1. Remove the front bumper.

2. Remove the valance panel attachments to the fender.

3. Remove the fender attaching screws.

4. Remove the headlight filler and fender extension-to-fender attaching screws.

5. Remove the hood hinge-to-fender attaching screws.

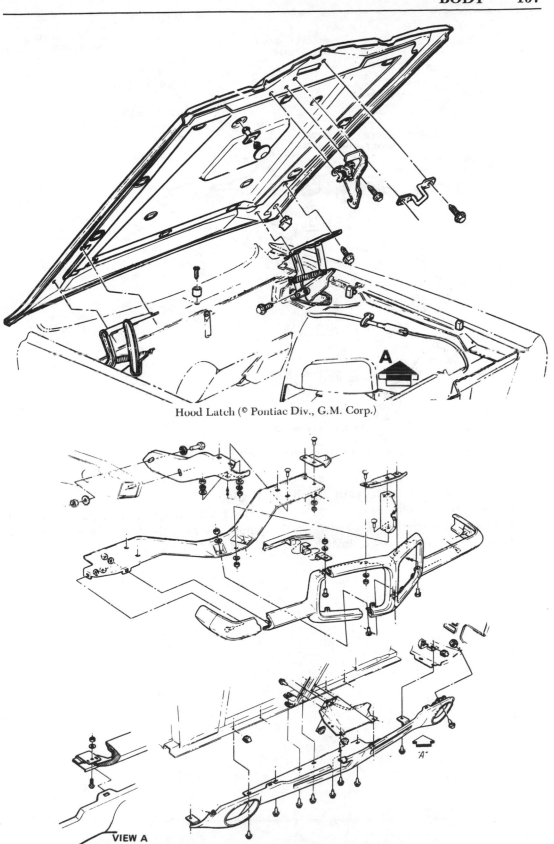

Hood Latch (© Pontiac Div., G.M. Corp.)

VIEW A

Front Bumper—GTO (© Pontiac Div., G.M. Corp.)

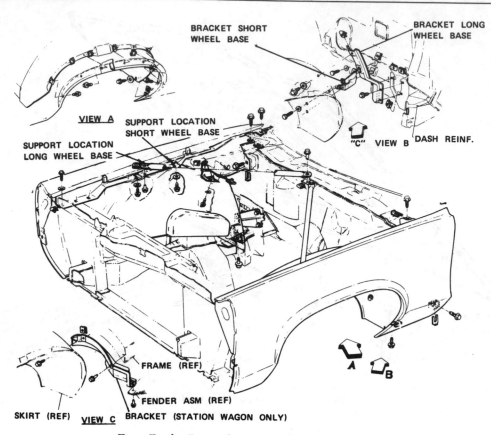

BRACKET SHORT WHEEL BASE

BRACKET LONG WHEEL BASE

VIEW A

SUPPORT LOCATION SHORT WHEEL BASE

SUPPORT LOCATION LONG WHEEL BASE

"C"   VIEW B   DASH REINF.

A

B

FRAME (REF)

FENDER ASM (REF)

SKIRT (REF)   VIEW C   BRACKET (STATION WAGON ONLY)

Front Fender Removal (© Pontiac Div., G.M. Corp.)

6. Remove the fender inner skirt attaching screws at the wheelhouse.

7. Remove the fender.

8. Reverse the procedures to install.

Alignment

To adjust, insert shims at the attachment points, through the large holes at the rear of the fender.

Appendix

General Conversion Table

Multiply by	To convert	To	
2.54	Inches	Centimeters	.3937
30.48	Feet	Centimeters	.0328
.914	Yards	Meters	1.094
1.609	Miles	Kilometers	.621
6.45	Square inches	Square cm.	.155
.836	Square yards	Square meters	1.196
16.39	Cubic inches	Cubic cm.	.061
28.3	Cubic feet	Liters	.0353
.4536	Pounds	Kilograms	2.2045
3.785	Gallons	Liters	.264
.068	Lbs./sq. in. (psi)	Atmospheres	14.7
.138	Foot pounds	Kg. m.	7.23
1.014	H.P. (DIN)	H.P. (SAE)	.9861
—	To obtain	From	Multiply by

Note: 1 cm. equals 10 mm.; 1 mm. equals .0394".

Conversion—Common Fractions to Decimals and Millimeters

Common Fractions	Decimal Fractions	Millimeters (approx.)	Common Fractions	Decimal Fractions	Millimeters (approx.)	Common Fractions	Decimal Fractions	Millimeters (approx.)
1/128	.008	0.20	11/32	.344	8.73	43/64	.672	17.07
1/64	.016	0.40	23/64	.359	9.13	11/16	.688	17.46
1/32	.031	0.79	3/8	.375	9.53	45/64	.703	17.86
3/64	.047	1.19	25/64	.391	9.92	23/32	.719	18.26
1/16	.063	1.59	13/32	.406	10.32	47/64	.734	18.65
5/64	.078	1.98	27/64	.422	10.72	3/4	.750	19.05
3/32	.094	2.38	7/16	.438	11.11	49/64	.766	19.45
7/64	.109	2.78	29/64	.453	11.51	25/32	.781	19.84
1/8	.125	3.18	15/32	.469	11.91	51/64	.797	20.24
9/64	.141	3.57	31/64	.484	12.30	13/16	.813	20.64
5/32	.156	3.97	1/2	.500	12.70	53/64	.828	21.03
11/64	.172	4.37	33/64	.516	13.10	27/32	.844	21.43
3/16	.188	4.76	17/32	.531	13.49	55/64	.859	21.83
13/64	.203	5.16	35/64	.547	13.89	7/8	.875	22.23
7/32	.219	5.56	9/16	.563	14.29	57/64	.891	22.62
15/64	.234	5.95	37/64	.578	14.68	29/32	.906	23.02
1/4	.250	6.35	19/32	.594	15.08	59/64	.922	23.42
17/64	.266	6.75	39/64	.609	15.48	15/16	.938	23.81
9/32	.281	7.14	5/8	.625	15.88	61/64	.953	24.21
19/64	.297	7.54	41/64	.641	16.27	31/32	.969	24.61
5/16	.313	7.94	21/32	.656	16.67	63/64	.984	25.00
21/64	.328	8.33						

Conversion—Millimeters to Decimal Inches

mm	inches	mm	inches	mm	inches	mm	inches	mm	inches
1	.039 370	31	1.220 470	61	2.401 570	91	3.582 670	210	8.267 700
2	.078 740	32	1.259 840	62	2.440 940	92	3.622 040	220	8.661 400
3	.118 110	33	1.299 210	63	2.480 310	93	3.661 410	230	9.055 100
4	.157 480	34	1.338 580	64	2.519 680	94	3.700 780	240	9.448 800
5	.196 850	35	1.377 949	65	2.559 050	95	3.740 150	250	9.842 500
6	.236 220	36	1.417 319	66	2.598 420	96	3.779 520	260	10.236 200
7	.275 590	37	1.456 689	67	2.637 790	97	3.818 890	270	10.629 900
8	.314 960	38	1.496 050	68	2.677 160	98	3.858 260	280	11.032 600
9	.354 330	39	1.535 430	69	2.716 530	99	3.897 630	290	11.417 300
10	.393 700	40	1.574 800	70	2.755 900	100	3.937 000	300	11.811 000
11	.433 070	41	1.614 170	71	2.795 270	105	4.133 848	310	12.204 700
12	.472 440	42	1.653 540	72	2.834 640	110	4.330 700	320	12.598 400
13	.511 810	43	1.692 910	73	2.874 010	115	4.527 550	330	12.992 100
14	.551 180	44	1.732 280	74	2.913 380	120	4.724 400	340	13.385 800
15	.590 550	45	1.771 650	75	2.952 750	125	4.921 250	350	13.779 500
16	.629 920	46	1.811 020	76	2.992 120	130	5.118 100	360	14.173 200
17	.669 290	47	1.850 390	77	3.031 490	135	5.314 950	370	14.566 900
18	.708 660	48	1.889 760	78	3.070 860	140	5.511 800	380	14.960 600
19	.748 030	49	1.929 130	79	3.110 230	145	5.708 650	390	15.354 300
20	.787 400	50	1.968 500	80	3.149 600	150	5.905 500	400	15.748 000
21	.826 770	51	2.007 870	81	3.188 970	155	6.102 350	500	19.685 000
22	.866 140	52	2.047 240	82	3.228 340	160	6.299 200	600	23.622 000
23	.905 510	53	2.086 610	83	3.267 710	165	6.496 050	700	27.559 000
24	.944 880	54	2.125 980	84	3.307 080	170	6.692 900	800	31.496 000
25	.984 250	55	2.165 350	85	3.346 450	175	6.889 750	900	35.433 000
26	1.023 620	56	2.204 720	86	3.385 820	180	7.086 600	1000	39.370 000
27	1.062 990	57	2.244 090	87	3.425 190	185	7.283 450	2000	78.740 000
28	1.102 360	58	2.283 460	88	3.464 560	190 .	7.480 300	3000	118.110 000
29	1.141 730	59	2.322 830	89	3.503 903	195	7.677 150	4000	157.480 000
30	1.181 100	60	2.362 200	90	3.543 300	200	7.874 000	5000	196.850 000

To change decimal millimeters to decimal inches, position the decimal point where desired on either side of the millimeter measurement shown and reset the inches decimal by the same number of digits in the same direction. For example, to convert .001 mm into decimal inches, reset the decimal behind the 1 mm (shown on the chart) to .001; change the decimal inch equivalent (.039″ shown) to .000039″.

Tap Drill Sizes

National Fine or S.A.E.			National Coarse or U.S.S.		
Screw & Tap Size	Threads Per Inch	Use Drill Number	Screw & Tap Size	Threads Per Inch	Use Drill Number
No. 5	44	37	No. 5	40	39
No. 6	40	33	No. 6	32	36
No. 8	36	29	No. 8	32	29
No. 10	32	21	No. 10	24	25
No. 12	28	15	No. 12	24	17
1/4	28	3	1/4	20	8
5/16	24	1	5/16	18	F
3/8	24	Q	3/8	16	5/16
7/16	20	W	7/16	14	U
1/2	20	29/64	1/2	13	27/64
9/16	18	33/64	9/16	12	31/64
5/8	18	37/64	5/8	11	17/32
3/4	16	11/16	3/4	10	21/32
7/8	14	13/16	7/8	9	49/64
1 1/8	12	1 3/64	1	8	7/8
1 1/4	12	1 11/64	1 1/8	7	63/64
1 1/2	12	1 27/64	1 1/4	7	1 7/64
			1 1/2	6	1 11/32

Decimal Equivalent Size of the Number Drills

Drill No.	Decimal Equivalent	Drill No.	Decimal Equivalent	Drill No.	Decimal Equivalent
80	.0135	53	.0595	26	.1470
79	.0145	52	.0635	25	.1495
78	.0160	51	.0670	24	.1520
77	.0180	50	.0700	23	.1540
76	.0200	49	.0730	22	.1570
75	.0210	48	.0760	21	.1590
74	.0225	47	.0785	20	.1610
73	.0240	46	.0810	19	.1660
72	.0250	45	.0820	18	.1695
71	.0260	44	.0860	17	.1730
70	.0280	43	.0890	16	.1770
69	.0292	42	.0935	15	.1800
68	.0310	41	.0960	14	.1820
67	.0320	40	.0980	13	.1850
66	.0330	39	.0995	12	.1890
65	.0350	38	.1015	11	.1910
64	.0360	37	.1040	10	.1935
63	.0370	36	.1065	9	.1960
62	.0380	35	.1100	8	.1990
61	.0390	34	.1110	7	.2010
60	.0400	33	.1130	6	.2040
59	.0410	32	.1160	5	.2055
58	.0420	31	.1200	4	.2090
57	.0430	30	.1285	3	.2130
56	.0465	29	.1360	2	.2210
55	.0520	28	.1405	1	.2280
54	.0550	27	.1440		

Decimal Equivalent Size of the Letter Drills

Letter Drill	Decimal Equivalent	Letter Drill	Decimal Equivalent	Letter Drill	Decimal Equivalent
A	.234	J	.277	S	.348
B	.238	K	.281	T	.358
C	.242	L	.290	U	.368
D	.246	M	.295	V	.377
E	.250	N	.302	W	.386
F	.257	O	.316	X	.397
G	.261	P	.323	Y	.404
H	.266	Q	.332	Z	.413
I	.272	R	.339		

ANTI-FREEZE INFORMATION

Freezing and Boiling Points of Solutions
According to Percentage of Alcohol or Ethylene Glycol

Freezing Point of Solution	Alcohol Volume %	Alcohol Solution Boils at	Ethylene Glycol Volume %	Ethylene Glycol Solution Boils at
20°F.	12	196°F.	16	216°F.
10°F.	20	189°F.	25	218°F.
0°F.	27	184°F.	33	220°F.
−10°F.	32	181°F.	39	222°F.
−20°F.	38	178°F.	44	224°F.
−30°F.	42	176°F.	48	225°F.

Note: above boiling points are at sea level. For every 1,000 feet of altitude, boiling points are approximately 2°F. lower than those shown. For every pound of pressure exerted by the pressure cap, the boiling points are approximately 3°F. higher than those shown.

ANTI-FREEZE CHART

Temperatures Shown in Degrees Fahrenheit
+32 is Freezing

Cooling System Capacity Quarts	Quarts of ETHYLENE GLYCOL Needed for Protection to Temperatures Shown Below													
	1	2	3	4	5	6	7	8	9	10	11	12	13	14
10	+24°	+16°	+ 4°	−12°	−34°	−62°								
11	+25	+18	+ 8	− 6	−23	−47								
12	+26	+19	+10	0	−15	−34	−57°							
13	+27	+21	+13	+ 3	− 9	−25	−45							
14			+15	+ 6	− 5	−18	−34							
15			+16	+ 8	0	−12	−26							
16			+17	+10	+ 2	− 8	−19	−34	−52°					
17			+18	+12	+ 5	− 4	−14	−27	−42					
18			+19	+14	+ 7	0	−10	−21	−34	−50°				
19			+20	+15	+ 9	+ 2	− 7	−16	−28	−42				
20				+16	+10	+ 4	− 3	−12	−22	−34	−48°			
21				+17	+12	+ 6	0	− 9	−17	−28	−41			
22				+18	+13	+ 8	+ 2	− 6	−14	−23	−34	−47°		
23				+19	+14	+ 9	+ 4	− 3	−10	−19	−29	−40		
24				+19	+15	+10	+ 5	0	− 8	−15	−23	−34	−46°	
25				+20	+16	+12	+ 7	+ 1	− 5	−12	−20	−29	−40	−50°
26					+17	+13	+ 8	+ 3	− 3	− 9	−16	−25	−34	−44
27					+18	+14	+ 9	+ 5	− 1	− 7	−13	−21	−29	−39
28					+18	+15	+10	+ 6	+ 1	− 5	−11	−18	−25	−34
29					+19	+16	+12	+ 7	+ 2	− 3	− 8	−15	−22	−29
30					+20	+17	+13	+ 8	+ 4	− 1	− 6	−12	−18	−25

For capacities over 30 quarts divide true capacity by 3. Find quarts Anti-Freeze for the 1/3 and multiply by 3 for quarts to add.

For capacities under 10 quarts multiply true capacity by 3. Find quarts Anti-Freeze for the tripled volume and divide by 3 for quarts to add.

To Increase the Freezing Protection of Anti-Freeze Solutions Already Installed

Cooling System Capacity Quarts	Number of Quarts of ETHYLENE GLYCOL Anti-Freeze Required to Increase Protection													
	From +20°F. to					From +10°F. to					From 0°F. to			
	0°	−10°	−20°	−30°	−40°	0°	−10°	−20°	−30°	−40°	−10°	−20°	−30°	−40°
10	1 3/4	2 1/4	3	3 1/2	3 3/4	3/4	1 1/2	2 1/4	2 3/4	3 1/4	3/4	1 1/2	2	2 1/2
12	2	2 3/4	3 1/2	4	4 1/2	1	1 3/4	2 1/2	3 1/4	3 3/4	1	1 3/4	2 1/2	3 1/4
14	2 1/4	3 1/4	4	4 3/4	5 1/2	1 1/4	2	3	3 3/4	4 1/2	1	2	3	3 1/2
16	2 1/2	3 1/2	4 1/2	5 1/4	6	1 1/4	2 1/2	3 1/2	4 1/4	5 1/4	1 1/4	2 1/4	3 1/4	4
18	3	4	5	6	7	1 1/2	2 3/4	4	5	5 3/4	1 1/2	2 1/2	3 3/4	4 3/4
20	3 1/4	4 1/2	5 3/4	6 3/4	7 1/2	1 3/4	3	4 1/4	5 1/2	6 1/2	1 1/2	2 3/4	4 1/4	5 1/4
22	3 1/2	5	6 1/4	7 1/4	8 1/4	1 3/4	3 1/4	4 3/4	6	7 1/4	1 3/4	3 1/4	4 1/2	5 1/2
24	4	5 1/2	7	8	9	2	3 1/2	5	6 1/2	7 1/2	1 3/4	3 1/2	5	6
26	4 1/4	6	7 1/2	8 3/4	10	2	4	5 1/2	7	8 1/4	2	3 3/4	5 1/2	6 3/4
28	4 1/2	6 1/4	8	9 1/2	10 1/2	2 1/4	4 1/4	6	7 1/2	9	2	4	5 3/4	7 1/4
30	5	6 3/4	8 1/2	10	11 1/2	2 1/2	4 1/2	6 1/2	8	9 1/2	2 1/4	4 1/4	6 1/4	7 3/4

Test radiator solution with proper hydrometer. Determine from the table the number of quarts of solution to be drawn off from a full cooling system and replace with undiluted anti-freeze, to give the desired increased protection. For example, to increase protection of a 22-quart cooling system containing Ethylene Glycol (permanent type) anti-freeze, from +20°F. to −20°F. will require the replacement of 6 1/4 quarts of solution with undiluted anti-freeze.

Chilton's Repair & Tune-Up Guides

The complete line covers domestic cars, imports, trucks, vans, RV's and 4-wheel drive vehicles.

BOOK CODE	TITLE	BOOK CODE	TITLE
#7199	AMC 75-82; all models inc. Eagle	#6937	Granada 75-80
#7163	Aries 81-82	#5905	GTO 68-73
#7032	Arrow Pick-Up 79-81	#5821	GTX 68-73
#6637	Aspen 76-80	#6980	Honda 73-82
#5902	Audi 70-73	#6845	Horizon 78-82
#7028	Audi 4000/5000 77-81	#5912	International Scout 67-73
#6337	Audi Fox 73-75	#5998	Jaguar 69-74
#5807	Barracuda 65-72	#7136	Jeep CJ 1945-81
#6931	Blazer 69-82	#6739	Jeep Wagoneer, Commando, Cherokee 66-79
#5576	BMW 59-70	#6962	Jetta 1980
#6844	BMW 70-79	#6931	Jimmy 69-82
#5821	Belvedere 68-73	#7059	J-2000 1982
#7027	Bobcat	#5905	Le Mans 68-73
#7045	Camaro 67-81	#7055	Lynx 81-82 inc. EXP & LN-7
#6695	Capri 70-77	#6634	Maverick 70-77
#6963	Capri 79-82	#6981	Mazda 71-82
#7059	Cavalier 1982	#7031	Mazda RX-7 79-81
#5807	Challenger 65-72	#6065	Mercedes-Benz 59-70
#7037	Challenger (Import) 71-81	#5907	Mercedes-Benz 68-73
#7041	Champ 78-81	#6809	Mercedes-Benz 74-79
#6316	Charger 71-75	#7128	Mercury 68-71 all full sized models
#7162	Chevette 76-82 inc. diesel	#6696	Mercury Mid-Size 71-81 inc. T-Bird, Montego & Cougar
#7135	Chevrolet 68-81 all full size models		
#6936	Chevrolet/GMC Pick-Ups 70-82	#6780	MG 61-81
#6930	Chevrolet/GMC Vans 67-82	#6973	Monarch 75-80
#7051	Chevy Luv 72-81 inc. 4wd	#6542	Mustang 65-73
#7056	Chevy Mid-Size 64-82 inc. El Camino, Chevelle, Laguna, Malibu & Monte Carlo	#6812	Mustang II 74-78
		#6963	Mustang 79-82
#6841	Chevy II 62-79	#6841	Nova 69-79
#7059	Cimarron 1982	#7049	Omega 81-82
#7049	Citation 80-81	#6845	Omni 78-82
#7037	Colt 71-81	#5792	Opel 64-70
#6634	Comet 70-77	#6575	Opel 71-75
#6316	Coronet 71-75	#5982	Peugeot 70-74
#6691	Corvair 60-69 inc. Turbo	#7049	Phoenix 81-82
#6576	Corvette 53-62	#7027	Pinto 71-80
#6843	Corvette 63-82	#8552	Plymouth 68-76 full sized models
#6933	Cutlass 70-82	#6934	Plymouth Vans 67-82
#6324	Dart 68-76	#5822	Porche 69-73
#6962	Dasher 74-80	#7048	Porche 924 & 928 76-81 inc. Turbo
#5790	Datsun 61-72	#6962	Rabbit 75-80
#7196	Datsun F10, 310, Nissan Stanza 77-82	#6331	Ramcharger/Trail Duster 74-75
#7170	Datsun 200SX, 510, 610, 710, 810 73-82	#7163	Reliant 81-82
#7197	Datsun 210 and 1200 73-82	#5821	Roadrunner 68-73
#6932	Datsun Z & ZX 70-82	#5988	Saab 69-75
#7050	Datsun Pick-Ups 70-81 inc. 4wd	#7041	Sapporo 78-81
#6324	Demon 68-76	#5821	Satellite 68-73
#6554	Dodge 68-77 all full sized models	#6962	Scirocco 75-80
#6486	Dodge Charger 67-70	#7059	Skyhawk 1982
#6934	Dodge Vans 67-82	#7049	Skylark 80-81
#6326	Duster 68-76	#6982	Subaru 70-82
#7055	Escort 81-82 inc. EXP & LN-7	#5905	Tempest 68-73
#6320	Fairlane 62-75	#6320	Torino 62-75
#6965	Fairmont 78-80	#5795	Toyota 66-70
#6485	Fiat 64-70	#7043	Toyota Celica & Supra 71-81
#7042	Fiat 69-81	#7036	Toyota Corolla, Carina, Tercel, Starlet 70-81
#6846	Fiesta 78-80	#7044	Toyota Corona, Cressida, Crown, Mark II 70-81
#7046	Firebird 67-81	#7035	Toyota Pick-Ups 70-81
#7059	Firenza 1982	#5910	Triumph 69-73
#7128	Ford 68-81 all full sized models	#7162	T-1000 1982
#7140	Ford Bronco 66-81	#6326	Valiant 68-76
#6983	Ford Courier 72-80	#5796	Volkswagen 49-71
#6696	Ford Mid-Size 71-78 inc. Torino, Gran Torino, Ranchero, Elite & LTD II	#6837	Volkswagen 70-81
		#6637	Volaré 76-80
#6913	Ford Pick-Ups 65-82 inc. 4wd	#6529	Volvo 56-69
#6849	Ford Vans 61-82	#7040	Volvo 70-80
#6935	GM Sub-compact 71-81 inc. Vega, Monza, Astre, Sunbird, Starfire & Skyhawk	#6965	Zephyr 78-80

Chilton's Repair & Tune-Up Guides are available at your local retailer or by mailing a check or money order for **$9.95** plus **$1.00** to cover postage and handling to:

**Chilton Book Company
Dept. DM
Radnor, PA 19089**

NOTE: When ordering be sure to include your name & address, book code & title.